Praise for *Pioneers*

"In an era where we're all pioneers navigating unfamiliar territory, Karra Sillaman's *Pioneers* serves as an essential guidebook for thriving in our rapidly evolving world. Whether you're crossing geographical borders or adapting to seismic shifts in your industry, this book will show you how to design your own path in a world that's new to us all."

—Ayse Birsel
cofounder, Birsel + Seck, and author of
Design the Life You Love

"At a time when immigrants are being viewed with suspicion in many parts of the world, Karra Sillaman's book comes as a breath of fresh air. She has brought together inspirational stories of immigrant entrepreneurs from around the world shining a light on their tenacity, appetite for risk, and capacity for hard work, and how it translates into success. This book is not just for immigrants though. All entrepreneurs would do well to read it."

—Kamal Munir
Pro-Vice-Chancellor and Professor of Strategy and
Policy, University of Cambridge

PIONEERS

8 PRINCIPLES OF BUSINESS LONGEVITY FROM IMMIGRANT ENTREPRENEURS

PIONEERS

NERI KARRA SILLAMAN

WILEY

For general information on our other products and services or for technical support, please contact our Customer Care Department within the United States at (800) 762-2974, outside the United States at (317) 572-3993 or fax (317) 572-4002.

Wiley also publishes its books in a variety of electronic formats. Some content that appears in print may not be available in electronic formats. For more information about Wiley products, visit our website at www.wiley.com.

Library of Congress Cataloging-in-Publication Data is Available:

ISBN: 9781394304059 (Cloth)
ISBN: 9781394304066 (ePub)
ISBN: 9781394304073 (ePDF)

Cover Design: Wiley
Cover Image: © Claire Sullivan
Author Photo: Andrea Sunderland
SKY10099952_031225

To those who came before us:

Şehri and Halil Karaoğlu

Bedriye and Fahri Yaşar

Mary Ann and James Sillaman

Ilona (Helen) and Peter Tellocolo

Contents

Preface
*Entrepreneurs Will Change
Your Life*

Picture the scene: It was my freshman year at the University of Miami in the late 1990s and I was staring wide-eyed in amazement at a mysterious and magical contraption in the corner of the room while my roommate from Alabama was staring open-mouthed in equal amazement at me.

"Don't they have *computers* where you come from?" It was a genuine question, but her distinctive drawl also carried more than a hint of scorn.

She was right to ask though. They didn't have computers where I came from. Born into a persecuted Turkish ethnic minority in communist Bulgaria, my family had fled from our little town, Asenovgrad, when I was just 11. Entering Turkey with only two suitcases to our names, I spent the rest of my childhood first in a refugee camp, and then in a rough and rundown neighborhood of Istanbul.

Living in communist Bulgaria and then in Istanbul, we sometimes caught glimpses of colorful places outside the confines of our own grid of streets: a discarded can of Pepsi that was treated by the local kids like a fallen piece of the moon; a video of Michael Jackson dancing that seemed beamed in from outer space. But never in the 18 years before I arrived in Florida had I ever seen this machine whose rows and rows of keys opened doors to an infinite variety of new worlds.

That computer was far from the only thing that was new to me when financial aid took me straight from our modest apartment in Istanbul to the palm-tree-lined streets of Miami. Some days it seemed like everything was unsettlingly new, from the slick cars my classmates drove to the confident and carefree ways they joked with the professors. Much like the discarded Pepsi can, I felt as if I'd been dropped out of the sky onto another planet—where the sun always seemed to shine but could never fully pierce the dark clouds gathered around my heart.

Some things in Miami filled me with fascination; other things filled me with anxiety; many things did both at the same time. And underlying everything always were the host of voices in my head that undermined me at every opportunity: "You'll never speak English like the rest, you'll never fit in, how stupid you were to ever dream of making it in America. You are simply not good enough."

It was in the computer lab where my fears seemed most acute. Where my classmates, who all had PCs at home, seemed most at ease and I least. Where my struggles with a new language were compounded by my struggles with new technology as I typed with furrowed brow and one finger on the keyboard and watched unfamiliar words appear on the screen.

Our professor tried to help; he was a kindly, elderly man who delighted the students with his countless stories and an anecdote about how his best friend helped inspire *Seinfeld*. But their laughter only made me feel even more alienated—I didn't have a clue who or what Seinfeld was.

But then one day, in the same computer lab, I made a startling discovery that changed my life. My unease around the computer was gradually turning to a fascination with it and its "World Wide Web" which could answer any conceivable question, provided you had the patience to wait 20 minutes while the page loaded.

And as I tried to find out more about computers, I slowly started to discover how they worked. And that's when I learned that the chip inside them that was making all their magic happen had been developed by a man named Andrew Grove whose work for Intel had made the personal computing revolution possible.

But what was the best thing I discovered about Andrew Grove? That he was an immigrant, just like me.

If the creator of the very device that was confounding me had also come here from elsewhere, why couldn't I master it and make it in America too?

I was inspired, and in the weeks that followed, it was as if I was breathing in new air and finally able to exhale the clouds that had built up inside me.

Discovering Andrew Grove's story was a transformative moment. Much of my subsequent success, from teaching at some of the world's leading universities to founding a multimillion-dollar fashion label, can be traced back to the confidence boost that it gave me.

But the impact of that discovery was about much more than just boosting the confidence of a young immigrant; it inspired me to look deeper into the whole world of immigrant entrepreneurs, and through those studies, I discovered that there is something going on within immigrant entrepreneurship that the rest of the business world urgently needs to know about. Stories of immigrants building successful brands are not merely feel-good tales of triumph over adversity, nor are they just evidence of the enormous economic contributions migrants make; they also contain lessons from which everyone trying to create a business that lasts can learn.

Consider these simple facts: Immigrants make up 13% of the U.S. population but 28% of its entrepreneurs.[1] Among the Fortune 500 companies, 45% were founded by immigrants;[2] 80% of billion-dollar startups have a founder or leading executive who is a first- or second-generation immigrant.[3] And despite often starting with limited resources, immigrant-founded companies grow faster and survive longer than those founded by natives.[4]

In a world in which 90% of startups fail,[5] the success rates of immigrant businesses are striking. And at a time when the old rules of business longevity, derived from studying hoary companies created in centuries gone by, no longer apply, we need to explore how immigrant-led startups are disrupting every industry with innovations that work in the 21st century.

In *Pioneers*, I draw on my own experience, my academic career, and my interviews with prominent immigrant entrepreneurs to chart a route to business longevity based on the unique skillsets and strategies deployed by the most successful businesspeople in the world: immigrants. Along the way, we'll both explore the history of immigrant entrepreneurship and meet the migrants behind such modern-day success stories as WhatsApp, Duolingo, Chobani. BioNTech, Calendly, and the Cronut. Filling a huge gap in the current literature, this is the first book to reveal how immigrant entrepreneurship creates sustainable businesses from the perspective of immigrant entrepreneurs themselves.

Through their stories and the evidence accumulated through empirical research into their endeavors, I will present the eight principles that underpin the success of immigrant entrepreneurs. Each of these principles can be applied by any entrepreneur, irrespective of whether they have migrated or not and regardless of what resources they have at their disposal. So, if you want to learn from the world's leading experts about how to build a business that lasts from scratch, then this book is for you.

But I want to conclude this preface with an important caveat, explaining who this book is not for. In *Pioneers*, I focus on building iconic, sustainable brands—one of the central obsessions that has driven my career. But if your idea of business longevity is simply about producing profit year after year after year, then the principles in this book will not help you do that. That's because my research into the immigrant entrepreneur experience consistently reveals one key element that is at the heart of real business success: the desire to build a legacy that transcends profit.

By my definition, a legacy is most definitely not just the bank balance that you pass to the next generations. A legacy is something that you can be proud of, that changes the world in a beneficial way, something that you can look back on at the end of your journey and say, "It was all worthwhile." Because real longevity does not come from the money you take but from the difference you make. That's why, when I think about Andrew Grove, I don't picture Intel's balance sheet but rather how his computers revolutionized our world. The best of immigrant entrepreneurs understand that true longevity is a positive legacy and have found the ways to turn that principle into a reality. *Pioneers* explains how you can join them.

PART

I Departure

The Refugee

1.

Every minute
has its countless cities
and skies,
briefly illuminated clouds,
windows lit by the sunset...
Every minute
has its secret corridors
leading to dark rooms.

Who lives there?
What would we have said to each other?
How would we have lived there?
I don't know.

Every minute I pass
endless doors
to eternal life....

2.

My soul,
we have guilty knowledge
of our loneliness, of the end.
And our guilt keeps us
from Paradise.

The clock is that cherub
with two swords
which guards
the paths of minutes
we might have traveled
to Eternity.

—Vladimir Levchev

Courtesy of Vladimir Levchev

1 | The Myths and Reality of Business Longevity

During the 20th century, more than 100 million people were
forced to flee their countries; this is the story of just one of them ...

Budapest, Hungary, 1956

"Andris, you must *go!*"[1]

András Grof, a lean and striking 20-year-old student, looked up from
his book and his half-empty coffee cup with a shiver of shock. Of course,
he'd been expecting to hear those words for weeks now as the noose
tightened around his city, his home, his neck, but there is a world of
difference between living in a nightmare and discovering it is real.

The young man didn't always hear everything well, a bout of scarlet
fever when he was four having left him with ears severely damaged and an
unusually active imagination. But he heard these words with piercing clarity
and instantly felt their weight, a weight that came from the identity of the
speaker: his Aunt Manci, the only member of her family to return from
Auschwitz, a hell that had shriveled her skin till it clung tight to her bones.

3

Manci understood the darkest corners of the human heart and had come to tell Andris, as his family called him, that it was now his time to flee.

It was far from the first time that András's young life had been in danger; indeed, he was born into hatred, a Jewish baby in Hungary's homegrown fascist dictatorship. When he was seven, his homeland was occupied by Hitler as the Third Reich entered its death throes and its "Final Solution" intensified. To avoid persecution, he and his mother assumed false identities and hid in friends' houses, but his father was not so lucky and was taken to a labor camp, tortured, and barely survived. András would not see his father until after the war ended. Shortly after his eighth birthday, he endured the Soviet Union's siege of Budapest, and his life since then had been lived beneath the boots of a series of repressive Communist regimes, which targeted András's family as bourgeoise entrepreneurs because of the modest dairy his father had run before the war.

But this time, the threat to András was both imminent and somehow crueler because it was coming in the immediate wake of hope. Just weeks before, in the early autumn of 1956, Budapest was full of falling leaves and the scent of revolution was in the air. Students, wired on strong Hungarian coffee and the wild optimism of youth, debated outside cafes long into the night about the new world that would dawn after the long Soviet night had melted away. Incredibly, the students' dreams seemed to be turning into reality; protests outside the parliament building had escalated into the overthrow of the Russian-backed regime, the appointment of a new prime minister, and the dissolution of the hated secret police.

But those autumnal dreams were soon to die. Responding to the danger, the Soviet Union reacted in the only way it knew how: lashing out with the full force of "the People's Army" to crush the people. Russian tanks encircled Budapest once again and began the process of strangling the newborn revolution.

The students outside the cafes dissipated like the steam from their coffees. And the lights across the city went out as an eerie autumn fog descended, pierced only by the harsh headlights of the tanks on the city's grand boulevards and the flaming arcs of burning bottles thrown in response from the darkened side streets; their lights both as bright and as brief as the doomed revolution they sought to defend.

Every life has tipping points, where a decision that takes seconds to make profoundly alters everything that follows. For András, the choice was both deceptively simple—stay or go—and infinitely complex, to lose every aspect of the life he knew in the hope of finding a new world in the utterly unknown spaces beyond the Iron Curtain.

Even the act of escape contained the chance of losing everything he had, but András remained determined to control his own fate. So, in the face of those who would stamp on him for the rest of his life, and with his family's encouragement ringing in his ears, he chose to risk the 120-mile journey west to the Austrian border and freedom.

Every yard of that journey contained danger. Boarding a steam train from Budapest alongside his closest school friend, András resolved to take it as close to the border as he dared, each turn of the wheels taking him further from his old life and deeper into an uncertain future. Throughout the journey dark rumors swirled: police checkpoints blocked all routes; Soviet forces bound Hungary's borders and detained anyone trying to escape the country's fate. Their insides gnawed away by paranoia, András and his friend made a desperate decision. Leaving the train, they placed their lives in the hands of a hunchbacked smuggler who promised to lead them to freedom via obscure paths unknown by the invaders.

Hours later, after night had fallen, András lay in the cold, dark mud of a field in the middle of nowhere. Even with his broken ears, he could still hear above the beating of his own heart the boots marching on the twisted lanes surrounding the fields and the dogs howling at the moon. Or were they howling at him? Suddenly a shout cut through the darkness, a voice barking at him to identify himself. The worst thing: the question came in Hungarian. The blood in András's veins froze in fear and overwhelming questions raced in his mind: Had their guide betrayed them? After 120 miles of terror, had they been caught within yards of freedom?

Summoning the remains of his spent courage, András replied with the question of a man cut loose from all the bindings of his life: "Where am I?" The answer consisted of a single Hungarian word: "Ausztria."

András's new life was born that second, but it would take many more years and struggles before it reached maturity. Despite being penniless and barely able to speak English, he set himself a goal of reaching the United States, where he had relatives in New York City. Rejected for admission to the United States at an initial interview by representatives of the International Rescue Committee in Austria, he refused to take *no* for an answer.

Securing himself a second interview the next day, the panting and profusely sweating András threw every English word he knew at the interviewer in a semi-coherent torrent that he hoped would secure his passage across the Atlantic. Incredibly, it worked. Unknown to everyone, the interviewer's decision to take pity on the desperate Hungarian chemistry student changed the world.

Arriving in New York, the young András found employment as a busboy, helping waiters clear tables and wash dishes. But he never lost his passion for learning and his determination to succeed in his new home. Despite his hearing problems, he mastered English and his success at university earned him a mention in *The New York Times* in a brief article entitled "Refugee Heading Engineers' Class."[2]

Many more mentions in the press were to come. By 1968, the young engineer became the third employee of a tiny tech startup making semiconductors from its base in Mountain View, California. By 1987, he had risen to be the CEO of the company, which by then was ranked the tenth biggest in the world in its industry. Under András's leadership, it rose to number one. By 1997, *Time* magazine named him its "Man of the Year,"[3] describing András as "the person most responsible for the amazing growth in the power and the innovative potential of microchips." The man who had fled the violence following a failed revolution in one country was now leading a peaceful revolution around the whole world.

It's hard to identify another company that has had more influence on creating our modern age than the computer firm that András helped to found and later led. That company is Intel, whose chips still power two-thirds of all computers today (including the one on which I am writing this). And András Grof, who died in 2016, is known to history by the name he adopted upon arriving in America: Andrew Grove.

America was the country that made him, but Grove also helped to make America the world tech leader that it is today. And he never lost his gratitude to his adopted home or forgot his immigrant roots. "It is a very important truism," he once told *Esquire*, "that immigrants and immigration are what made America what it is. We must be vigilant as a nation to have a tolerance for differences, a tolerance for new people."[4]

On one level, Grove's story is exceptional, but on another, it is illustrative of the broader phenomenon of immigrant entrepreneurship. Few people from any background achieve his level of success, but the fact remains that immigrants, despite all the odds stacked against them, are more likely than native-born citizens to succeed as entrepreneurs. This book is about explaining why that is and showing you what you can learn from immigrant entrepreneurs so you, too, can build businesses that succeed and create an impact in the long term. But before turning to that, let's start by trying to understand why debates about business longevity to date have failed to focus on the crucial lessons that immigrant entrepreneurs can teach.

Why the Conventional Wisdom on Business Longevity Gets It Wrong

As a refugee from a communist country myself, an entrepreneur, and a professor of entrepreneurship, I've long been fascinated by the question of business longevity: Why do some brands survive and thrive when so many good ideas die young? Growing up in Bulgaria in the 1980s, where brands simply didn't exist, meant that when I finally arrived in America in the late 1990s, I was utterly in thrall to these brash and bright companies that seemed to dominate the corporate world. And so I studied them, obsessively, to learn their secrets and see what I could take away to guide the building of my own brand: the business back in Istanbul turning discarded bits of Italian leather into bags and accessories that my family and I were dreaming of making into a global luxury brand.

Studying the literature on business longevity was at first a dizzying experience. Classics of the genre like Robert H. Waterman Jr. and Tom Peters's *In Search of Excellence*[5] turned my head with their promise that the principles of business success could be distilled into a blueprint that would work anywhere and anytime it was applied. It was thrilling to read, and its successors, like James C. Collins and Jerry I. Porras's *Built to Last*,[6] inspired me to believe that I, too, could build a business that would stand the test of time and achieve the iconic status of the designers whose work I loved. And when I found myself facing struggles, books like Collins's *Good to Great*[7] reassured me that the timeless principles of business success had now been revealed, and all I needed to do was follow them to make the leap from mediocrity to longevity.

But soon I came to feel like something wasn't quite right. For some reason, the situations and strategies recommended by these bestselling classics didn't seem to match up to the real-life scenarios that Neri Karra, the company, was facing on the streets of Istanbul. Companies like Philip Morris, Walmart, and Disney, it turned out, had little to teach a tiny, refugee-founded company in Turkey struggling with a lack of resources and forced to find ways to get the maximum value out of everything we had. ("You have to fry in your own oil," my grandfather never tired of reminding me, which wasn't advice that I could find from reading about the likes of 3M, IBM, or General Electric.)

Like me, it seemed like the authors of the famous bestsellers had been seduced by the glamor of the biggest brands and consequently were focusing on companies whose day-to-day dealings bore no relation to the struggles of startups equipped with little more than dreams and ideas. Could it be that the "timeless principles" of success were hard to apply when it came to the contexts in which my family and I, and millions of others like us, were trying to build our businesses?

The more I studied the business longevity literature and measured it against my own lived experience, the deeper my disillusionment grew. I started to realize that the bestselling classics, and much of the rest of the academic research, simply didn't reflect what was going on in the real world. The deeper reasons for this disconnect slowly started to dawn on me, and they were not just due to the authors focusing on giant firms that inhabited different ecosystems. Researchers could only pontificate about firms' long-term successes when they looked at companies that were started a long time ago. But the past, as L.P. Hartley famously wrote, is a foreign country,[8] and it's becoming more and more foreign by the day as the pace of change accelerates further and further. In a world characterized by constant disruption, how could we imagine that what worked even as relatively recently as the 1980s could be transposed into the twenty-first century?

And the flaws of the business longevity literature were not even just restricted to size and time. Space was an issue, too. Specifically, many of the studies, I came to realize, were overgeneralizing the experiences of particular places, confidently proclaiming, perhaps implicitly, that what worked in the U.S. Midwest would equally work in the Middle East. Similarly, stories from particular industries, from tobacco to tech, were being sold as universal answers to the challenge faced in very different contexts.

A perceptive piece by Nick Forster in the *Journal of Business Perspective* neatly summed up what I was realizing about the business longevity literature.[9] Despite being well-written, inspirational, and seemingly full of solid advice, it was based on research with too many methodological flaws to be valuable. In addition to the problems related to size, space, and time already mentioned, Forster also skewered other fundamental flaws, ranging from a lack of longitudinal data to failures to account for external variables—factors like market conditions, changing technology, and geopolitics that have more influence over our businesses than we'd like to believe. As Forster concluded, inconsistent definitions of success led to conflicting recommendations about how companies should act. And because the books' suggested strategies were rarely tested in different cultural or organizational settings, they left serious questions about the extent to which a route to success in one place can be replicated in another.

Taking a look around at what had happened to the companies lionized in the bestsellers in the years since they were held up as examples to the rest of us also produced some interesting insights. Of the 30 exceptional enterprises featured in *In Search of Excellence* in 1982, only 9 were performing above average 20 years later (and the same number were outright failures).[10] Similarly, of the 18 firms featured in *Built to Last* in 1994, only 8 were performing above average in 2014. And of the 11 companies celebrated in *Good to Great* in 2001, only 6 were bigger in 2023 than they were when the book was written, 2 were in major trouble, and 1 had gone bankrupt, which didn't seem all that, well, great (or even particularly good).[11]

My general disillusionment with the business longevity research coalesced into a realization that it was selling easy answers and, in the process, propagating myths that could be, ultimately, harmful to budding entrepreneurs like myself. I've compiled a list of these myths below, alongside a description of the reality that each one obscures.

The Eight Main Myths of Business Longevity

Myth 1: You don't need a great idea to start a company

Reality: While many researchers have argued against the importance of individual big ideas in business, reality tells a different tale. Compelling initial ideas that address specific market needs often form the cornerstones of long-lasting businesses. It's true that adaptability and continuous improvement are indispensable for survival and growth, but dismissing the impact of the foundational idea oversimplifies the complexities of entrepreneurship. These original ideas, which stem from unique insights into unresolved problems, disrupt industries, redefine norms, and create lasting legacies.

Myth 2: Business longevity is about maintaining stability at all costs

Reality: True longevity comes from balancing stability with adaptability to changing market conditions, customer needs, and technological capabilities. Many venerable firms have faced near-catastrophic challenges, with some teetering on the brink of bankruptcy before pivotal adaptations spurred recovery and renewal. My own research shows that business longevity isn't about constantly finding calm waters in which to sail but rather about being able to navigate fierce storms; adaptability and evolution in response to challenges are key.

Myth 3: Only companies with large capital and resources can achieve longevity

Reality: Endurance in business isn't solely dependent on starting big. Many long-lasting companies have started small and grown over time through strategic decisions, customer loyalty, and organic growth. In fact, starting a business with an abundance of resources may not always be a good idea as it can stifle creativity. Small companies thrive by leveraging their limitations as strengths, using their small size to maneuver swiftly and respond to changes more effectively than their larger, more cumbersome counterparts.

Myth 4: Continual growth is a must for longevity

Reality: Sustainable growth is more important than continual growth. Companies that focus on sustainable practices tend to last longer because they manage resources wisely, avoid overextension, and maintain financial health. Sustainable growth is strategic and measured, prioritizing long-term stability over short-term gains. It involves making decisions that are economically, socially, and environmentally responsible, ensuring that the business does not exhaust its resources faster than they can be replenished.

Myth 5: You must be successful in the market where your business is founded first

Reality: Historically, the big companies that tend to feature in the business longevity literature, like Coca-Cola, Procter & Gamble, and Levi's, proved themselves first in their local markets before expanding internationally. But this no longer needs to be the case. Modern technology and the shrinking of the world have enabled firms to be global from day one (a phenomenon sometimes referred to as "born global"), making their abilities to build bridges across cultures and countries a business superpower.

Myth 6: The best companies are always the top players in their market

Reality: Being a market leader is less important than having a solid strategy for resilience and adaptability. Many enduring companies thrive by carving out strong niches or comfortably maintaining a second or third position in their industries. These companies often benefit from "the giant's shadow" effect, where being slightly less visible allows them more flexibility to innovate without the constant scrutiny faced by market leaders. Operating in niche markets can help companies develop deep expertise and strong customer loyalty.

Myth 7: Having more customers always results in a longer-lasting business

Reality: The quality of relationships often trumps quantity. Businesses that last tend to focus on deepening relationships with existing customers through excellent service rather than just increasing customer numbers. This focus on customer satisfaction creates a solid foundation of loyal clients who are not only likely to continue doing business but are also inclined to become advocates for the brand. As online reviews become increasingly fundamental components of success, such advocates are crucial drivers of business growth.

Myth 8: Business longevity is mainly about competitive advantage in products or services

Reality: Enduring success is as much about corporate culture and employee engagement as it is about products or services. Companies that invest in their people and foster a positive work environment are more likely to be innovative and efficient and thrive in the long term. These businesses understand that employees who feel valued and see their workplace as a supportive community perform better and remain with the company, reducing turnover and building institutional knowledge.

Immigrant Entrepreneurs and the Real
Principles of Business Longevity

At the same time as I was becoming increasingly disillusioned with the mythical nature of the business longevity literature, I was becoming increasingly inspired by what was happening in my own life in the real world of business. Neri Karra the company was taking off, and my family and I were achieving success by doing things that none of the big business books talked about or that they actively discouraged. We were going straight from our base in Istanbul to working across cultures on the international stage, we were focusing on building community rather than chasing profit, and we were prioritizing sustainability in every aspect of our operations rather than chasing growth ("Frying in our own oil," much to my grandfather's delight).

And, crucially, these things were working. We employed 750 craftsmen in our factory in Istanbul, opened another manufacturing operation in Bulgaria, and expanded very rapidly across Eastern Europe, Russia, and Central Asia. At the time I was working on my PhD thesis, and when I mentioned that we simply trusted our distributors and did not ask for money up front when building the business, this came as a surprise to my professors. It was not how one did business. And that's when I realized something that had been missing from all the literature that I'd been reading on business longevity. The things that we were doing were those things that came naturally to us as immigrants. They derived from our experiences and the particular worldviews and survival strategies that having to rebuild our lives in a new land had taught us. It all seemed so simple and so obvious. People who are survivors are better placed to build businesses that survive. People who have shown the resilience and adaptability to move to new countries and start again from scratch are better able to weather the inevitable storms of entrepreneurship and start businesses that last. And people who have experienced deep hardships in their lives are more likely to want to create companies that have positive impacts and leave a better world for all.

I was reminded of the story of Andrew Grove, which had inspired me when I first moved from my adopted home of Turkey to study in Miami. And revisiting his story, I was struck by how it contains some of the reasons for the remarkable success of immigrant entrepreneurs. In his own writing, Grove talked about the importance of "strategic inflection points," those key moments at which businesses must adapt or die; parallels can be drawn, of course, between the decision faced by Grove himself in Hungary, and by hundreds of millions of refugees the world over, when the choice was between life-threatening danger at home and the risk of starting again from nothing abroad. Even those people who emigrate in peaceful times, rather than fleeing as refugees, still must make bold decisions at a strategic inflection point when they choose to surrender their old life and risk all the pain associated with birthing a new life in an unfamiliar place.

The story of Grove's subsequent escape from Hungary to Austria and, ultimately, the United States correlates to the key decisions businesses have to make to survive. Just like Grove, they must know when the time is right to change, set a clear vision of where they wish to go (in his memoir, Grove tells how during his escape from Hungary he didn't take his eyes from the lights that the smuggler tells them to be Austria "and trudged towards them as if they were a magnet"), and plan methodically how to achieve that vision while also retaining the flexibility to improvise rapidly when circumstances dictate (as Grove did by choosing when to leave the train heading to the border and throwing his life into the hands of the smuggler who offered him a new route to freedom). Any entrepreneur needs to know, just as Grove did, when to call on the help of others, like the friend who joined him on his escape and his family in New York who welcomed him there. And immigrant entrepreneurs, like Grove, generally understand much better than their native counterparts the enormous importance of community for success because it's only when you lose something that you truly realize its value, and it's only when you are starting anew with nothing that you come to appreciate how every connection increases your strength.

Thinking about my experiences and Grove's, I was inspired to look deeper into the stories of other immigrant entrepreneurs and to further research the whole phenomenon of immigrant entrepreneurship itself. And that's when I discovered the facts that provide the foundation of this book.[12]

- Immigrants are more than twice as likely as native-born residents to be entrepreneurs.
- Nearly half of Fortune 500 companies were founded by immigrants.
- Fortune 500 companies founded by immigrants or their children generated more than $7 trillion in revenue in 2022, more than the GDP of every country in the world apart from the U.S. and China.

- Four out of five billion-dollar startups have founders or leading executives who are first- or second-generation immigrants.
- Immigrant-founded businesses grow faster and survive longer than those founded by natives.

But despite everything I was discovering, when I looked in the business literature for accounts of the lessons that could be learned from immigrant entrepreneurship, they simply weren't there. True, there has been research on immigrant entrepreneurs, but most of it focuses on the weaknesses of immigrants: the things that they lack and the ways in which they compensate. And these are important issues to examine because, as I will argue throughout this book, the strategies immigrants devise to overcome their disadvantages are so successful that everyone can learn from them.

However, solely focusing on immigrants' weaknesses and their compensation strategies diverts attention from an equally important element of immigrant entrepreneurs' successes: the inherent strengths that they bring, which native entrepreneurs can also learn from. These include their greater capacity for innovation, the power of diverse perspectives, and the ability to build cross-cultural bridges in a globalized world, all of which we will also examine in detail in this book.

Finally, none of the business literature has gone beyond looking at why immigrants start enterprises to understanding why they are more likely than their native counterparts to build businesses that *last*. In this book, I set out to do just that, focusing on what everyone can learn from immigrants' creative ways of overcoming weaknesses and the fundamental strengths that they bring to their new countries.

To inform my conclusions, I have engaged with and studied some of the leading immigrant entrepreneurs of our times, including the people behind such modern-day success stories as Calendly, Chobani, Udemy, BioNTech, Wondery, Duolingo, and WhatsApp among others, to create a rich tapestry of immigrant entrepreneurial stories across a wide spectrum of industries and cultural backgrounds. Their stories are not only inspirational but also filled with actionable insights that I have distilled into the eight principles of immigrant entrepreneurship success that form the core of this book, principles which, when correctly applied, can help any business to improve and last longer.

Mindful of the critiques of the established literature on business longevity, I have been very careful to avoid falling into the same traps as previous authors. To avoid only focusing on big firms, I have selected companies with a wide range of sizes in a variety of different stages of development. To avoid paying too much attention to particular geographies and industries, I have examined a diverse range of businesses that reflect the breadth of the immigrant entrepreneur experience, from traditional craft companies to tech startups. And, perhaps most crucially, to check the practical value of my findings, I have applied the recommendations derived from my interviews with a wide range of leading immigrant entrepreneurs in my work with startups striving to build long-lasting businesses around the world.

In the following two chapters, I set the foundation for the rest of this book. In Chapter 2, I use the story of the Statue of Liberty as a way to introduce the history of immigrant entrepreneurship internationally and explore the contributions that immigrants have made to making the American Dream a reality. In Chapter 3, I use the inspiring stories of two great contemporary immigrant entrepreneurs to reveal what research can tell us about why immigrants are so entrepreneurial and explain how *Pioneers* goes beyond that to explain why they build businesses that last. This crucial contextual material prepares us for our exploration of the eight principles of success from immigrant entrepreneurs that follow in Part II.

But before we get into the details of my findings, I want to really emphasize two key points, which are absolutely fundamental to understanding the rest of *Pioneers*. The first point is a quick one that concerns what I am hoping to achieve by writing this book. The second one is a little more complex and concerns what I hope you will achieve after reading it.

Let's take the simpler point first. Unlike some writers on business longevity, I want to make it absolutely clear that I do not believe that there is a simple blueprint for success that can be copied and pasted into any circumstances. Because if the stories of immigrant entrepreneurs teach us anything it is about the importance of adaptability—to new circumstances, new contexts, new countries. So, this book is not about blueprints but about inspiration and ideas that can influence your own journeys and point you toward success. This book is about learning from the world's most successful entrepreneurs—immigrants—and looking at what has worked for them and thinking about how you can apply it to your own business to help it grow, survive, and thrive. In other words, following the advice contained within these pages should help increase the longevity of your business. But I can't give you all the answers; it's down to you to take the pieces that work for you and put them together in such a way that creates success in your context.

The second point concerns the precise meaning of success. And this is crucial because it's my contention that the definition of success is the number-one thing that the literature on business longevity gets wrong. But to illustrate that, let's turn to the story of another immigrant entrepreneur who, more than 100 years before Andrew Grove left Hungary, fashioned a career that exemplifies true business longevity with achievements that still resonate in the world today.

Lincolnshire, England, 1837

Snow was solemnly falling on silent English fields on the bitter morning when Charles bid farewell to his mother. For just a few seconds, it seemed like the stagecoach would remain stuck in the dirty sludge on the roadside, but some sharp blows from the driver to his horse stirred it to drag the reluctant wheel onto the track. Steam clouds shot from the horse's nostrils as it shook its head and the wheel free, and a tear rolled down young Charles's cheek as the sight of his mother waving receded into the mist and was lost. Charles turned away and sunk his head deep into his chest to avoid the blank stares of his fellow passengers because an English boy should never be seen crying.

And, after all, the boy now had to be a man. A 13-year-old man who had to leave his mother less than a year after his father had left them both—the once successful solicitor having drunk and gambled away the family's wealth. And now Charles was taking a huge gamble of his own, leaving everyone and everything he knew to try and supplement the pitiful income his mother earned from her new job as a housekeeper.

True, the sensitive young boy wasn't leaving for another country, but it must have felt like it. With a liberally applied whip, the horse pulling the stagecoach took a painful 12 hours to haul its passengers the 102 miles that separated Charles's home in Bourne, Lincolnshire, from London—a modern traveler would get from Bucharest to New York City in the same time. And England in 1837 must have seemed much more of a patchwork of little countries than it does today, with dialects, dress, and customs each of their own. And London itself, the smog-filled global metropolis that presided over a land still mostly made up of fields and farms, must have appeared to be a different planet to the wide-eyed Lincolnshire lad spat out of the stage-coach on that cold winter's night.

Charles hadn't gone to London to seek his fortune but just to survive. With his education cut short by the sudden change in his family's circum-stances, he hardly had the luxury to expect a good job, and he was grateful to find work as an apprentice in a linen drapery shop named Swan and Edgar, just off Regent Street, which sold fine fabrics to a wealthy clientele. His gratitude was not for the pay, because when he started there was none, but because the shop provided him with a little food and a place to sleep—on the floor under the benches—to keep away the chill of London's dark streets.

Life in London was hard, between empty stomachs, restless nights, and homesickness, but Charles found beauty there, too. The majestic National Gallery was just a short walk from the workshop he toiled and slept in, and on his rare breaks he'd take himself there and into another world, where he'd stare at the gigantic portraits of the nation's grandees, the cleaner boy in his rough-cut clothing admiring the opulent gowns of different classes and long-gone times. In the drapery, too, Charles became fascinated with the fabrics that surrounded him, the way they looked, the way they felt, even the rustling sounds they made when held. His keen eye for detail eventually brought a slight improvement in his career as he started sewing and providing advice on garments to Swan and Edgar's rich customers.

Eventually, Charles's passion for beauty and clothes led him to take an even greater risk than leaving his childhood home for London. Seduced by what he'd heard about French fashions, he impulsively boarded a boat across the Channel and followed his heart to Paris in 1846, age 20, arriving in his new home with just five pounds in his pocket and barely a word of French on his lips.

But against any possible expectation, Paris was the making of Charles and, in one sense, the young Englishman was the maker of Paris. The City of Lights has made many stars, but few have risen with such speed as Charles. Two years after arriving, he was an assistant draper at a textile house. Within six years, his designs helped his employer win a gold medal at London's Great Exhibition. Within 13 years, he had his own fashion house in Paris. Within 15 years, he had princesses and empresses queuing for his creations, which mixed the classical and avant-garde in ways that have been compared to the great artists of his age. "So extraordinary were his clothes," said the Empress Eugénie, the wife of Napoleon III, "that he became our master."[13] For a journalist watching him at work in 1883, Charles was "the only absolute monarch left in Europe."[14]

Charles Frederick Worth was much more than just a wildly successful designer—he was the creator of the entire modern fashion industry.[15] If you are now wearing clothes with a designer's name on them, you have bought from a company still under the influence of Worth, who created the concept of the celebrity designer and the designer label, effectively signing his creations in the style of an artist. And that was far from the only innovation that Worth introduced to the world of fashion; everything from seasonal collections to catwalk shows can be attributed to the boy who rose from such humble circumstances to become the father of haute couture. Solidifying his place in history, he founded the forerunner of today's *Fédération de la Haute Couture et de la Mode,* which continues to govern the entire French fashion industry and has done much to preserve Paris's status as that industry's world capital.

Worth's innovations and the institution he founded may have lasted, but ironically, his own business did not. Shortly after his death, in 1895, the House of Worth was divided between his sons who had opposing visions of traditionalism and innovation. They soon came under sustained pressure from a host of disruptive competitors inspired by Worth's own creative legacy. Even before the First World War, the House of Worth's sun was being eclipsed, and although the business lumbered on until the 1950s, it became an increasingly irrelevant element of the world Worth himself had made. Perhaps it was a victim of his own genius; the seasonality that he had introduced to fashion fostered a relentless pursuit of the new and novel. Later designers, many of whom were also immigrants lured by Parisian glamor, mastered the art of reinvention and found ways to intertwine rich heritages with innovative designs that resonated with each new generation.

The House of Worth never found a way to achieve that delicate balance and fell as a result. But does that ultimately matter? No business lasts forever; even Kongo Gumi, the over-1,000-year-old renovator of Japanese temples, became just a subsidiary of another construction firm in 2006. And in the modern world where human lifespans are ever increasing, those of firms are forever falling: companies on Standard & Poor's 500 list now only live for an average of 18 years, compared to 61 for the same cohort in 1958.[16]

And if what Worth, the poor immigrant entrepreneur, achieved in making the entire modern fashion industry, worth $1.7 trillion a year today, is not to be considered creating longevity, then what is? What he did is worth more, in my mind, than building a business that keeps turning a profit for years after your death but fails to revolutionize the world. Real longevity comes from making changes that last long after your last balance sheet has been filed. Because if all you did was take money and never make a change, then all you did was worthless.

And, as the story of Charles Worth illustrates, I am absolutely clear that success is about much more than just continually striving for profit: it's about building a company that you can be proud of and that makes a difference in the long term. And the difference you make isn't just about what your products or services do but also about how you conduct yourself as a company. My research on business longevity has shown that companies that make the biggest difference are those that think long term, shy away from fast growth and expansion, treat their staff well, focus on their communities, and believe in creating value for all their stakeholders. And these are characteristics that, as we shall see, are particularly common in immigrant-founded and -led businesses.

If you agree with me about the real nature of business success, then read on. Because that's what the rest of this book is about. In it, we'll learn from immigrant entrepreneurs like Grove, Worth, and a whole host of contemporary innovators and disrupters about what success really means and how you and your business can have a real *impact* that lasts.

Prospective Immigrants Please Note

Either you will
go through this door
or you will not go through.

If you go through
there is always the risk
of remembering your name.

Things look at you doubly
and you must look back
and let them happen.

If you do not go through
it is possible
to live worthily

to maintain your attitudes
to hold your position
to die bravely

but much will blind you,
much will evade you,
at what cost who knows?

The door itself makes no promises.
It is only a door.

—Adrienne Rich

2 | Immigrant Entrepreneurship and the American Dream

New York, New York, 2017

The first time I saw the world's most famous immigrant was one of the most powerful moments of my life.

It was an early morning in New York on a winter's day in 2017, and the first rays of the sun were yet to break free from the clouds and clear away the mist that had threaded itself through the city streets in the night. My boyfriend and I held each other tightly against the remains of the chill as we waited patiently in line with the rest of the sightseers ready to take the morning's first boat into the Upper New York Bay. Around us, couples quietly debated their itineraries for the day, trying to remember which Broadway show they'd booked, their voices occasionally drowned out by the cawing of seagulls caught up in a sweeping battle over a discarded bagel.

What happened next is hard to put into words. It began as the boat slipped from its moorings and into the bay. My boyfriend and I sipped our coffees for a little extra warmth as we stood against the railing on the deck while he shared with me the story of his maternal grandmother, Ilona

(Helen), who aged 11, had left her home in Hungary to properly meet for the first time her parents who had emigrated to America in search of a better life when she was a newborn. Helen and her siblings had traveled from Hungary to Amsterdam and then on by boat to New York, arriving in the very same harbor we had just departed. And they had traveled alone save for a chicken that her relatives had provided as food but which Helen likely held on to as a last reminder of the place that she had called home. Helen eventually built a life in the U.S. and met and married my boyfriend's grandfather, himself a second-generation immigrant from Poland. And their daughter eventually married the son of two Scots-Irish immigrants whose families had settled in Western Pennsylvania generations before and gave birth to my boyfriend.

Suddenly, listening to his stories and the whispers of the waves around us, I was filled with an overwhelming sensation of the lives of the millions upon millions who had made this journey in reverse, entering the harbor we'd just left. And while our sightseeing trip would take only a few hours, their travels would have taken days or even weeks as they crossed the inhospitable Atlantic in search of a new home, leaving behind everything they had known with the knowledge that they would probably never return. Many of them were fleeing oppression, as I had as an 11-year-old with my family when we crossed the border from Bulgaria to Turkey as refugees with just two suitcases to our name. Many of them were just hoping for something better than the poverty they lived in, as I had when I left Istanbul for the University of Miami to pursue my dream of education. All of them were united by a determination to build something better than what they had left behind.

And it was just then, as my own memories of the pain and possibilities of immigration mixed with my imagination of the lives, hopes, and dreams of the millions of others who had crossed this same waterway, that I caught my first glimpse of her. Libertas, Lady Liberty, a Roman goddess who had herself left the old world and found her perfect new home here, at the mouth of the harbor, watching over and welcoming the brave immigrants as they arrived at their destination, "tempest-tost" as Emma Lazarus put it in her famous poem inscribed on the statue's base. And even if some of those immigrants did not experience literal tempests over the water, they must have been through great storms of emotion as they said goodbye to home and family to step into an unknown future on a continent that probably seemed as distant as the moon. Looking up at Lady Liberty, I imagined how they must have felt, to arrive in a country that did not put up walls but instead welcomed immigrants with this mighty statue that declared here you are welcome and here you are free to be who you want to be and chase all your dreams.

I watched her transfixed, barely aware that the sun was starting to break its way through the clouds until I saw its rays start to light up the torch above her head, which suddenly seemed to be catching fire, "imprisoned lightning" as Lazarus put it. And again, I was struck with the emotion that came from the collective impact of art, place, memory, and imagination as I thought of the immigrants themselves as the imprisoned lightning, about to be set free and unleash their potential in the new land that they would build and help elevate to the status of the world's leading country in so many ways.

This book is about harnessing the power of the lightning that immigrants bring. But it does not take the form of a case for more immigration or differing policies to encourage different types of immigrants, political issues that are beyond my scope. Instead, it will illustrate how you can learn from the successes of the most entrepreneurial of immigrants to build businesses that last.

But before we turn to that, it's essential to understand who immigrant entrepreneurs are and why they are worth learning from. And the best way to gain that understanding is by reviewing some of the history of immigrant entrepreneurship, especially in America, the country that launched a million ships full of dreamers. And when considering the history of American immigration, I think there is no better starting place than at the foot of Lady Liberty herself, whose own story can teach us much about immigration and the power of unlocking imprisoned lightning.

Liberty Comes to New York

Is there any better symbol of the power of immigration than the Statue of Liberty? After all, Lady Liberty was not just built to symbolize the immigration that has shaped and defined the United States; she is herself an immigrant. She was conceived and created in France and only pieced together into her final, world-famous form on the other side of the Atlantic. Thus, she is not just a symbol of the country's openness to immigration but an epitome of how the process of immigration creates something new and glorious. In other words, because she does not come from America but found her home there, she is the perfect symbol of the United States.

Like all immigrants, the story of how she came to be in her new home is fascinating and worth exploring. In 1865, 11 years before the United States' 100th birthday, the French historian, politician, poet, and anti-slavery activist Édouard de Laboulaye conceived of a grand idea to celebrate the two nations' friendship and common values: a giant statue representing freedom. A long fundraising campaign was required before the statue was eventually built in France, deconstructed, and shipped in bits and pieces to New York in 1885, where it was welcomed by a crowd of 200,000 and reconstructed on Liberty (nee Bedloe's) Island where it stands today.

But the Statue of Liberty (officially titled "Liberty Enlightening the World") represents even more than just the friendship of two countries and their common commitment to freedom. The task of turning the vision into reality was given to Laboulaye's friend, the sculptor Frédéric Auguste Bartholdi, with support from Gustave Eiffel (whose eponymous tower was completed four years after the statue). And Bartholdi drew his influences for the work from a diverse range of sources inspired by his travels in Egypt and Italy, to which he added a touch of his own home.

In addition to those influences, the statue's skin is made of copper sourced from Norwegian mines, her pedestal features elements influenced by Greek and Aztec architecture, and the funds for construction came partly from the donations of thousands of regular New Yorkers, many of whom would have been immigrants in a city that was receiving an average of about a quarter of a million new arrivals annually in the late 19th century. Thus, it all came together to produce something much grander than its constituent parts. Through its conception, its design, and its construction, the Statue of Liberty symbolizes the connection between the United States' ideals and its reality as a nation built and continually revitalized by immigrants.

Who Are Immigrant Entrepreneurs? Defining Migration Around the World

With 50 million residents born outside the country, the United States remains, by far, the country with the highest number of immigrants (second and third place are taken by Germany and Saudi Arabia, with 16 and 13 million, respectively). When you add in the children of those immigrants, the country's "immigrant stock" currently numbers around 84 million people, about a quarter of the total population, according to the latest edition of the University of California's *Immigrant America*.[1] It is also probably not unrelated that the United States remains one of the world's most innovative countries, scoring highest in the Global Innovation Index's 2023 ratings for global research and development investments, venture capital received, and total unicorn value (with 54% of the world's total 1,206 unicorns based there).[2]

Although we will return time and again to the stories of immigrants in the United States, this book is about immigrant entrepreneurship as a worldwide phenomenon. Indeed, although the United States is perhaps the best example of a country built by immigrants, the global history of emigration far predates the Declaration of Independence on July 4, 1776, the arrival of the Mayflower on November 11, 1620, or even the "discovery" of the Americas on October 12, 1492.

The roots of migration can be traced back as far as humans have ever existed—we are, after all, a migratory species, which walked the African savannah in search of food. And eventually, some 100,000 or so years ago, some members of that species walked out of our ancestral home in search of better opportunities elsewhere and populated the rest of the world. As Gloria Steinem once wrote, "In many languages, even the word for human being is 'one who goes on migrations.'"[3] Even the very first Americans arrived there as migrants from Asia, walking from Siberia into Alaska across a frozen Bering Strait around 11,000 years ago, and spreading from there to the southernmost tip of South America within 1,000 years.

Over time, as countries and nation–states formed, our natural tendency to move and wander eventually became formalized into a process whereby one "immigrated" into another country. Remarkably, we can date linguistically when this transition happened; it was in 1828 when Noah Webster (of Merriam-Webster fame) published *An American Dictionary of the English Language*, which included the first recorded instance of the word "immigrate."[4] The word did not feature in Dr. Johnson's groundbreaking *Dictionary of the English Language* (published in London in 1755),[5] but "migration" did, defined simply as "the act of moving from place to place." Webster's first attempt at a dictionary mostly followed Johnson's, but by 1828 he was branching out with some of his own words, including "immigrate," which he defined as "to remove into a country for the purpose of permanent residence." According to historian Neil Larry Shumsky, Webster's introduction of the concept of crossing international borders to stay permanently "shaped the way millions of citizens have thought about a phenomenon that, perhaps more than any other, has defined [America]."[6]

That originally American definition of *immigration* and, by extension, *immigrant* has gone on to be adopted around the world. As noted by Oxford University's Migration Observatory,[7] some dictionaries distinguish between "immigrants" (who are settled or plan to be settled in their new country) and "migrants" (who are only temporary residents), but the terms are often used interchangeably even by researchers. For the purposes of this book, I don't distinguish between the two terms and largely follow the inclusive definition used by the United Nations' International Organization for Migration, which refers to a migrant (or immigrant) as "any person who is moving or has moved across an international border or within a State away from his/her habitual place of residence, regardless of the person's legal status; whether the movement is voluntary or involuntary; what the causes for the movement are [or] what the length of the stay is."[8]

That definition, you will notice, is also inclusive of refugees and asylum seekers, two (related) categories of immigrant that attract particular attention from commentators on the subject of migration. Refugees are individuals forced to flee their countries due to threats of persecution, conflict, or violence. Their status is legally recognized under international law, which obligates host countries to provide protection and rights, including the right to work, which can lead to entrepreneurial activities. Asylum seekers are people engaged in the legal process of seeking refugee status within a country.

I want to highlight here two ways in which I deviate from the UN's definition of a migrant. The first relates to a category that I do not cover in this study and the second to a category that I do. When talking about migrants/immigrants in this book, I am only focusing on people who have crossed international borders. I recognize that internal displacement or movement from one region to another within a diverse country can sometimes be an experience as unsettling and challenging as international migration, particularly when people are displaced by conflict or natural disasters. However, including people who have migrated internally in the book would make its scope too wide and also incorporate many cases in which people made moves within a country that did not require them to develop or exhibit the special skills that epitomize the immigrant entrepreneur.

Interestingly, the UN itself applies the same distinction between people moving within a state and those moving internationally when calculating its statistics on migration. Specifically, it reports that there are 281 million international migrants around the world (people living outside the country in which they were born). Of those, the majority are in Europe (86.7 million), followed by Asia (85.6 million), and North America (58.7 million), with the vast majority of those 58.7 million found in the United States.[9]

My second variation from the UN definition of *migrant/immigrant* is that I do also include some people who are the children of immigrants (i.e., "second-generation immigrants"). The reason for that is, as I shall discuss further in Part II, people who are born into a country and a culture that differs from that of their parents can epitomize some of the key qualities of the immigrant entrepreneur, especially the ability to act as a bridge between two worlds.

After applying those two qualifications, the definition of *immigrant entrepreneur* used for this book is still broad and inclusive. It encompasses a vast range of categories of people and different experiences: from the rich, Indian student starting at an Ivy League university to the Syrian refugee arriving in Germany without a word of the language, and from the tech specialist leading a Silicon Valley startup to the daughter of Vietnamese immigrants trying to grow a nail salon in Texas. What interests me for the purpose of this book are the characteristics that link such diverse and dynamic groups together because it is my contention that all immigrants, regardless of their backgrounds, abilities, and current statuses, are more likely to have certain characteristics that increase their chances of enjoying entrepreneurial success. Throughout Part II, I will identify those characteristics so that every entrepreneur, whether immigrant or otherwise, can learn from them.

And in my search for a way to describe something that is common to the experience of all immigrant entrepreneurs, regardless of their background or future aspirations, I came across the words of Adrienne Rich in her 1962 poem "Prospective Immigrants Please Note," which I quote in full at the start of this chapter. In it, Rich implicitly defines an immigrant as someone who has gone through a door—a door that "itself makes no promises." And this going through a door, from one country to another, from one life to another, with no guarantees of finding success or anything on the other side, is the common experience that defines all the immigrant entrepreneurs you will meet in this book. For "entrepreneur," we can use the definition of Merriam-Webster, "one who organizes, manages, and assumes the risks of a business or enterprise."[10]

The immigrant entrepreneur is, therefore, a pioneer who has gone through a door while understanding that it is what they do on the other side, how they make the best use of the resources that they have, that makes the difference. They risk failure, of course, but so does the person who remains behind and who holds on to their identity at the cost of not exploring the opportunities that life offers on the other side. And the immigrant entrepreneur who steps through to that side can, if they can remain resourceful, hopeful, and resilient, find the success that the door alone never promised.

Of course, you could argue that so broad a definition of a migrant means that everyone is one. And on one level, that is true. All of us, throughout our lives, go through experiences that act as doors into new worlds—going to university, changing jobs, moving house, starting a new relationship, getting married, having children—all of which can cause disruption that feels like a migration. As Rumi put it, "Notice how everyone has just arrived here from a journey."[11] And even a person who only ever stayed in the same place and tried to keep their life as steady as possible might ultimately, in our rapidly changing modern world, end up feeling like they've migrated because of the way in which everything around them had shifted.

Nevertheless, in this book, I focus on those who have gone through the door of moving country, because it is that group that is most likely to demonstrate the qualities of entrepreneurial success that make great contributions to society. And it is to those contributions that I now turn, with the story of a man who was born in Sweden in 1871, when the Statue of Liberty was still just a drawing in Paris, and who became one of the first immigrants to sail beneath the statue when he passed through New York's Golden Door 16 years later. A man whose story would come to epitomize not only the American Dream but the dream of all immigrants.

Johan, Mohamad, and the American Dream

Johan was born into a bitterly cold winter in the northern Swedish village of Alvik, where the sun would only shine for four hours each day. His harsh life on the family farm, which stands at roughly the same latitude as Anchorage, Alaska, got much worse when his father died when Johan was just eight. As his family struggled, young Johan was pulled out of school three years later to start earning what little money he could to help keep the chill and hunger from the door.

With his prospects for achieving success seemingly as frozen as the ponds around his farm in winter, 16-year-old Johan made a radical decision: to board a boat to New York in search of a new life away from the poverty and rigid class restrictions that bound the European peasantry in their place. Answering the call that Emma Lazarus placed on the lips of the Statue of Liberty—"Give me your tired, your poor, / Your huddled masses yearning to breathe free, / The wretched refuse of your teeming shore."—he arrived on Ellis Island in 1887 with only $5 in his pocket, no resources, and not even a contact to call on. The bravery, or desperation, behind such a decision we can barely fathom. But Johan was far from alone; by that time migration to the United States was becoming a human tidal wave, with the upsurge that began in 1880 eventually bringing 23 million new immigrants to the United States in just 40 years.[12]

Like many in that wave, Johan did not speak English when he arrived. Deprived of words, he fell back on jobs that required the strength and resilience he'd developed from working on a sub-arctic farm. He worked in lumber camps, on railroads, and down iron mines, toiling for bare pay on

America's rapidly growing frontiers in places where, as he put it, "no American would work… greenhorns like us were the only ones they could get."[13] Through years of tough work, careful saving, and a continual willingness to undergo hardship in pursuit of new opportunities, Johan eventually purchased a small potato farm in Arlington, just north of Seattle in the Pacific Northwest.

When the 25-year-old Johan arrived in Seattle in 1896, it was a town of around 60,000 people which was rapidly growing; in 1871, the year Johan was born, its population was 1,100. Shortly following Johan's arrival, its population growth exploded after the S.S. Portland docked in Puget Sound on July 14, 1897, carrying "a ton of gold" from Alaska and Canada's neighboring Yukon Province. Johan was among the millions caught up in the subsequent gold rush, which transformed Seattle and his life.

The Klondike Gold Rush (named after the Yukon River where the gold was first found) made a few fortunes and broke many more men. Of course, Johan was helped by having grown up among harsh weather and icy streams. Nevertheless, the grueling conditions tested even his mettle and although he did, after two years of trying, eventually strike gold, it was not enough to make his fortune for life. But what matters is what he did with the money that he brought back from the wilderness into Seattle in the last weeks of the 19th century.

Wisely choosing not to squander his very hard-earned money, Johan invested it in opening a small shoe store in Seattle, hoping to take advantage of the city's ongoing economic boom. From the start he prioritized one thing in his store: customer satisfaction, which he aimed to guarantee through a mixture of high-quality products, exceptional service, and out-standing value.

From those simple beginnings, the business founded by Johan (who by that time had anglicized his name to John) has spread to more than 360 stores worldwide and has a net worth of $3.7 billion. The company expanded from just selling shoes in 1963, but it still epitomizes the values of quality and customer service instilled in it by its emigrant founder whose name the company continues to carry: John W. Nordstrom.

Nearly 100 years separate Nordstrom's arrival into New York by boat and the arrival of another immigrant from a very different part of the world into JFK airport in 1981. Mohamad was traveling with his mother from

Guyana, the rainforest-dense South American country that sits just on top of the equator between Brazil and Venezuela. At the time, Guyana was a dictatorship allied with the Soviet Union. Seeking a better life for his family away from the poverty the government inflicted on the people, Mohamad's father had left for the United States in 1980. A year later, 11-year-old Mohamad and his mother went to New York to join him. They had just $34 when they arrived, and they were both immediately confronted, inside the airport, with a perplexing problem. Facing an iron stairway that moved, they both had no idea how they were meant to get on and off it safely. It wasn't too long before they learned that this strange staircase had a name—an escalator—and being able to work out how to deal with it was the first step, literally, in Mohamad's journey toward success.

From such inauspicious beginnings, Mohamad eventually thrived in his new home. Despite growing up poor in New York City, he went on to become Hewlett Packard's chief strategy officer and the CEO of the data protection company Carbonite and the market intelligence firm IDG. He is currently a senior vice president and head of IBM Consulting. Just like Nordstrom, 100 years before him, Mohamad Ali's journey epitomizes the American Dream. And it shows that although the countries from which migrants come to America may have diversified, their dreams remain the same.

It's also important to remember that America does not just make immigrants' dreams come true; the reverse is also correct: immigrants make America's dream a reality too, the dream of the founding fathers that it would act as a beacon to the rest of the world for prosperity and progress. As Mohamad Ali put it in an article for the *Harvard Business Review*, "The U.S. draws its global competitive advantage from its openness to new people and new ideas … From my personal experience … I firmly believe that curtailing immigration will make it harder to sustain America's vibrant, creative mix."[14]

Those beliefs are borne out by evidence from studies of immigration that have looked both at the time of Nordstrom and the time of Ali. For example, recent research by academics from Harvard, the London School of Economics, and Northwestern University found that the great wave of immigration that Nordstrom was part of (from the late 19th to the early 20th centuries) produced major, long-term economic benefits for the

United States, without creating long-term social costs. These benefits not only increased productivity but also increased innovation (measured by applications for patents for new inventions and products).[15]

That research is important because it takes a long-term perspective on the impacts of immigration. But equally important is more recent research that contradicts the current popular notion that immigration has become less beneficial. For example, Ran Abramitzky and Leah Boustan's book *Streets of Gold*[16] shows that modern immigrants from Asia and Latin America become successful at the same rate as immigrants did following the predominantly European waves of immigration in the past. Analyzing vast datasets on immigration in the United States, the authors show that even the children of immigrants from poor countries like Guatemala and Laos are more likely to be successful than the children of native-born families with similar income levels. The same data also proves, however, that the fabled rise "from rags to riches" has traditionally taken a long time and continues to do so. Whether immigrant entrepreneurs specifically offer an exception to that rule, we will explore in subsequent chapters.

I want to conclude this discussion about the impact of the American Dream by highlighting that it does not only inspire immigrants inside America itself. The notion, still revolutionary in parts of the world, that your abilities and your attitude matter much more than the accident of your birth when it comes to determining your status in society, motivates people to try to break old class structures or to seek opportunities in places where they can thrive away from the restrictions they encountered at home. My own company was founded 6,000 miles away from America in Istanbul, but it was infused with the ideals of the American Dream that I carried home with me after my experience as a student in Miami. Indeed, the idea that I could create such a company despite my own humble background and status as an immigrant in Turkey was born in America.

But Why Are Immigrant Entrepreneurs So Successful?

As we have seen, immigration has a long history and research has shed considerable light on the contributions that immigrants make to their new countries. I also recognize that despite the many studies showing immigrants' contributions, there is a real lack of research showing *how* they make those contributions. To fill that gap, I will focus on the facts about immigrant entrepreneurs to highlight the lessons that everyone, immigrant or otherwise, can learn from their successes.

Before turning to that, however, it's important to get a sense of what else the existing research can tell us about immigrant entrepreneurs beyond the contribution that they make to society. And that research is the subject of the following chapter, which surveys the literature to discover the truth about what makes immigrants so entrepreneurial.

The New Colossus

Not like the brazen giant of Greek fame,
With conquering limbs astride from land to land;
Here at our sea-washed, sunset gates shall stand
A mighty woman with a torch, whose flame
Is the imprisoned lightning, and her name
Mother of Exiles. From her beacon-hand
Glows world-wide welcome; her mild eyes command
The air-bridged harbor that twin cities frame.
"Keep, ancient lands, your storied pomp!" cries she
With silent lips. "Give me your tired, your poor,
Your huddled masses yearning to breathe free,
The wretched refuse of your teeming shore.
Send these, the homeless, tempest-tost to me,
I lift my lamp beside the golden door!"

—Emma Lazarus

3

Who Are Immigrant Entrepreneurs?

When Isaac[1] caught sight of Mourtaza advancing again down the alleyway, his heart felt like it was trying to beat its way out of his body and his mouth turned as dry as the desert. Despite his preparation in anticipation of this moment, nothing had prepared the young boy for the sensation that he was about to face his fate.

The alleyway cut through the Tehran slums surrounding Isaac's house, a one-bedroom shack that made up for what it lacked in water, heating, and light by being full of people: his parents, uncles, and cousins. Ever since he moved to Tehran from Isfahan at the age of four, this alleyway had been one of the main thoroughfares of Isaac's life. It was both his playground and his route into the rest of the city where he'd walked since age nine looking for jobs, anything from washing dishes to carrying bags, to try to bring a few rials home to supplement the tiny income his mother made making dresses for their neighbors.

Isaac knew every stone of that alleyway and the rest of the twisting network of alleys that threaded through the labyrinthine local slums. But today that knowledge counted for nothing. Mourtaza was a creature of the slums too, and running away would do Isaac no good. The biggest kid in the neighborhood would catch him again and beat him again till the tears flowed from his eyes and the blood from his nose. And the other kids would laugh and taunt him again, the skinny Jewish boy beaten and bloodied once more. And when he crawled back to his house, he would have to face his mother, who had told him the last time he'd been beaten up, "If you ever come home bleeding again, I'll hit you too."

She had told him that the last time it had happened, and those words had sparked a change in Isaac. Determined to not be beaten again, by Mourtaza or anybody, he'd turned two old bricks into dumbbells and practiced with them religiously, every day lifting them and himself a little higher. But there comes a moment when practice is over and it's time for the real deal. And as Isaac heard Mourtaza spitting his latest insult and the shouts of an eager crowd gathering, he realized that moment was now.

Mourtaza advanced and landed the first blow, which hit Isaac with the force of an avalanche. But to his, and everyone's, surprise, this time he didn't go down. He took the blow and returned it with more force. And again and again, and soon it was Mourtaza on the ground. And when Isaac extended his hand to lift up his enemy, a new friendship was born from mutual respect.

It wasn't the only thing that was born that day. Isaac would always trace his new life back to that moment when he learned that when life hits you, you get stronger, you strive for better, and you hit back. And Mourtaza was just the first, but far from the only, biggest kid in the neighborhood that Isaac would have to overcome on his road from the Tehran slums to the stars.

"When you are 17, and you have grown up with hardship," Isaac says, "you have a feeling of invincibility." It must have been that feeling that inspired him in 1971, at 17, to buy a one-way ticket for the United States despite not knowing anyone there, not speaking English, and having only $753 in his pocket. Feeling invincible doesn't mean you can't feel sadness, though, and Isaac cried all the way to Los Angeles, covering the yellow blanket his mother had made for him as a parting gift with his tears.

The flight attendants who tried to comfort the young man were right to be concerned. His American dream turned out to be a nightmare. The $753 his mother had laboriously pieced together by borrowing from her brothers evaporated in the Californian heat in just a fraction of the time it had taken to collect. In desperation, Isaac tried the approach that had worked in Tehran, walking everywhere asking for work. But LA is no city for a pedestrian and his long hikes on the smoggy streets between gas stations, stores, and restaurants brought him nothing but blisters and sunburn.

This was not the America he expected from the Hollywood movies he'd seen on shared TVs in Tehran as a child.

The combination of no money and very little help eventually became too much to bear. And Isaac, feeling utterly lost, found himself in tears sitting on the hot pavement outside Spires restaurant, which had just become the latest place to tell him "Sorry, no." Then he felt a hand on his shoulder and heard a single word that, like Andrew Grove when he crossed the Austrian border, would change his life. The word was a question, "Iranian?" And the speaker was the chef from the restaurant, who had been listening to Isaac's pleading with the manager for a job.

In Iran, Isaac had been part of a discriminated minority. In LA, he was recognized just as a fellow Iranian, with no stigma attached. Looking up through eyes blurry with tears, he nodded to the chef, who told him "Come back here tonight after we've closed, and I'll cook you liver and onions." Isaac, who hadn't eaten a proper meal in weeks, gratefully accepted. And when he returned, the chef, almost apologetically, made him an offer, "Look, the only job we have is a graveyard shift washing dishes, it pays $1.65 an hour." When you feel like your life is over, discovering you're only in the graveyard rather than already under the ground is a feeling of overwhelming relief. Isaac's eyes lit up; earning $1.65 seemed like a dream coming true.

That job was the start of Isaac Larian's American dream. From washing dishes, he was promoted to being a busboy and then a waiter, using English skills he picked up from watching TV. Saving his meager earnings, he put himself through a civil engineering program at Los Angeles Southwest College. But his ambitions lay elsewhere, "I knew I was meant to be an entrepreneur. It's what I learned working in my father's shop in Iran."

Isaac's entrepreneurial journey began by selling imported Asian brass products from out of his apartment in LA. He moved from that into imported electronics, and by the late 1980s, he was the first official American distributor of Nintendo's Game and Watch handheld video games. From there he moved into toys, which became the serious money earner for his company, MGA Entertainment, especially after the launch in 2001 of the "anti-Barbie" Bratz dolls, which became a multi-billion-dollar global success.

Becoming a billionaire was not the end of Isaac's troubles, however. Just as he'd had to face the biggest kid on the block in Tehran, in America, he found himself targeted by Mattel, the makers of Barbie and market leaders in the doll world. Being sued by Barbie nearly ruined him, but thanks perhaps to the toughness he learned in the Iranian slums, he's fought through everything to remain at the top of the game. Today, MGA Entertainment, the company founded by an Iranian immigrant who once wept with joy to earn $1.65 an hour, is the largest privately owned toy company in the world.

And through all his success, Isaac Larian has never forgotten his roots or the people who helped make him. He still has the yellow blanket his mother gave him when he left for Los Angeles. And, just once in a while, he still returns to Spires restaurant (founded by a Greek immigrant) for a plate of liver and onions to remind him of the kindness that set him on his way in the States.

The scale of Larian's success makes his story exceptional, but in another way it illustrates some of the common threads that run through the stories of so many immigrant entrepreneurs. Of course, not all grow up with the level of hardship he faced, but many do. And many, like him, are motivated by dreams of another country that are cruelly shown to not match reality when they finally arrive there.

I strongly associate with that from my own experience as a child fleeing from my native Bulgaria to neighboring Turkey. As members of a centuries-old Turkish ethnic minority, we carried within us dreams of the land our ancestors had left behind. But unlike Larian, whose image of America came from Hollywood movies, our pictures of Turkey were a kind of folk memory, transfigured by the passage of time.

"Istanbul," my grandmother would tell us, "is the greatest city in the world, built by the sultans of fairytales; there water flows from faucets made of gold and the people walk on streets paved with marble." When we arrived in Istanbul, fleeing from the Bulgarian communist government's "Process of Rebirth," which aimed to wipe away any traces of Turkish-ness from Bulgaria, the contrast between her words and the world we found was stark. I searched in vain for the golden faucets, in fact even finding running water from a regular faucet was hard enough; with none in our home, we had to walk every day to the neighborhood mosque to fill our plastic buckets. And the streets we walked to get there were not paved with marble. In fact, they were not paved at all. The marble, it seemed, had long since been removed, or never existed in the first place.

Many years later, when I visited the Ellis Island National Museum of Immigration in New York, I was struck by how our experience as refugees in Turkey in the 1990s resonated with the experiences of the millions who had crossed the Atlantic to seek new lives in America. A quote written on the wall there caught my eye, attributed to an unknown Italian immigrant:

"I came to America because I heard the streets were paved with gold. When I got here, I found out three things: First, the streets weren't paved with gold; second, they weren't paved at all; and third, I was expected to pave them."

Traditionally, academics would classify the stories of Isaac Larian, my family, and many other immigrants who found that the reality of a new country didn't match their dreams as examples of the phenomenon of "necessity entrepreneurship." That's the idea that immigrants become entrepreneurs because they don't have other options in the land they just arrived in, where they often lack connections, language skills, or recognized qualifications.

As you'll soon see, I am not a fan of overly focusing on necessity entrepreneurship because it is a rather simplistic way to categorize many immigrant entrepreneurs who *did* have other options (Larian, after all, was a qualified civil engineer, who chose entrepreneurship). But because it plays such a prominent role in the literature, it seems like an appropriate place to start our review of what academics say about immigrant entrepreneurship. I've organized that review under the headings of the five main themes that I see in that literature: necessity entrepreneurship; immigrant entrepreneurs' skills, resources, and capabilities; their personality traits; the influence of family; and the importance of ethnic ties and networks.

But before getting into each of those disparate themes, I'd like to highlight something that links them all together. It's an observable fact that immigrants are more entrepreneurial than people who still live in the country where they were born. But, regrettably, most of the literature on immigrant entrepreneurship only focuses on explaining why they are so entrepreneurial without going beyond that to ask why they build businesses that last and make an impact. Nevertheless, before getting on to how we can answer that most important question, let's see what the existing research says about the forces that turn immigrants into entrepreneurs.

Necessity Entrepreneurship

Answers to the question of why immigrants are so entrepreneurial can basically be divided into two main categories: the disadvantage theory and the cultural theory. The disadvantage theory says that immigrants' positions in their new host countries tend to be so poor that they are forced into entrepreneurship for lack of other options, the phenomenon referred to as necessity entrepreneurship. The cultural theory approaches the same question from a more positive perspective, looking at how specific traits make immigrants more likely to open their own companies and influence the types of industries that they tend to go into. But let's start with necessity entrepreneurship first.

The central idea at the heart of necessity entrepreneurship is very neatly and directly stated in one of the questions in the survey of the Global Entrepreneurship Monitor (GEM): "Are you involved in this start-up to take advantage of a business opportunity or because you have no better choices for work?" This casts necessity entrepreneurship as the opposite of opportunity entrepreneurship (i.e., choosing to pursue an opportunity you have spotted rather than being forced to look for any opportunity that you can find). Necessity entrepreneurship occurs when barriers to entering the local labor market are insurmountably high, forcing immigrants to search for other options. Such barriers can come from things like discrimination, a lack of language skills, or the absence of recognized qualifications in a new country.

Necessity entrepreneurship has something of a bad name, being associated more with the limitations that immigrants face rather than the positives that they bring. When thinking of immigrants forced into entrepreneurship, the popular imagination might conjure up images of people with few resources trying to eke a living out of a very small business that generates marginal profits and has a limited economic impact. I would argue that the theory of necessity entrepreneurship deserves its bad name, being both unfairly pejorative and overly crude. Of course, I'm not saying that immigrants are never forced into entrepreneurship by their limited resources and lack of other opportunities. But what I am saying is that the idea of necessity entrepreneurship is applied to far too many cases, obscuring the various options that immigrants do have (and create for themselves) and leading to too much of a focus on what immigrants lack rather than what they add.

To truly understand the origins of entrepreneurial activity among immigrants, we need to move away from overly simplistic notions of necessity and do more to examine individual characteristics, the support and resources available within social and ethnic networks, and labor market dynamics in their host countries. These factors are intricately linked with broader migration motives and strategies, which influence both the types of industries that immigrants are likely to enter and the business models that they are likely to use.

During immigrants' entrepreneurial journeys, there's a frequent initial tendency to establish businesses that serve their own ethnic communities. Such decisions are typically influenced by familiarity and perceived lower uncertainty. Moreover, immigrants often leverage their unique competencies to compete effectively in markets with low entry barriers. However, as migration patterns and the global business landscape evolve, so too does the diversity of immigrant-led business ventures. This shift challenges traditional views and stereotypes about immigrant entrepreneurship, suggesting a broader, more nuanced understanding is necessary to appreciate the full scope of their economic contributions and the challenges they face. Let's move into that discussion by looking at what the literature has to say about more positive aspects of immigrant entrepreneurs—the skills, resources, and capabilities that they bring to their new homes.

The Skills, Resources, and Capabilities of Immigrant Entrepreneurs

When Hamdi first left his remote home in northeastern Turkey for New York, he must have felt like he was entering a new world where nothing he had learned before had any value. The world that he came from was once the cradle of civilization, the land between the rivers Euphrates and Tigris that was known as the Fertile Crescent because of its fecundity. By the time Hamdi was born into a Kurdish shepherd family on an uncertain date sometime in 1972, the fertility was long gone. His family and everyone he knew eked out a semi-nomadic living herding sheep and goats along the banks of the river and up the dry mountain paths in search of pasture. When he moved to Long Island in New York to study English in 1994, Hamdi was confronted by a world of concrete, crowds, ever-flowing rivers of traffic, and stores offering a dizzying array of products that could take hours to navigate. Although none of the seeming infinity of mass-produced options could match the simple and wholesome flavors of the yogurts and cheeses that he had taken for granted back home.

Lost in this new world, Hamdi found himself struggling in his English classes when asked to write an assignment about something he knew. Searching for something familiar, he instinctively thought of home and wrote an essay about making cheese, something he'd started to learn even before he knew how to write. I don't know how well Hamdi wrote his assignment, whether it was full of errors or what grade it got. But by one very important metric, it was probably one of the greatest essays ever written because it ultimately was the steppingstone that turned Hamdi Ulukaya into a billionaire.

His teacher was astounded by Hamdi's knowledge of dairy farming, a skill that few in the United States had but which for Hamdi was as natural as operating a TV remote was for an American. Hamdi's story shows how immigrants don't just bring a wide range of skills that are, for whatever reason, scarce within their new host country. Initially, those skills only earned Hamdi free accommodation on his teacher's farm in Upstate New York in return for helping to take care of the cows, shoveling manure, and making cheese. But over time, he realized that the special skills that he brought could be turned into a business after he spotted an opportunity in the market. A visit from his dad, who was shocked by the terrible quality of the feta in the United States, inspired Hamdi to think: Why not bring the dairy products he loved from home to the U.S. market to see if there was an appetite for the taste he loved?

Initially, Hamdi tried what seemed like the simpler option: importing feta cheese from Turkey. But the complexities of international trade meant that he struggled just to break even. After two challenging years, he made the bold decision to purchase a defunct yogurt factory that had been abandoned by Kraft Foods. His attorney and business advisor tried to persuade the struggling entrepreneur to stay away from the big investment. But Hamdi went ahead anyway, and by 2007, his new company Chobani (its name inspired by the Turkish word for shepherd: *çoban*) was born. Its first sales were a few hundred crates of yogurt to a grocer on Long Island, the same part of New York where Hamdi had first studied. By 2012, he was making more than $1 billion in annual sales.

We will return to the story of Hamdi Ulukaya and his business philosophy later as it has much to say about how the attitudes, innovations, and community spirit of immigrant entrepreneurs lead to success. But for now, let us just focus on what it shows us about why immigrants become entrepreneurs. In contrast to the claims of the necessity entrepreneurship theory, Hamdi's story shows how immigrant entrepreneurs can spot opportunities to make use of the skill sets that they bring, especially when those skills, which might be common and unremarkable back home, are scarce in their new home.

The current research on immigrant entrepreneurship[2] has, rightly, picked up on the issue of immigrants' skills and resources. But in my opinion, it still does not go far enough into a full understanding of the complexities of the issue. For example, it fails to go beyond looking at why immigrants' unique skills encourage them to set up businesses to identifying how those skills help those businesses to survive and thrive in the long term, a topic that I will have much more to say about in subsequent chapters.

The existing research also fails to recognize the complexities that characterize the relationships between immigrants' skills and the places where they put them to use when building new businesses. Or to put it another way, immigrants' identities and their entrepreneurial decisions are influenced by a complex interplay of cultural, social, and economic factors that derive from their original, adopted, and other contexts. For example, when my own family arrived in Turkey as refugees from Bulgaria, we found opportunities that existed because of the connections we were able to make in other post-communist countries in the wake of the fall of the Berlin Wall. In other words, the shared identity that came from the common experience of communism helped to forge connections in third places beyond our host country, and those connections became the foundation of our success. In an increasingly globalized world, opportunities for new businesses are not limited to their host countries. This complexity, and the special ways in which immigrant entrepreneurs navigate it, is another issue that I will return to throughout this book.

Finally, some of the research on why immigrants are more entrepreneurial looks at the issue of their skills in the context of selective immigration policies. Such studies argue that differences in immigrants' and natives' tendencies toward entrepreneurship can be explained by governments' decisions to permit only the most talented people to come and settle. There is obviously some truth to the argument that selective immigration policies will lead to a pool of more highly qualified immigrants. But, as the stories of many of the immigrant entrepreneurs that we will consider here show, the immigrants who have gone on to demonstrate the greatest entrepreneurial abilities were not necessarily permitted to enter their new host country because of exceptional talents they had shown at home. For example, neither Isaac Larian nor Hamdi Ulukaya had achieved anything before coming to America that would even hint at the successes they would enjoy. When trying to explain the roots of immigrants' tendencies toward entrepreneurship (and their likelihood to be more successful than natives) we must look further than selective immigration policies for answers.

Personality Traits

Another aspect that features heavily in the current research is how immigrants' personalities influence their decisions to pursue entrepreneurship. One particular personality trait that has been much discussed is immigrants' predisposition toward taking risks. The logic here seems straightforward: a willingness to stake everything on a move to an unfamiliar land suggests a mindset that is comfortable with risk. Certainly, the ability to tolerate risk is a prerequisite for entering the world of entrepreneurship, where 90% of new startups fail, with 10% not even making it through their first year.

There are, however, a few problems with the argument that immigrants are always people who have chosen the riskier path of pursuing a new life in another country. Most significantly, it ignores the experiences of the very many people who migrated only when they had no other choice. As the British Somali poet Warsan Shire put it in her poem "Home," "No one leaves home unless / home is the mouth of a shark / you only run for the border / when you see the whole city running as well."[3] Still, perhaps even in such cases, the experience of being forced to run to save your life might make you more inclined to take risks in other parts of your life in the future.

Other personality traits that have been prominently discussed in the literature include adaptability and being comfortable with uncertainty and operating in multiple cultures concurrently. Immigrants' cross-cultural experiences and knowledge often provide the foundations for their businesses as we have already seen with Hamdi Ulukaya. Another example of how products and services are influenced by overseas experiences comes from Starbucks, which changed its business model and kickstarted its world dominance under new owner Howard Schultz after his trips to Italy inspired him with a new vision for coffee culture in the United States. Schultz himself, incidentally, descends from an immigrant family of Ashkenazi Jews in New York.

Other personality traits that featured heavily include courage, willpower, and positivity. Interestingly, some of the literature highlights the role that family plays in transmitting such personality traits and important values to immigrant entrepreneurs. And it is to the more general influence of family on immigrant entrepreneurship that we turn next.

The Influence of Family

Another characteristic of many immigrant entrepreneurs, or at least those coming to the West from other cultures, is their generally closer-knit family ties. These familial connections impact their entrepreneurial experiences in various ways and have been much commented on in the literature. For example, much emphasis has been placed on the fact that most immigrant enterprises are family-owned or at least start small. One recent study of a wide variety of papers about immigrant entrepreneurship in different contexts found that family was a common thread running through much of the immigrant entrepreneur experience. Of the articles examined in that study, 94% showed that family played key roles in identifying opportunities (think of Hamdi Ulukaya's dad expressing his displeasure at the taste of the feta cheese in America), providing funding, working for the new company, acting as role models, or providing a cultural influence that impacts the work of the entrepreneur.[4]

In keeping with the important roles families play in immigrant entrepreneurship, immigrant entrepreneurs are more likely than their native-born peers to hold on to their companies until they retire so that they can pass them on to their families. They are also more likely to say that they created their businesses to be closer to their families and provide jobs for family members rather than to seek public recognition.

Such research has been quoted as an indication that family is an important factor motivating immigrants to become entrepreneurs. But, again, few studies have focused on the strength that families add to immigrant entrepreneurs' businesses. And none, until now, have looked at what all entrepreneurs can learn from the ways in which immigrants use family and other ties to build businesses that last.

The experience of my own company and my previous research on family businesses have shown that immigrant entrepreneurs do not restrict their notions of family to their blood relatives. Therefore, the final main issue emerging from the literature on immigrant entrepreneurship is the important role played by ethnic ties and networks.

Ethnic Ties and Networks

When the Hollywood actress Tippi Hedren (star of Alfred Hitchcock's *The Birds*) visited Hope Village, a Vietnamese refugee camp in California, in 1975, she could hardly have guessed that her nails were about to inspire a business revolution. The ladies in the camp almost certainly didn't know the star from her movie career, but they were highly impressed by her manicure, to such an extent that Hedren arranged for Dusty Coots, her personal manicurist, to visit the camp and help teach 20 of the Vietnamese women the trade. With further support from Hedren, the 20 trainees subsequently established their initial businesses in locations across southern California. From that small start 50 years ago, Vietnamese Americans currently run 50% of all the salons in the United States' billion-dollar nail industry.[5]

The term that researchers use to explain the reasons why the Vietnamese came to dominate the nail industry is *homophily*, which is basically an academic way of saying "birds of a feather flock together." The networks that naturally form between people who come from the same background and speak the same language translate into safety nets for new migrants, offering them opportunities for work. For immigrant entrepreneurs, their networks provide them with potential customers and staff, and when those staff have been trained and gained experience, some of them go off and create their own businesses and replicate the model of searching for staff among the people in their well-established ethnic networks.

As with the first Vietnamese manicurists or the female Syrian entrepreneurs featured in Andrew Leon Hanna's *25 Million Sparks*,[6] these networks can be forged in the pressured environment of refugee camps, which bring people of the same ethnicity together in challenging contexts that can act as a stimulus for creative entrepreneurship. Or they can be created in those neighborhoods that become home to many people of the same ethnicity as new arrivals are drawn to the areas where people from their home country already live (the many Chinatowns and similar that we find in cities all around the world). The same phenomenon can also be witnessed in high-tech industries, with the clustering of Indian and Chinese entrepreneurs in Silicon Valley. Previous research has focused on the roles that immigrant entrepreneurs' strong networks play in overcoming challenges like limited access to opportunities and financial resources.

This all helps to explain not only why immigrants become entrepreneurs but also why they are more likely to enter certain fields in which members of their own ethnic group are already well established. But now let's turn to the big issue that the research tells us very little about.

The Big Gap in the Literature: Why Are Immigrant Entrepreneurs So Successful?

As we have seen, academic research has many interesting things to tell us about the reasons why immigrants become entrepreneurs. Major factors that researchers have identified include necessity; the skills, resources, and capabilities immigrants bring; the influences of their families; and the ethnic ties and networks that can help guide people into particular fields. But, as I have repeatedly highlighted, the literature has much less to say about why immigrants are so successful (and even less to say about what we can all learn from that). When statistics clearly show the long-term success of immigrant-founded and -managed businesses, ignoring the reasons why seems to be an enormous oversight.

To answer the question of why immigrant entrepreneurs outperform their native-born counterparts, I studied a group of more than 50 such entrepreneurs[7] whose diversity of experience is linked by the common threads of their immigrant origins and their subsequent success. To make the connections between immigrant entrepreneurship and business longevity, I generally focused on individuals who have built businesses that have lasted at least 15 years (although some of the companies studied are more than a century old). Fifteen years may not seem a long time when thinking about business longevity, but the advantage is that I could still speak to the founders who could give the real story of how their business was built (something that can't usually be achieved when the company is already more than 100 years old).

Also, as I argue repeatedly throughout this book, the true mark of longevity is not how long your company lasts but how long your impact does, and many of these even relatively new firms have already changed the world in ways that will persist far into the foreseeable future even if the company closes its doors tomorrow. In fact, when I started my research, I set out to understand the principles of business longevity, but halfway through my interviews, it became clear to me that NONE of the entrepreneurs I was interviewing were concerned with creating a "business that lasts." They wanted to make an impact, to leave a legacy, to be of use, and bring value to the world.

Reflecting the diversity of the immigrant entrepreneur experience, the companies I studied spanned a great range of industries from beauty and entertainment to restaurants, real estate, and tech. They also cover a diversity of sizes, from mega-corporations to boutique fashion and jewelry houses. Studying these companies and the people behind them took me on many journeys, from the Far and Middle East to Central Asia, West Africa, Eastern Europe, South and Central America, and many places in the United States, taking in just a few of the many contexts from which immigrant entrepreneurs come and in which they successfully operate.

Despite being a successful immigrant entrepreneur myself, and an academic expert in entrepreneurship, what I learned from my research surprised and even shocked me. Time and time again, the immigrant entrepreneurs I studied and spoke with emphasized the importance of elements of business practice that don't appear in any of the standard texts on business longevity. I was excited to make these discoveries, but they also filled me with doubts. Could it be that the conventional wisdom on creating long-term success was missing some fundamental elements?

I had to find the answer to that question. To verify that what I was learning from these entrepreneurs would still work in the real world of today, I took the principles I derived from my research and applied them with a group of contemporary startup founders. Some of those founders were my students at Oxford, others were people I either advise or have invested in; all of them were linked by the fact they had just created companies and were looking for the secrets that would turn their startups into well-established firms.

The verification process was even more exciting than doing the initial research as I got to share my findings with the startup founders and witness in real time the difference those findings made to their businesses. What I learned from that process has given me the confidence to formulate the eight principles of success, which I share in Part II of this book. Of course, none of these things guarantee success, but every one of them has contributed significantly to the success of the least-studied but most successful group of entrepreneurs of our times: immigrants. Every one of them is worth considering and trying to see if it works for you in your own business now. And, as you will discover, each of the principles questions the conventional wisdom on immigrant entrepreneurship and business longevity in ways that could have radical implications for how people build companies that last.

But before turning to that, I want to reemphasize an important caveat. In this book, I am not promising a foolproof path to business longevity. Any research, no matter how robust, always has limitations. And no principles written down on paper are worth much until you try to put them into action for yourself, so you can see what works for you and refine the way you use it so that it suits the particular and ever-changing circumstances of your own company.

When writing these caveats, I'm reminded of the words of Larry Liu, the founder of Weee! whom you'll read much more about later. "There are so many management books, and so many wise people out there. They give talks. Can you really learn from that? … It's just one piece of information. When I read a book now, I see it as one data point, one piece of information. I have to actually do it or be in the process of doing it, then revisit the concept I learned on paper and try to connect that concept to my real experience to make it part of my own. But without the doing part, the information is just a piece of information, nothing more."[8]

So, please remember when reading the principles that follow that each is just one data point. They are distilled from the experience of some of the most successful immigrant entrepreneurs in the world, they have been tested with real startups that have found them to work, and they are presented here so that that everyone can benefit from them. But it's down to you to try them out in your own business to see what works for you, retain what does, and refine, or reject, what doesn't. And please let me know what you find, because I'd love to hear about your lived experience of these principles so that together we can improve them to keep helping businesses make impacts that change the world. And in that spirit of openness and collaboration to make the world a better place, I give you the eight principles of business longevity from immigrant entrepreneurs.

II

Exploration: The 8 Principles

1989, Crossing

My life is a borrowed whisper—
an accent pieced together,
like the chocolates I once stole
when even bread was a splurge.

In 1989, under Istanbul's scornful gaze,
my mother counted pennies for bread,
her hands hopeful, shaping our future.

My life: a series of border lines,
tangled tongues, misunderstood names.
Home? A ghost that never quite solidifies,
a haunting echoed in my misspoken words.

Every year, my identity—
borrowed, reinvented, tested.
I've learned to navigate these crossings,
crafting survival from necessity.
Do you recognize my accent?
It's one I've had to steal to survive.

—Neri Karra Sillaman

4

Principle 1: Be a Bridge Across Cultures

Beauvais, France, 1994

Thhwacckk! Hssss! "Owww!"

Again! It had happened again! There Dominique was, minding his own business as usual, carefully rolling out croissant dough on the pastry board, when it happened again, a great big whack on the side of his head with a heated spatula. "Owww!" he screamed as he felt the blow and then the burn and whirled round to face the assailant who was, once again, the same sadistic, always snarling sous-chef who had taken an intense dislike to the young newcomer.

Perhaps fortunately, it was not the first time life had dealt Dominique a few knocks around the head. Born in the 1970s into a working-class family in the unglamorous French town of Beauvais, just over an hour north of Paris, the aspiring pastry chef had had a tough upbringing. He left school at 15 to help provide for his family who struggled in the second half of each month to put food on the table.

The free culinary school in Beauvais was supposed to be Dominique's route out of that poverty, but at first, it just presented him with more problems.

53

The work experience element of the program had placed him in that small local restaurant where the cruel sous-chef led the bullying, which started with name-calling and progressed to physical violence—blows with the hot spatula and even cuts with knives. At times, Dominique was treated as roughly as a piece of dough being twisted and bashed into shape. But the teenager was made of stern stuff: "Quitting was not an option," he later reflected on the abuse. "You stick with it no matter what."

Relief came when the restaurant changed hands and the new owner took Dominique under his wing and taught him how to prepare food with love and care. The young pastry chef was soon ready to fly. His first overseas opportunity came as a result of France's mandatory military service, which he chose to do as a cook in French Guiana (not far from where Mohamad Ali, whom we met in Chapter 2, grew up in the independent country of Guyana). After his service, he spent a year there on a community program, teaching local people the skills that he had learned in culinary school.

Returning from the South American rainforest to Beauvais, Dominique's horizons had been expanded and he decided it was time to move again and learn more skills for himself. He bought a car for $1,000 and he headed to Paris with a firm conviction in his mind: "I was just a young kid from a small town, [but] I knew what I wanted to do, I wanted to learn from the best." Like Charles Worth 150 years before him, Dominique arrived in Paris not knowing a soul but with a determination to succeed. And like Isaac Larian during his early days in LA, he took himself around to every potential employer he could find, asking for work and leaving resumes at every restaurant and bakery (and in Paris, that means going to a lot of places).

Eventually, his determination was rewarded with a seasonal job at Fauchon, one of the city's oldest patisseries, which was founded in the days when Charles Worth was still the king of Parisian fashion. During seven years there, Dominique rose to be responsible for the patisserie's international expansion, helping to set up new shops in locations ranging from Russia to Kuwait.

Confident in the skills he learned at Fauchon, and with his eyes open to international possibilities, Dominique decided his next move would be to emigrate to the immigrant city par excellence, New York, where he worked under the celebrated French chef Daniel Boulud, best known for his twice-Michelin-starred restaurant Daniel. But Dominique did not settle for even such a high-profile post, and, inspired by his own entrepreneurial spirit, he set out to make his own bakery where he would rise or fall on his own merits.

At first, it felt like he was going from the Michelin stars to the gutter, literally. Squeezed by expensive Manhattan rent and tight margins, Dominique and his girlfriend did everything themselves with a remit that went far beyond making pastries to encompass fixing broken generators and cleaning toilets. It was a struggle, as Dominique told me when I interviewed him for this book:

> Back when I opened up the Bakery in 2011, New York was all about cheesecake and cupcakes. A lot of people told me a French-stye bakery would never make it. But I had envisioned a French bakery that was modern and welcoming, and I described it as "not having any chandeliers."

Then, on Mother's Day 2013, everything changed.

Deciding to put out a special that he hoped might lure a few extra customers to the bakery, Dominique came up with a culinary creation that mixed his native culture with that of his new home. From the Mother's Day liaison of the French croissant and the American donut, a love child was born: the Cronut. Soon there were daily lines around the block to pay homage to the newborn, which spoke to the local people's love of French food and their home-grown cuisine. With a new flavor introduced every month, Dominique continued to innovate in ways that combined flavors from different cultures with his French American base.

The Cronut craze eventually got so strong that Dominique was forced to hire security to manage the crowds, and his cross-cultural creation received rave reviews on shows ranging from *Good Morning America*[1] to *Late Night with Jimmy Fallon*.[2] *Time* magazine celebrated it as one of the "25 best inventions of 2013,"[3] the *New York Post* called Dominique "the Willy Wonka of NYC,"[4] and the World's 50 Best Restaurant awards named the humble boy from Beauvais as the "World's Best Pastry Chef"[5] in 2017. But despite all the accolades and success, Dominique has never forgotten what it felt like to grow up in a family that couldn't always put food on the table, which is why sales of the Cronut have helped raise hundreds of thousands of dollars for charities fighting hunger in New York City.

Bridging Cultures: The Superpower of the Immigrant Entrepreneur

The story of Dominique Ansel and the Cronut is the perfect way to start our examination of how immigrant entrepreneurs enjoy success by bridging and mixing cultures. And that's not only because of the success the Cronut has enjoyed but also because food itself is a wonderful example of how different cultures are always combining to create fabulous new things. On the subject of food and culture, we've already talked about Hamdi Ulukaya's Turkish yogurts being made in Upstate New York; other examples of dishes that have combined different worlds to become iconic range from Tex-Mex cuisine to the meal that has been called "the U.K.'s national dish:" chicken tikka masala (an Indian recipe adapted to British tastes).

Just as culinary fusion can create something so cherished that it becomes part of a national identity, immigrant entrepreneurs are uniquely well-placed to mix different cultural elements in all sorts of fields to create innovations that consumers love. The ability to be a bridge between cultures is a superpower of the immigrant entrepreneur. And many of the entrepreneurs that we meet in this book have deployed that superpower to great effect, building businesses that take something from one culture and make it work in another.

Some do that by combining two distinct cultural elements into something new as Dominique Ansel did with the Cronut. Describing that process to me, he said:

> For me, my understanding of pastry is rooted in French technique and so it is always honoring those roots. The innovation comes in applying the same techniques in different ways but it's foundations and chemistry remain the same.

Other immigrant entrepreneurs import a product from their family's original country but give it a marketing twist to make it work in their new home. An example of the latter approach comes from Numi Organic Tea, the creation of brother-and-sister team Ahmed Rahim and Reem Hassani. Brought up in Cleveland as the children of Iraqi immigrants, the siblings would visit Iraq regularly in the summer and every night when they got home from school, as Reem explained to me when I interviewed her for this book:

> I always used to say that we lived in two worlds. Our house was an Iraqi home, and outside was the American culture. Inside was like a little Iraq. [Our parents] spoke to us only in Arabic because they wanted us to learn the language ... And at the same time, they wanted to integrate with the culture and do well at school. They had flourishing careers outside the home. So, we were surrounded by both worlds.

By the early 1990s, the brother and sister were living far apart (Reem working in California as a teacher and Ahmed running a teahouse in Prague), but their minds were on the same page when they separately but simultaneously came up with a business idea. The inspiration came from their childhood trips to Baghdad, where they would drink a steeped dried desert lime tea that was so common there but unknown in the United States. Often the siblings thought, "Somebody should sell this in the States. It's so different and nothing like this exists." The business idea they had can be summarized as "Why don't we be that somebody?"

The siblings didn't just import Iraqi tea, they also originally maintained the Middle Eastern practice of not putting the leaves into bags as a way of preserving their full flavor. This went against the norm in America, where tea bags were used for greater convenience. But Reem and Ahmed's decision helped maintain the quality of the product and establish it as a connoisseur's choice. However, they did cleverly adapt to the American context in other ways as can be seen through their marketing and their slogan, "Activating Purpose," which resonates with a contemporary American audience. Also, much of their brand identity and packaging is inspired by Reem's work as an artist following her studies at the Lorenzo de Medici Art Institute in Florence and in JFK University's Arts and Consciousness Studies course in California. Mixing such disparate influences, the siblings have created a brand that has its roots in the tea culture of the Iraqi desert but appeals all over the United States.

A third category of immigrant entrepreneurs starts by importing goods from their original home country and then moves on to creating fusion products that combine qualities from there and their new homes. A great example of that comes from the British Indian businessman Karan Bilimoria. Born into a Zoroastrian Parsi family in Hyderabad, Bilimoria moved to England for his studies and organized Cambridge University's polo team's first tour of India. During the tour, he noticed how superior the Indian-made polo sticks were to the ones being used by the Cambridge students, and he enjoyed his first business success importing them to sell in the U.K.

Polo sticks, however, are never likely to be more than a niche concern, so Bilimoria branched out into another field that has a much broader appeal in the U.K.—beer. But his Cobra Beer brand did not try to take on the behemoths of the British brewing industry directly. Instead, Bilimoria cleverly crafted a product that mixed Britain and India and was designed to appeal to the U.K.'s flourishing Indian restaurant market. And the origins of that idea and his subsequent business were, as he told me:

> … very much based on my feeling equally at home in India as I do in the U.K. And that feeling comfortable with both countries and wanting to put both countries together was the genesis of my business because Cobra Beer is very much an Indo-British brand. I came up with the idea in the U.K. I manufactured first in India. It's a beer of Indian origin. I'm somebody from India, born in India, brought up in India, lived here [in the U.K.]. So, that living bridge concept. I'm very much like my own product, if you know what I mean.

This is yet one more example of how immigrant entrepreneurs act as cultural bridges and can use that position to either import products from one context to another or create fusions that take inspiration from one place to create something that works in another market.

These stories also illustrate how some of the immigrant entrepreneurs who have acted as cross-cultural bridges only came to their new country as adults, like Dominique Ansel. Whereas others, like Ahmed Rahim and Reem Hassani, were second-generation migrants, brought up in the land that their parents moved to. People who lived from childhood onward in a country different from the one where their parents grew up are most likely to face the challenges that come from the feeling of being caught between two cultures but perhaps also best placed to act as bridges in ways that enable them to create something new and activate entrepreneurial success. The challenges and opportunities that come with that aspect of the immigrant experience are neatly encapsulated by the Indian Canadian writer Rupi Kaur:

> being an immigrant is a funny little thing. i grew up … teeter-tottering
> two very different worlds … [and] i realized being an immigrant feels
> like being a bridge between both countries. i can't fully step into and
> just belong to one. i'm somewhere in the middle. being an immigrant is
> being the bridge between the last generation and the next. and damn.
> that's a beautiful thing.[6]

However, although such immigrant entrepreneurs are particularly likely to possess the cultural bridge superpower, sometimes people who have not emigrated at all can enjoy similar successes by adapting products encountered on their travels for the markets back home. An example of that comes from the Austrian businessman Dietrich Mateschitz, who discovered when jet lagged on a trip to Thailand in the 1980s a local energizing drink named Krating Daeng, a favorite of Thai truck drivers. The drink not only cured his jet lag but also made him a billionaire after he adapted it for the alternative clubbing scene back home where he sold it, with great success, as Red Bull.

Mateschitz's story reminds us that the principles that drive the success of immigrant entrepreneurs can be applied to great effect by anybody who is open-minded enough. The transition from being a bridge to creating a successful business is divided into three parts: identifying and developing an opportunity, building the cross-cultural connections that can take advantage of that opportunity, and adapting to the inflection points created by cultural change.

Opportunity Identification and Development

Traditional research on entrepreneurship has placed great emphasis on the importance of entrepreneurs' abilities to spot opportunities to create value. What it hasn't commented on, surprisingly, is the special ability of immigrant entrepreneurs to identify and develop opportunities that their native-born counterparts are oblivious to, even when such opportunities are "hiding in plain sight." In other words, one of the distinct benefits of immigrant entrepreneurs' cross-cultural experiences is that they can look at the same situation as a native-born entrepreneur but see something different. And sometimes, what they see makes their fortune. A great example of this comes from Jane Wurwand.[7]

Jane was born in Edinburgh, Scotland, in the late 1950s into a working-class family which was tragically torn apart when her father died when she was just two years old. As Jane's family struggled during her childhood, her mother always emphasized the importance of learning a trade that would enable her to earn money wherever she went. Following that advice, Jane trained as a beautician, beginning her career as a "Saturday girl" working part-time in a local salon. One day, during one of those long, gray summers that the U.K. specializes in, Jane spotted an ad looking for beauticians to go work in sunny South Africa. Answering the ad was the first major step on the road to changing her life. In South Africa, she refined her skills and cultivated the knowledge that would help her when she made her next move—to the United States.

Arriving in the United States, Jane began to spot opportunities that were, literally, staring her in the face: American beauty salons were big on makeup but placed no emphasis on skincare. And then she realized there were no American-made salon products; everything was being imported from Europe. Drawing on her experience from the U.K. and South Africa, Jane recognized the possibilities that existed in the United States and realized that there was a huge opportunity to "teach how to do skincare correctly and … sell this equipment to the people that we're training."

So, in 1986, when Jane was just 28, Dermalogica was born with an initial investment of just $14,000. Interestingly, looking back, Jane attributes her ability to spot the opportunity to the fact that she was an immigrant:

> We did the classic immigrant thing where [we] look[ed] at the population [and said] it takes 1% of the population to buy one product and it's already enormous, bigger than it ever could be in the U.K.

Jane started by selling to her own students in the beauty salons, and in their first year, she sold more than $1 million worth of products to that market. And that was just the start. By 2015, when Jane sold the brand to Unilever, Dermalogica had risen to become the number-one skincare brand not just in the United States but in the world. Jane has continued to use her experience as an immigrant entrepreneur to inspire others through her nonprofit FOUND/LA, which provides funding, education, and mentorship for aspiring entrepreneurs in her adopted home of Los Angeles. She was also appointed the U.S. Global Ambassador for Entrepreneurship by President Obama. Not bad for the Saturday girl from Edinburgh.

As we have seen, cross-cultural experiences can increase people's ability to spot opportunities and develop ideas that will take advantage of those opportunities. Living in different cultures exposes them to different solutions to customer problems, which they can then transfer to new contexts in the form of innovative products and services. Of course, as I have highlighted previously with the examples of Red Bull and (in the previous chapter) Starbucks, you don't have to be an emigrant to take advantage of such opportunities, but it helps.

My own research on this topic shows that entrepreneurs identify opportunities in three ways. The first is through active search, where the entrepreneur chooses to use their superior ability to scan the environment for gaps in the market (as we saw with the case of Hamdi Ulukaya and Chobani). The second is passive search, which can also be termed *fortuitous discovery*, where an entrepreneur is not looking for an opportunity but stumbles upon one that is obvious to them thanks to their specific experiences and knowledge (which is what happened with Isaac Larian and Bratz dolls).

Finally, entrepreneurs can use their imagination and creativity to identify an opportunity that is not immediately obvious to anyone (for example, Dominique Ansel's creation of the Cronut). Immigrant entrepreneurs, as we have seen, particularly excel at creatively combining resources from different contexts to make something new that works. However, it's important to remember that the academic classification of three types of opportunity identification does not necessarily match the messiness of the real world; in reality, all three elements often combine and the process of spotting an opportunity can move back and forth between imagination, active search, and fortuitous discoveries.

The way in which entrepreneurs move messily between the three types of opportunity identification is neatly illustrated by the story of Larry Liu, the founder of America's largest online Asian grocery store Weee! Liu's journey began with a sort of fortuitous discovery; when he was a student in China, he attended a talk by a representative of EachNet, an online retailer founded by Harvard-educated Chinese students who had been inspired to bring the eBay model to their home country. After the talk, Liu decided to start selling on EachNet as a hobby. After he emigrated to the

United States to work as an engineer for Andrew Grove's old company Intel, Liu maintained that hobby on eBay itself. And as his interest in business deepened, what started as a bit of fun was generating enough money to pay for his entire MBA studies.

The advent of WeChat was a cultural change that created opportunities as it facilitated the formation of groups of Chinese immigrants interested in bulk buying products from home that were hard to get or expensive in the United States. By now, Larry was actively looking for his own business idea and was able to use his creativity and cross-cultural knowledge to create a platform that acted as the infrastructure for social messaging groups in the same way as Amazon provides an infrastructure for e-commerce.

Basically, Larry combined cross-cultural inspiration from Amazon, Walmart Grocery, and the types of Chinese e-commerce practices that were common on WeChat and other online retailers like Pinduoduo to create Weee! in 2015. In 2017, he pivoted away from facilitating group buying to providing a comprehensive delivery service for Asian groceries, ranging from food to skincare. Within just five years, and supercharged by the COVID-19 lockdowns, the California-based startup was generating hundreds of millions of dollars in revenue. (The company's unusual name, incidentally, comes from the happy noise Liu's young daughters would make when going down a slide).

It remains important to stress that taking advantage of opportunities can be more complex for immigrant entrepreneurs because those opportunities are likely to lie across international boundaries. In other words, immigrant entrepreneurs like Larry Liu often need international understanding and awareness that is not required in traditional domestic entrepreneurship. We will look at this in more detail in the following section. But, for now, it is sufficient to say that it is precisely because of immigrant entrepreneurs' cross-cultural understanding and awareness that they are better placed to identify opportunities in the first place. They look at something and spot an element that no one else has seen, like a secret door to another world that everybody else is walking straight past.

Of course, the mere fact of having lived in multiple countries is not enough to help the aspiring entrepreneur identify opportunities that will bring success, although it is an advantage. Any entrepreneur still needs to come up with creative insights to turn their stocks of international knowledge into a business that works. They also need to be able to analyze whether an opportunity can be translated across different cultures; obviously, not everything that works in one place will work somewhere else even if it is adapted with the new target market in mind. All of this raises the question of how entrepreneurs, especially those from non-immigrant backgrounds, can develop their cultural knowledge, creativity, and analytical abilities.

Building Cross-Cultural Connections to Take Advantage of the Opportunity

Immigrant entrepreneurs' abilities to act as bridges between cultures don't just help them with identifying an opportunity but also with building the cross-cultural teams, institutions, and partnerships that enable them to take advantage of that opportunity. Thanks to their backgrounds, immigrant entrepreneurs are particularly expert in building ties with partners from different countries that can form complex international supply chains that combine the best elements of the places that they link together.

My research on this subject has shown that there are two key parts to successful collaboration across cultures. First, you have to be able to identify and select the right partners—the people and organizations that have the knowledge and skills you need to make your product or service a success. However, just having the right people in your network is not enough unless you have the right systems and processes in place to coordinate them.

Putting together those systems and processes can be challenging because they often have to deal with information in different languages while also tackling the complexities of cross-cultural communication; even if you understand literally what someone is saying in another language, you may not understand the real meaning that might be hidden beneath the words. Interpreting that meaning can require the sort of detailed cultural knowledge that comes naturally to immigrant entrepreneurs.

Karan Bilimoria's success is also a good example of how cross-cultural connections help to make immigrant entrepreneurs' businesses work. When launching his first business importing polo sticks from India, he worked with a friend from his hometown of Hyderabad and used his own fluency with English culture, which came partly from his studies at Cambridge, to forge sales connections in London. As he put it when recalling those early days as an immigrant entrepreneur:

> I knew from my days running for office at Cambridge that when it comes to selling, there's no shortcut. You have to go door-to-door with your pitch. Soon Harrods and Lillywhites were clients, and we'd expanded into other traditional Indian goods, including leather, silks, and garments.

When Bilimoria made the move from that to create the company that really made his name, Cobra Beer, he benefited from his ability to harness expertise in India and his knowledge of the British market to make a product that would work in the latter. While sitting in a pub in Cambridge, England, he came up with the idea of a less fizzy lager that would team well with Indian food. Then, on a trip to India, he and his business partner were:

> introduced by chance to India's largest independent brewer, in Bangalore. It employed the country's finest brewmaster, an Indian biochemist who had studied in Prague, but it had never exported its product. I seized the opening and explained my idea. The company first suggested that we import two of its brands to the UK: Pals and Knock Out. But the former shared the name of a British dog food, and the latter—suggesting a boxer's punch—wasn't what we had in mind. Amazingly, the company agreed to let us develop our own brand. I already had the taste in my mind; the brewmaster and I just needed to sit in the laboratory and come up with the recipe.[8]

This illustrates so much about how cross-cultural knowledge helps immigrants to develop successful products. For example, it tells us that the brewer himself had once been a migrant, learning his trade in the capital of one of the world's leading beer-producing nations: the Czech Republic. As an Indian himself, Bilimoria was ideally well-placed to create a relationship with the brewery, but his knowledge of England's culture also allowed him to identify that their product names would not work there. Working together, the brewmaster and Bilimoria could combine their different cultural knowledge, from India, the Czech Republic, and the U.K., to produce an Indian version of a European lager that would work in Britain's curry houses. It's a great example of how cross-cultural partnering works to turn an identified opportunity into an exploited one.

The second key part to successful collaboration across cultures is being able to span what academics call the "institutional distance" between them. This refers to how the environments in which a company operates change from one country to another, which can include everything from laws and regulations to consumer preferences. Bridging institutional distance is a key capability for any entrepreneur operating across countries, but again immigrant entrepreneurs are particularly well equipped to do that.

Karan Bilimoria bridged institutional distance by making sure that his Indian-produced beer complied with all of the U.K.'s alcohol production, distribution, and advertising regulations. When he eventually decided to shift brewing operations to the U.K., as part of his efforts to scale up his business, he only did so when it was clear that the customers were choosing his beer because of the taste, which could be replicated elsewhere, rather than because of its country of origin. Again, this shows his understanding of another key aspect of the context in which he was operating—consumer preferences.

Bilimoria's work also exemplifies another way in which immigrant entrepreneurs can build connections that help reduce the institutional distance between different cultures: by literally creating institutions that help countries to do business together in ways that are mutually beneficial. As he told me:

> For 21 years, I've held official positions of chairing UK–India government initiatives. I founded the UK–India Business Council. I was the co-chair of the Indo-British partnership. I've just become the co-chair of the India All-Party Parliamentary Group. So, it [making a bridge between different cultures] is a big part, it is very much the essence of it.

Sir Stelios Haji-Ioannou is the Greek Cypriot founder of the London-based airline easyJet. Haji-Ioannou based the business model for his European low-cost airline on his detailed studies of Southwest Airlines in the United States. Nevertheless, he had to adopt that model to fit in with the different regulatory requirements of the 35 countries in which easyJet now operates. Equally importantly, he had to find ways to convince European travelers that the low-cost model, which was almost entirely new to them in the mid-1990s, did not involve compromising on reliability or safety. The fact that the brand is currently worth more than $4 billion is a great testament to his success.

Closely related to the issue of institutional distance is the question of where you choose to locate your business. Although some might argue that location is becoming less important as the ever-more connected world increasingly facilitates remote working, business success can still sometimes come down to where you are based. That's illustrated by the story of Turkish entrepreneur Eden Bali and his company Udemy. One of the keys to the success of his online education business was his decision to shift operations from Turkey to San Francisco. After his first attempt in Turkey floundered, Bali realized that his idea wouldn't work where he was—he needed to go to Silicon Valley. Hundreds of millions of learners later, his radical decision to change location has been vindicated.

I believe that effective institutional bridging has three elements. Immigrant entrepreneurs are particularly likely to possess all three, but that doesn't mean that they don't have to work on them too. It also doesn't mean that non-immigrant entrepreneurs can't also find ways to bring together all three elements to create successful bridges across institutional distance.

First, entrepreneurs must develop detailed social and cultural knowledge about the markets they wish to enter. Specifically, they must have:

(1) knowledge about potential customers and their buying behavior, so that products and services can be customized to local needs;
(2) cultural knowledge about the norms and practices that underpin commercial transactions; and
(3) knowledge of the legal and regulatory environment, both formal and informal.

Second, successful bridging requires the development of networks of key actors in the entrepreneur's target markets. Karan Bilimoria cultivated alliances with local entrepreneurs who acted as distributors, but linkages with established local firms may also play a significant role in helping entrepreneurs bridge institutional distance. Such links are particularly important because entrepreneurs operating outside their home countries are liable to suffer from problems of credibility, and alliances with local actors can confer legitimacy. But they can also provide another key benefit—helping entrepreneurs to gain the requisite market knowledge as discussed above.

Finally, entrepreneurs need to attract talented local workers in every country where they operate. Doing that requires them to adopt ways of working that align with local expectations and traditions. However, that can pose major challenges when the institutional distance between the entrepreneur's host context and the target context is particularly great. In such cases, entrepreneurs may need to adapt their practices and/or business models to align their operations with their host country's conditions.

And that provides a neat link into the third stage of the process of using cross-cultural knowledge to create entrepreneurial success. The final stage is being ready to adapt to all the inevitable but unpredictable challenges that the world will throw at your best-laid plans. And here, we'll see how the sort of knowledge possessed by immigrant entrepreneurs can also help you to adapt to changes, even when they affect a whole culture.

Inflection Points: "How to Read Tomorrow's Newspaper Today"

You've spotted an opportunity to create a new cross-cultural product, and you can't believe that nobody thought of it before. And you're super excited about the partners you've found and the team you've created, which balances all the cross-cultural knowledge and skills required to take advantage of that opportunity. You've even got the systems and processes in place that are going to facilitate that collaboration, smooth over any cultural differences, and help your team realize their collective potential. So, everything should be clear sailing from now on, right? Of course not.

No amount of preparation can prepare a ship for all the storms and obstacles it will encounter on the sea. And that's how it is with your entrepreneurial journey. Every business, just like every life, faces challenges that will make or break it—sometimes multiple ones at the same time. Andrew Grove, a man who dealt with many such challenges in his business and personal life, described them as "strategic inflection points." That's a term that we will return to throughout this book, but here I want to focus on the inflection points that come from cultural change and how immigrant entrepreneurs are particularly skilled at dealing with them.[9]

What is an inflection point in the business context? It is an event that creates major changes in the development course of a company or even a whole industry. As Andrew Grove put it, an inflection point "changes the way we think and act." Such events can stem from a change inside a company or in the world outside, and they can come in many shapes and sizes;

sometimes something that seems just like a minor ripple can turn into a savage whirlpool that threatens to sink your entire ship. Of course, how we act strategically in response to such events has a major bearing on whether their impacts are positive or negative.

But the key thing I want to emphasize here is that the crucial factor that determines the impact of an inflection point is how we respond to it *before it happens*. Because no matter how sudden it may seem, cultural change is never random; it is always the culmination of factors that have been building for some time—the pot bubbles before it boils over. The key as a leader is to recognize when the bubbles are building so that you can react in the right way at the right time with the right resources. Immigrant entrepreneurs' cross-cultural knowledge makes them uniquely well-equipped to anticipate cultural change before it occurs. And my research on this subject has shown that that elusive ability is essential if you want to achieve large-scale, long-term business success and impact.

Andrew Grove always emphasized the importance of recognizing that an inflection point is approaching and understanding when to act in response to it. From my reading of his memoir *Swimming Across*, I am convinced that he developed his thinking based on his own experience of having to flee Hungary and seek refuge in another country. As we saw in Chapter 1, Grove recognized that the Soviet Union's response to the Hungarian revolution was an inflection point that demanded immediate and drastic action. I'm sure his experience of responding to that helped inform the subsequent decisions and chances he took throughout his stellar career in tech, one of the world's most volatile industries. Under his leadership, and subsequently, Intel has responded to multiple major inflection points and managed to remain at the top of its game.

In my previous book, *Fashion Entrepreneurship: The Creation of the Global Fashion Industry*,[10] one of the main questions I explored was why some designers endure while others, once giants, fall from grace. To illustrate this, I examined the story of Paul Poiret, who succeeded Charles Worth as the king of Parisian fashion by liberating women from restrictive corsets. Poiret's success during Paris's Belle Époque was such that his lavish parties, where he sat enthroned like an Ottoman sultan or Zeus, became synonymous with opulence. However, just before World War I, Poiret faced competition from a young woman, Coco Chanel, who could see the cultural changes that he could not. Her designs, emphasizing chic simplicity and famously "making poverty fashionable," directly opposed Poiret's luxurious, Oriental-inspired creations.

Chanel sensed that the world of fashion was ready for something new, and her ability to adapt led to her enduring success, while Poiret's inability to evolve caused his downfall. By 1929, Poiret's fashion house had collapsed, and he ended up selling drawings in Paris cafes for a few francs. Chanel, however, became a symbol of adaptability, and her brand still thrives today with a value of $19.4 billion in 2023. While Chanel wasn't an immigrant, she embodied the characteristics of an outsider who could read and adapt to cultural shifts—qualities that are particularly common among immigrant entrepreneurs, who often have an acute sense of change.

There are plenty of current examples as well that show why immigrants can be so good at reading and adapting to cultural change before it happens and the benefits that can bring.

Hernan Lopez was very nearly my contemporary at the University of Miami—he started his MBA there the year I graduated from my bachelor's degree. Like me, he came from a humble background, in his case, in Buenos Aires, Argentina, where his father ran an auto parts store. Like me, he spent most of his childhood under a dictatorship. Like me, English was not his first language, in fact, he barely spoke it until he was in his early twenties. And also like me, he traveled to the United States in pursuit of his dream.

Hernan had first shown his entrepreneurial streak as a teenager in Argentina when he bought airtime on a neighborhood radio station with four friends and financed it by selling advertising. Unfortunately the show, which was the equivalent of a modern podcast, was not a runaway success; in fact, according to Hernan, it only attracted ten listeners, "assuming that [we all] got both of our parents to listen."[11]

Low listener figures were not the only reason the show didn't last—Hernan soon got a proper job at an Argentinian cable and radio company. His success selling advertising there eventually earned Hernan a move to the United States to work for Fox International Channels, where he rose up the ranks with almost unbelievable speed. By 2000, at the age of 30, the man who could barely speak English a decade before was senior vice president for Fox Latin America, responsible for adapting American shows for a Spanish-speaking audience. Three years later, he was the president of Fox Latin America and general manager of its U.K. operations. By 2011, Hernan was the CEO of Fox International Channels, a position he held for five years.

But often even a high-profile and successful career is not sufficient to suppress the calling to be an entrepreneur. So, in 2016, Hernan, whose own short-lived radio career had only brought him 10 listeners, took the bold decision to quit Fox and leave TV behind to found his own company, Wondery, with the intention of getting into a still relatively niche industry known as podcasting.

What inspired that seemingly reckless change of direction? Hearing the first very highly successful podcast, *Serial*, had changed Hernan's life because he didn't just hear the words being spoken but also something that very few others at the time could: an inflection point for the whole audio industry. Hernan knew as well as anybody how TV had been revolutionized by the introduction of TiVo, which made it easy to watch whole series on demand. That technology had empowered writers and producers to craft increasingly complex, multi-layered shows (HBO's *The Sopranos* was an early example of this), confident that their audience would be able to follow because they could watch (and rewatch) back-to-back episodes without having to wait weeks for the next installment.

With Wondery, Hernan spotted the potential to do the same for the nascent podcasting industry. If TiVo had enabled the golden age of television, wasn't there an inflection point looming that could lead to a golden age of audio? Hernan gambled that there was, and he focused his efforts on launching a service that offered listeners access to a library of podcasts, in the same way as Netflix does with visual content. Hernan struggled at first, but after he scored his first big hit with a suitably complex and bingeworthy podcast, *Dirty John*, he was ultimately proved right.

Following Amazon's recent $300 million acquisition of Wondery, Hernan stepped down as CEO and has moved on to his new company offering management consultancy services to media firms: Owl & Co. Crediting his success to "others who lifted me up along the way," he also invests money and time in his foundation that provides mentorship and leadership training to young diverse professionals.

Fascinatingly, Hernan attributes his ability to spot inflection points before they occur precisely to his cross-cultural experience:

> If you work in international, you [can] "read tomorrow's newspaper" because you are in a country and you're seeing a trend. And that trend probably happened in some other country … before … so, you are much more able to predict [new] trends.

And when you can read tomorrow's newspaper today, that massively increases your chance of getting your timing right when responding to a strategic inflection point. Reflecting on his entrepreneurial successes, Hernan offers some important advice on timing: if you can't be right on time, it's better to catch a trend too early rather than too late.

Immigrant entrepreneurs' cross-cultural expertise gives them particular strengths in spotting approaching inflection points and responding to them. Hernan Lopez is an immigrant, but his story also shows how non-immigrants can cultivate such expertise too (for example, he attributes lots of his knowledge to working internationally, even in countries that he didn't migrate to, like the U.K.).

With that in mind, I've compiled some tips to help any entrepreneurs achieve the sort of cross-cultural knowledge that helps immigrants identify and take advantage of opportunities and strategic inflection points.

But before turning to those tips, I want to reemphasize one crucial point. Throughout this chapter, I have highlighted the importance of culture, and there is a reason why I chose that to be the subject of the first of my eight principles of success. Books and research about business don't place much emphasis on the importance of culture beyond the internal culture of a company itself. But all my research on the fashion industry and immigrant entrepreneurs has shown me that understanding and adapting to cultural change in the world around you is the crucial determinant of success. Opportunities exist in cultural contexts, and the never-ending process of cultural change drives strategic inflection points. So, and I can't emphasize this enough, you must always strive to understand all the cultures that you are operating in and, just as importantly, read the ways in which they are changing so that you can spot the bubbles rising through the water, attend to the pot before it boils over, and use the power of the boiling water to brew wonderful new ventures.

Strategies for building bridges between cultures:

(1) **Look to your own heritage for inspiration:** If you are an immigrant looking to become an entrepreneur, don't be afraid to look to your own heritage for inspiration. As so many of the stories in this chapter, and elsewhere, show, your ability to be a bridge between your heritage and your new home could well be your superpower. But also, don't feel that you have to limit yourself to

your own heritage, just like non-immigrant entrepreneurs, you should be prepared to look to other cultures for inspiration.

(2) Immerse yourself in other cultures: You can increase your chance of spotting cross-cultural entrepreneurial opportunities by traveling with an open mind and immersing yourself in another culture. If you have the opportunity, take long trips and leave the beaten track, learn a new language, and take chances to learn about a culture through its arts and media. All of this increases your likelihood of being able to "read tomorrow's newspaper" today.

(3) Look for chances to learn from others: Seek opportunities to work with and learn from people from different cultures; entrepreneurs learn most effectively through direct experience, experimentation, networking with others, and finding experienced mentors who have the expertise they are seeking.

(4) Ask questions: Don't be afraid to ask people questions about their culture; sometimes we feel rude to do so, but most people are very happy to talk, and open conversations are the best way to get beyond assumptions and approach the heart of another culture.

(5) Research your cross-cultural ideas carefully: After you have spotted an opportunity that bridges different cultures, do your research to check if someone else has already tried the same thing. If they haven't, maybe you need to work out why. And if they have tried, and failed, it's also important to analyze why. Doing so can help make sure that you don't underestimate the challenges of working across cultures, and it can help you formulate strategies that will overcome the challenges others have faced and lead you to success.

(6) Find the right partners: When seeking partners from another culture, I advise trying to partner with people who also understand your culture too as this can decrease the risk of miscommunication and misunderstandings (of course, this does not apply if you are also from their culture). Hiring a trusted intermediary who genuinely understands both cultures can also be a good way of smoothing over relations and avoiding cultural faux pas or miscommunication.

(7) Use your partners as teachers too: Make sure your partners or intermediaries are not just being a bridge for you but also teaching you about the culture; that way, you won't become dependent on them and can act as a bridge yourself even if you stop collaborating with them.

(8) Hire staff with cross-cultural experience: If you're already at the stage where you are employing other people for your business, look for multilingual staff and others with cross-cultural and international expertise. Organizational diversity is proven to enhance creativity, and it's especially important when working across cultures. Employee mobility programs can also give your staff valuable opportunities to work internationally.

(9) Create an inclusive environment: Create an environment in which your cross-cultural team can thrive. To do that requires respect for people from diverse cultures and the contributions they can each bring. Approaches like cultural sensitivity and bias training and celebrating different cultural events can all help to build a more inclusive environment. It's also important to make openness and curiosity key parts of your corporate culture.

(10) Be authentic: Finally, and perhaps most importantly, be authentic. You will only really spot cross-cultural opportunities and be able to make the most of them if they are born out of a genuine love for the two cultures that you are bridging. Trying to fake this as a route to business success will simply not work. Immersing yourself in a culture and bringing what you love from it to another will not only inspire you but also your customers and help you to achieve the long-term success and impact that you are striving for as an entrepreneur.

Song of the Open Road

1

Afoot and light-hearted I take to the open road,
Healthy, free, the world before me,
The long brown path before me leading
wherever I choose.

Henceforth I ask not good-fortune, I myself am
good-fortune,
Henceforth I whimper no more, postpone no more,
need nothing,
Done with indoor complaints, libraries, querulous
criticisms,
Strong and content I travel the open road.
                                    —*Walt Whitman*

5

Principle 2: Build from the Past Forward and the Future Back

Kapıkule, Turkey, 1989

Once upon a time, there was a young girl who loved to read books and dream herself away from where she was. Some of the books she read were fairytales about princesses and witches, flying white horses and genies, and fire-breathing dragons who used their long tails to encircle their prey. But then, one day, the stories in the books seemed to come to life and the girl found herself and her family being pursued by dragons. Not real ones, of course, but they might as well have been because they were just as angry and dangerous and deadly. They must have been all of those things because why else would the girl's mother, with the girl in her arms, have had to jump from a third-story window onto a pile of firewood gathered against the encroaching winter and flee with her family into the surrounding forest for safety?

And the worst thing about the whole situation was that those dragons were the government of the country where the girl lived and the police and army of that country too. The very people who were meant to keep her and her family safe had turned against them because they had decided that she and hundreds of thousands of other people like her didn't really belong in the country that their families had lived in for centuries and should be forced to either be like all the other people in that country or leave.

So, the girl and her mother and father and little brother hid in her uncle's cabin in the forest, hoping the dragons would pass them by and not take their lives like they had those of 1,500 other people who had been prepared to stand up to them. Eventually, after a winter hidden away in the forest, the family emerged into the spring and fields fresh with flowers where white butterflies danced on the breeze.

But sadly, the dragons hadn't gone away, and soon the situation was worse than ever. The head of the dragons, Todor Zhivkov, decided it was time to force people like the girl and her family out of the country for good.

The girl still vividly remembers her family's final hours in their home-land: the suffocating heat in the air on that summer's day as she walked back from a library with a bag stuffed full of books; the tears in her mother's eyes when she told her she would have to instantaneously return them; the urgency and the crack in her father's voice when he announced it was time to leave; and the desperate hurry with which the whole family stuffed their lives into two suitcases and rushed for the border as if their lives depended on it. They left everything familiar behind: the rest of their family, their friends, their community, and the ghosts of generations of history in their homeland. Life as the girl knew it had ended at age 11.

A new life was born on that journey, and like all births, it was far from easy. The girl remembers the long hike to the border from the spot where a police officer friend of her father dropped them off. She remembers the forest they passed through where they snatched a few hours of sleep as a respite from the demands of the road. She remembers the sun breaking through the horizon, and her family resuming their journey surrounded by the heat that ambushed them as soon as they left the forest's shade. But most of all, she remembers how it ended, with the screams of her father as he ran like a wounded animal freed from a cage, two suitcases in his hands, and flung himself over the border and collapsed on the cement on the other side, kissing the hot ground then holding his two hands in the air, yelling, screaming, crying. And the chaos and the confusion all around as other families just like hers were also running to the border and falling on the other side.

And as the girl stood and watched all that, tears in her own eyes too, she had a very clear and simple vision. At that exact moment, she knew what she had to do with her life: "I have to get a good education" because education, she suddenly saw with absolute clarity, was the way to stop being a victim in the dragons' story and instead take control of the writing of her own.

And the reason you are reading this book now is because that girl, standing on the Bulgarian-Turkish border in the summer of 1989, had that vision. Because that girl was me, and that story was that of my family and our escape from the communist Bulgarian regime's "Process of Rebirth," which targeted the Turkish ethnic minority that we belonged to and aimed to wipe every trace of Turkishness out of the country.

And the intention I had then at the border to change my world into a better future that then only existed in my imagination, became a vision that has driven all of my subsequent life from Istanbul to Miami to Cambridge, Oxford, and Paris. And one of the results of that education and everything I've learned and taught is this book that you're holding in your hands now.

The Importance of Vision

As my own story shows, a clear, guiding vision can exert an enormously powerful influence on one's life and, by extension, one's business. In recognition of that power, it is a truism of any management 101 course that every organization needs a vision. In my journey of consulting many companies around the world, I've seen many mission and vision statements beautifully framed on office walls. But too often those words don't seem to live beyond those frames.

It seems to me that there are two main challenges with vision: the first is how do you create one that really means something; the second is how do you achieve it. My research with immigrant entrepreneurs has shown me that they are particularly skilled in both of those areas, and I believe that it is their aptitude for formulating and fulfilling visions that is one of the key drivers of their success, which is why I have made vision the second of my eight key principles.

Through my research with immigrant entrepreneurs, I have distilled their powerful, and perhaps unconscious, visioning process into the three simple steps that I call the 3-I framework for vision. This is a framework that links past, present, and future and leads to the creation of a compelling vision of what you hope to achieve that comes from intentions rooted in your own identity. Essentially, the framework shows you how to build a vision of the future that is deeply meaningful to you based on the foundations of your own past. Most importantly, it is a framework that anyone, immigrant or otherwise, can apply as they strive to create an authentic vision for their own entrepreneurial venture.

And the things we can learn from immigrant entrepreneurs about vision do not stop when the vision has been formed. Crucially, immigrant entrepreneurs are particularly adept at realizing their visions, using powerful tools that help them turn their imagined futures into present realities. I discuss tools like "planning from the future back" at the end of this chapter. But before getting to that, I'd like to introduce the 3-I framework with the story of a man who is hardly a household name but who envisioned an innovation that has become such an important part of the everyday life of billions; you probably use his innovation multiple times each day yourself. And what his story perfectly illustrates is the 3-I process, by which immigrant entrepreneurs use the identities that come from their pasts and their intentions to change the present to imagine and create better futures.

Mountain View, California, 1992

Jan was born in the mid-1970s in a small town outside Kyiv, Ukraine (at that time part of the USSR).[1] He was the only child of a housewife and a construction worker, and their simple home had no running water and often no electricity because household power was rationed by the government. As a member of Ukraine's Jewish minority, Jan and his family faced racism and discrimination, and the rising tide of antisemitism eventually influenced his parents' decision to take the family overseas by emigrating to the United States in 1992, shortly after the collapse of the Soviet Union.

Jan was 16 years old when he and his mother and grandmother arrived in Mountain View, California, where government assistance helped them to live in a small two-bedroom apartment in the heart of Silicon Valley. Jan's mother had stuffed their suitcases with pens and a stack of 20 Soviet-issued notebooks to avoid paying for school supplies in the United States. She took up babysitting, and Jan swept the floor of a grocery store to help make ends meet. His father intended to join them, but never made it, dying in Ukraine in 1997. When Jan's mother was diagnosed with cancer, they lived mainly off her disability allowance until she too died in 2000.

Like most immigrants, Jan always valued staying in touch with friends and family back home. But in the early 1990s, that was much more difficult, and costly, than it is today. He had to find a phone booth, make the call with AT&T, and hope the person he wanted to reach would be at the other end of the line to pick up. And from the first second, the price of the call would start ticking up and up, with conversations often cut off by their spiraling costs.

But when he did have the money for a call and was able to get through, Jan was connected, often over a bad line with delays and distortion, to the world he'd left behind. It was a world that lacked a lot—water and a consistent supply of electricity, for example—but some of the things it lacked Jan missed in the United States. Life in Ukraine had been free from the "noise" that characterized his every day in California; without TVs and the incessant interruptions of advertisements that screamed for attention, he had found it easier in Ukraine to focus on the things that mattered in life, especially his education. And throughout his childhood, Jan had forged deeper connections with people around him, based on the sort of open and honest communication that he found lacking in the United States, where most interactions never seemed to go beyond superficial friendliness.

For all that he missed his friends at home, Jan did not romanticize the communist world where he had grown up. There might have been less noise there, but there were always concerns about what the silence was hiding. The ever-present fear of phone tapping meant you never knew who might be covertly listening in to your calls. Jan remembered well how his mother would often have to interrupt the people she was talking to on the phone to remind them, "This is not a phone conversation. Let's talk face to face."

As someone who also grew up under communism, I remember well how paranoid the regime made everybody, and how that paranoia was a poison that ran through the veins of even everyday communication. Although we didn't even have a phone in my childhood home, my parents would often communicate in code or hushed tones because you never knew who might be listening in. And even to this day, when I call my mother, she never wants to speak on the phone about anything in the news and will often tell me, "We will speak about this in person" whenever the subject has even the slightest degree of sensitivity.

All the elements of Jan's experiences, from concern over being monitored to the need for connection, came together in the vision that eventually revolutionized his life and the world of communication. After working in tech for nine years with Yahoo! he had a vision that inspired him to create his own company in 2009. The company had one product, an app that was designed to address all the problems with communication that Jan had ever faced from growing up under communism to living as an immigrant in the United States.

The fear ingrained in him of having calls monitored convinced Jan to make all communication on his app encrypted, with complete privacy guaranteed. The childhood cost and complexity of calling home inspired him to make his app free and simple. The uncertainty of not knowing whether someone was available for a call persuaded him to add a feature that indicated if the person you wanted to reach was online or not. The noise and distractions of life in the United States motivated him to make the whole package ad-free.

And when you put that all together, Jan's vision became WhatsApp, a communication tool with more than three billion active users today. Just five years after its launch, Jan sold WhatsApp for $19 billion to Facebook, a company that had, ironically, once rejected his job application.

The story of Jan Koum and WhatsApp is a great illustration of an immigrant entrepreneur combining influences from different aspects of their life to create a vision that leads to success. But, of course, you don't have to be an immigrant to do that. Anyone can learn from such stories about how to create a powerful vision to deliver long-term impact.

Before sharing the three elements that must combine to create a vision that goes beyond mere words to inspire decisive action, I want to emphasize one aspect from Jan Koum's story that comes up time and again throughout this book. Despite selling it for $19 billion, Jan is adamant that he did not create WhatsApp with the intention of making money. His motivation, he insists, was only ever to solve a problem. So insistent is he on that point that he even angrily rejects the word "entrepreneur" because he thinks it denotes someone who is only interested in making money. He sees himself as simply a problem solver.

"He would say that," you might think. And some people might prefer to present themselves as being problem-focused rather than money-motivated. But my research on successful immigrant entrepreneurs shows the remarkable consistency with which they answer the question of motivation: it is never just, or even mainly, about money. Some of the entrepreneurs were genuinely shocked when I suggested that money might have been the factor that drove them to make all the sacrifices that they made along the road to realizing their vision.

As we shall see in this chapter, creating and following a vision that means something to you in your heart is a much surer way of achieving success, i.e., long-term impact, than having a vision that is just about making money anyway, anyhow. Finally, despite the importance of non-monetary motivations, I'm still absolutely clear that "entrepreneur" is the right word to use for all the people studied in this book, and that's because I use "entrepreneur" to emphasize the creative, visionary side of people who have a big idea and pursue it with passion to create impact, something that all the people in this book have excelled at.

With those important points made, it's now time to take a detailed look at vision and the 3-I framework that can help you, like Jan Koum, to turn your own past and the problems you see in the present into a revolutionary future.

The 3-I Framework for Vision: Identity, Intention, and Imagined Future

You start with vision by looking into the future, right? I would argue no. When you want to put together a vision for your company you start by looking into the *past*, your own past specifically. Because what the experience of Jan Koum, and immigrant entrepreneurs generally, shows is that the best path to success and real impact comes from understanding what deeply motivates the core of your **identity**—and the best way to understand that is to look deep inside yourself, into your roots, your history, your experiences, so you can distill the essential values and characteristics that are at the core of you.

I can't emphasize enough how much this crucial first step differs from the orthodox position on entrepreneurship that states that the place to start is by looking outwards to see where there are gaps in the market that you can fill. In complete contrast, the immigrant entrepreneurs I spoke with began by looking inward, into their own complex pasts and identities, to understand what really mattered to them and then made that the starting point of their vision. As Reem Hassani, of Numi Organic Tea, put it to me:

> A lot of people when they start businesses they try and find out what's going on out there in the world that they need to solve ... versus how do you find what's really true to you, what do you feel passionately about, what is the thing that you want to express to the world ... Entrepreneurs need to follow their heart and their vision and their passion first and then see what's out there, not the other way round.

When you have done that and deeply understand the forces from the past that have shaped your identity and core values, then you are ready to move to the next stage of the 3-I framework, which is when your focus shifts from the past to the present. Here, you look at the world around you and see how the things that you value as part of your identity are not always matched by the state of the world around you. And that disconnect is what gives you the **intention** to change something.

Again, immigrant entrepreneurs, with their complex cross-cultural backgrounds, are particularly likely to have a strong sense of a disconnect between their identities and the world in which they find themselves. But while some immigrants may have predominantly negative feelings associated with that disconnect, others are able to turn it to their enormous advantage by using it to ask questions and set intentions to change the world. It's important to stress, however, that those intentions do not necessarily have to be focused on addressing complex societal problems. Sometimes it is as simple as placing enormous value on a product that can't be found in another place, and through your passion for that product, setting an intention to make it available (although even in such cases, as we shall repeatedly see, immigrant entrepreneurs tend to mix such businesses with deeper messages about societal change and philanthropic efforts to change the world too).

When you are clear about what you intend to change, the final stage in the 3-I framework is to transfer that intention into an **imagined future** by visualizing the outcome of implementing your vision. The imagined future is a vivid, detailed picture of the desired outcome that the organization aims to achieve. It's a forward-looking element that extends beyond current capabilities and market positions, envisioning a future state that the organization strives to realize. And the beauty of following the 3-I framework is that the imagined future will express the values that you hold most dear as the core of your identity. Thus, the framework is circular in the sense that it binds together your past, the present in which you find yourself, and the future that you wish to create. And what you end up with at the end of that process is a vision that expresses your core values (i.e., your identity), what you want to change (i.e., your intention), and what the world will look like when you have fulfilled your intention (i.e., your imagined future).

I believe it is that connection between core values and imagined future that sometimes makes immigrant entrepreneurs so shocked when I ask them if their motivation for creating their business was money. For most of them, the money they made just appears to be a side effect of what they would have done anyway even if money was no object.

Another crucial point to emphasize here is the bridge that takes you from your intention to your imagined future. It is a bridge that is composed of questions, specifically the kind of "What if?" questions that encourage us to challenge existing assumptions and free ourselves from the bonds that the status quo imposes on our creative conceptualization of future possibilities.

But before getting into the practical detail of how you can apply the 3-I framework and use "what-if" questions to create your vision, let's first show the framework in action by mapping it to my experiences and those of Jan Koum.

In the story of how I came to my own vision of the paramount importance of education in my life, you can see how I was unconsciously using the steps of the 3-I framework. From the very first line of my story, my love of reading and learning was a key part of my identity. So was my family's pride in our heritage despite the attempts of the government to persecute people like us. But when measuring that identity against the state of the world in which I was living, I found a disconnect; the circumstances under which I was living, persecuted and in poverty, denied me the opportunity to fulfill my identity, and that disconnect informed my intention to change my world. Specifically, I wanted to stop being a victim in a story being written by someone else and to take control of my own story. And my vision for how to achieve that was to pursue the best education that I could, which would both resonate with the values that made up my identity and lead me into my imagined future, which looked very much like the life that I am privileged to lead now as an academic, consultant, entrepreneur, and author.

In Jan Koum's case, we can see how the things that he valued—which included friendship, privacy, and the ability to communicate freely and easily—were linked to his identity and experience of growing up under communism and emigrating to the United States. However, he found himself living in a world of "noise" where constant distractions and concerns about cost limited people's abilities to connect. So, he set the intention to change that. And the series of "what-if" questions he asked himself, which we will look at in more detail below, led him to his vision of an imagined future in which WhatsApp would address the disconnect between the things that he valued and the world around him—an imagined future that has now become a present reality for billions of people, thanks to Jan's big idea.

Having seen that the framework can lead to a big idea that works, let's turn to the detail of that and set out some of the questions that you can ask yourself as you seek to understand your identity, set your intentions, and visualize your imagined future.

Step 1: Identity

In the context of the 3-I framework, understanding your identity means knowing what your values are on a fundamental level. And when I use the word "value" I mean both the moral code that guides you and the things that you consider to be of worth.

Of course, discussions of immigrant identity typically focus on the internal confusion that comes from having to navigate multiple identities that derive from the cultural norms and practices of different places. I don't deny the reality of that challenge. But, as the previous chapter showed, when viewed from a positive perspective, cross-cultural identities can be a superpower of immigrant entrepreneurs.

Your identity is shaped by your past and strongly influences your present and future. It may become part of your company's competitive advantage, but that's not why it exists. Indeed, it consists of principles so fundamental that you would not betray them even if they cost you competitive advantage. It is your unshakeable foundation that persists through the hardest times. In other words, identity comes from an authentic place, not from strategic boards or consultants.

But because your core values are so ingrained in you, it can be challenging to articulate them. So, if you want to ensure that your vision is based on the heart of your identity, here are some questions that you can ask yourself:

- What did I value in my childhood that still plays a key role in my life now?
- When do I feel the most alive or most satisfied?
- What would I do with my life if money was no object?
- When faced with a critical decision, what considerations always take precedence?
- Which of my values would I never compromise on even if it would put me at a disadvantage when doing business?
- How do I want to be remembered?

Alternatively, if you're trying to reformulate a vision for a company that you have already established that seems to have lost its way, you could ask yourself the business-focused questions listed here:

- **What principles were important to you at the inception of the company?**
  - Reflect on the early days of your business. What beliefs and values were non-negotiable and have continued to guide your decisions?
- **What makes your organization unique in how it operates or interacts with its customers and the community?**
  - Analyze how your unique interactions are reflections of your deeper organizational values.

- **What are the values that every employee is expected to adhere to, no matter their position in the company?**
  - Universal expectations across the company often reflect its foundational values.
- **What are the behaviors and actions you consistently reward and recognize within your organization?**
  - The actions you incentivize can reveal the underlying values that drive your corporate culture.
- **When faced with critical business decisions, what considerations always take precedence?**
  - Understanding what takes priority in decision-making can highlight the core values that guide these choices.
- **What values are so crucial to your operations that you would continue to uphold them even if they became a competitive disadvantage in certain situations?**
  - This question helps identify values that are truly foundational, rather than those adopted for strategic advantage.
- **What commitments are you willing to make regardless of changes in the market or industry?**
  - Identifying commitments that are upheld irrespective of external changes can underline core principles.
- **In times of organizational crisis or change, what are the constants that you never question?**
  - Values that hold firm even in turbulent times are key indicators of core tenets.
- **How do you want your organization to be remembered in the distant future?**
  - Envisioning your company's legacy can help clarify the enduring values you wish to impart.

It is absolutely essential that whatever you end up with has to be authentic to you. Don't over-intellectualize it or hire someone else to come up with it. The point is that your identity and values are there all along. And when you have revealed the core of yourself, the next part of the framework asks you to place it into the context of the world around, so that you can set your intention to change not yourself but the world.

Step 2: Intention

When you understand your identity and that which you most deeply value, you are ideally placed to move to realizing what it is you intend to change. This is the stage at which you look outside at the world, and when you spot the disconnect between that and the things that you value as part of your identity, then you have found what you intend to change.

The key thing here is that you are not looking for customers but rather, as Jan Koum did with WhatsApp, looking for the right problem to solve. This is a point emphasized by Noubar Afeyan, the founder of Moderna, who was born in an Armenian family in Lebanon and subsequently emigrated to Canada and then the United States. Recalling his experience at MIT's Sloan School of Management, Noubar said:

> The folks at Sloan impressed upon me that far more interesting than finding customers … was finding problems that were worth solving. And so, I looked at a bunch of different things where we could apply engineering mindset problem-solving. And there were many because the field is so new.[2]

You are looking first for the problem rather than trying to think about where the customers are. If you find the right problem, then the customers will take care of themselves. That distinction is neatly illustrated by the story of Tope Awotona, a Nigerian entrepreneur who was born in Lagos. His father was an entrepreneur who was tragically killed in a carjacking witnessed by a 12-year-old Tope. Three years later he emigrated with his family to the United States, settling in Atlanta.

Inspired by his father, Tope tried to become an entrepreneur, but he failed three times. His first effort was a dating website that didn't get any love, then he tried an e-commerce website selling projectors that got rejected, and next, he turned to another site selling grills that failed to catch fire. But even after three failures, Tope showed the resilience that characterizes many immigrants and committed himself to an honest appraisal of where he was going wrong.

Eventually, he realized that his intention with each of those businesses was just to make money rather than to solve a real problem that people faced. Realigning his focus on problem-solving, he turned to an issue that had caused him great personal annoyance in his days working as a salesman for software companies: the endless back-and-forth of messages just to schedule a simple meeting. Applying his skills to a real problem that caused him discontent, Tope came up with a solution that he so believed in that he backed it by throwing away all the financial security he had (quitting his job and putting his life savings of $200,000 into his new company). With the right intention, Tope finally found the success he'd always sought, and by 2021 Calendly, the company he created in 2014, was worth $3 billion. His story, which is rooted in an entrepreneurial identity that comes from his father, is a potent illustration of the importance of setting an intention by finding the right problem to solve.

It's also important to note that sometimes when you have an established company with an intention, you can use it to work backward to discover how that intention sheds light on the identity and values that may unconsciously underpin that intention. For example, a company I consulted wanted to expand its lifestyle and hotel brand into fashion. So, I asked them, what is your intention behind that? If the answer is simply "Because our other partner is doing it," that is not good enough. Neither is "because we have seen that we make money from our lifestyle brand, and we want to expand it." Get to the core of your intention and there you will find your identity, which is both what makes you keep going and will also make people excited to work with you and partner with you.

Try this exercise if you want to trace the route back from intention to identity: List all the reasons you started your business and then keep asking yourself *why* each one was a reason. I did this exercise with a client of mine. She has a startup based in Germany and the U.K. that makes workbags, and her initial answer was "Because I could not find a bag I liked." Why? Ask again. Why is that important to you? "Because I want to empower women." Why do you want to empower women? "Because … etc." Until you get to the core.

Normally companies' attempts to create visions focus only on a vaguely described version of the future. But what I emphasize here is the absolute centrality of making the problem that you will solve the heart of the vision. But it is crucial that when you have found your problem you don't rush into trying to solve it too quickly—all too often it is just a fast track to failure. You need to take time to fully understand the problem and what solving it will lead to.

Finding the right problem involves asking the right questions, so you should pay a lot of attention to learning. Discuss the problem with experts so you understand it from a deep perspective. Then discuss it with people who know nothing about it so that you both check your ability to communicate it and benefit from the insights of people who bring wholly new perspectives to the problem. One of my clients included her grandmother on the team for her startup based on the well-known premise that when one of your grandparents gets your idea, it's clear and common sense.

And while accumulating your knowledge about the problem, think too about how the world will change after you have solved it. And that will lead you to the final step in the 3-I framework: the creation of an imagined future that will describe your vision and inspire the action required to realize it. And how do you move from the intention to change to the imagined future? By asking the simple question: "What if?"

Step 3: Imagined future

Noubar Afeyan argues for the crucial role that imagination plays "in accomplishing impossible missions,"[3] but that role is not just restricted to finding creative solutions to the problems you intend to solve. Before that, you must use your imagination to form your vision of the future that will exist when the problem is solved. When you have that powerful vision, you can use it to achieve three equally important things.

First, your imagined future can inspire other people to align with you so you can work together and overcome the inevitable challenges that will be encountered on the road because they are so committed to the ultimate destination. Second, establishing your imagined future is a crucial first step in the process of "planning from the future back," which will lead you from where you want to be back to the detail of the implementation plan that will get you there. Third, the imagined future inspires others to follow and aligns the efforts of your organization and its partners to achieve the required change.

Before we explore these three functions, let us start by looking at how you create a powerful imagined future in the first place. With your identity worked out and your intention clear, you start by asking questions that begin with two magical words: "What if…?"

"What if ..." is a powerful question that comes from the place of inno-vation, where ideas are born. It's also a question that seems to come naturally to immigrant entrepreneurs, perhaps because so many of them had to work out how to get out of a country in which they felt (or literally were) trapped. Or perhaps their fluency with the question comes from having to work out what to do when they arrived in a new place in which the possibilities may have seemed suddenly boundless or alternatively constricted as they tried to rebuild away from everything they once knew.

"What if" was the question that drove Andrew Grove in his escape from communist Hungary:

> Ever since the Russians had returned some three weeks ago, the number of young people who had set off to cross the border had grown by the week. Some clearly made it across because they sent back word from Austria. Others disappeared ... Our discussions were all of the: "What If" type: What if we could catch a ride on a truck on its way back to Austria? What if we got a travel permit to go to the vicinity of the border?[4]

In a business context, we can see how "what if" questions can act as the bridge between an intention to make a change and the big idea that will create your imagined future. For example, let's look at the sort of "what-if" questions Jan Koum might have asked on the way to creating WhatsApp:

- What if there was a way to communicate internationally without incurring huge fees?
- What if communication could be as instant and simple as sending an SMS, but across any platform or network globally?
- What if there was a messaging app that could guarantee privacy and security, keeping personal communications protected?
- What if people could stay connected with family and friends across the globe using only the internet?
- What if there was a way to make technology serve real human needs in a straightforward, uncluttered manner?
- What if you could see when your friends and family are online and when they have read your messages?
- And what if you could do all that without invasive ads or interruptions?

These questions are rooted in Jan's identity and in the intention to make a change that was inspired by the interaction of that identity and its value system with the world in which he found himself. "What-if" questions then led him from that intention into an imagined future in which something like WhatsApp would create a world that at that time only existed in his head.

As with the questions you ask when trying to understand your problem and set your intention for change, "what if" questions are particularly powerful when asked in a group. Such questions are open-ended and invite exploration and creativity. Just like at the intention stage, gather a group together to ask these questions. Expert input is good, but just as important are the inputs of your friends, family members, and trusted colleagues. Together with their varied inputs, you can work out an imagined future that is informed by expertise and inspiring to a diverse range of people. Also, try out multiple "what-if" options; don't be constrained initially to one imagined future, come up with multiple so you can select the one that will ultimately be the best way to achieve your intentions. And when "what-if" questions have finally led you to a clear imagined future, that vision has three key functions.

The first is that your visualization of what your success will look like will help to achieve it. Not only are immigrant entrepreneurs experts in dreaming of bigger, better lives for themselves and others but they are also the architects of those dreams. I know that from my own life; as a little girl standing at the border, I imagined and believed with my whole heart that I would get a good education. And I stayed with that vision even through life in refugee camps and struggling through realizing that the Turkish we had spoken in Bulgaria was incomprehensible in Turkey itself.

Jane Wurwand, whose story we looked at in the previous chapter, is also a great believer in the power of the sort of visualization that your imagined future enables:

> I believe that you need to fully visualize your success in order to achieve it. Dermalogica has been planned to be this success and even more. The skin therapists who built our brand are our "magic" and their endorsement to their clients has powered our growth.[5]

But, of course, belief alone, while important, is never enough. Any vision needs to be accompanied by a concrete plan to make it happen, and that is where the notion of "planning from the future back" comes in. One great advocate of that concept is Stéphane Bancel, the CEO of Moderna and, perhaps not incidentally, an immigrant too (having moved from his native France to the United States).

Seeking to escape the constraints of traditional linear approaches to thinking, which often restrict people's conceptions of possibility to what already exists, Bancel argues we should start by imaging a better future and then work backward from that to plan the detail of each step required to make the dream a reality. Using this technique, which he also calls "back-casting" or "reverse chronology,"[6] we can create a timeline from the future to the present that is not only free of current limitations but also systematic and detailed enough to be achievable.

The success of planning from the future back has been illustrated in the lives of many of the immigrant entrepreneurs I have interviewed. But equally important is the third function of the imagined future: providing a vision around which people can align. Without deep alignment, without everyone from the top down and bottom up buying into this vision and understanding their part in it, the strategy can stall. It's like having a map with no one to follow it.

Alignment can happen at all three levels of the 3-I framework: and it is most powerful when you align with people who share your identity, your intentions, and your imagined future. Throughout my research with immigrant entrepreneurs, I have been struck by the ways in which they worked with close friends and family members whose shared identities and perspectives linked them together as a powerful force. Maintaining that as your company grows is a challenge. But if you can integrate your identity, intentions, and imagined future into your recruitment and partner selection processes, then you can continue to work alongside people who will consistently pull together in the service of a shared vision.

When that alignment occurs, it becomes a powerful force, the inspiration that puts the wind in your sails and helps you overcome the inevitable storms you will encounter on the way to your imagined future. Ultimately, the difference between a company with a vision and a visionary company is having staff and partners who believe in the vision that comes from your identity, intention, and imagined future and are inspired every day to work to make it happen.

Strategies for building from the past forward and the future back:
(1) **Follow the 3-I framework step-by-step:** Don't try to rush straight to your imagined future. Take time to reflect on your identity and ask the right questions that will help you understand the problem that you intend to solve. Work with others to sense-check at every step of the process and you'll be much more likely to end up with an imagined future that will both inspire and be practically implementable.

(2) **Be a long-term thinker:** Realizing a vision and transforming it into reality is a process that unfolds over time, not overnight. As a leader, maintaining persistence and staying aligned with your vision is essential. This long-term dedication requires not just strategic foresight but also a deep belief in the vision's value, ensuring that every step taken is a building block toward the imagined future.

(3) **Plan based on your vision:** Shift your annual planning process from short-term financial targets to aligning with your long-term vision. Initiate your planning with a clear focus on your long-term vision so all strategic decisions, resource allocations, and individual actions are geared toward achieving the overarching objectives of your imagined future.

(4) **Make "what if" a part of any team planning session:** Begin your team meeting by proposing scenarios that stretch the imagination, such as, "What if we had no budget constraints?" or "What if we expanded into a new product line?" These questions push the team to think outside typical constraints and envision alternative approaches. The objective is to explore a range of perspectives that lead to a broader and richer understanding of the problem and the solution.

(5) **Use "what-if" questions to get buy-in:** The skillful use of "what-if" questions can persuade others to take ownership of the answer. Apple engineer Mike Bell persuaded Steve Jobs (the son,

incidentally, of an immigrant) to back his Apple TV idea by asking him "what if" questions that made Jobs feel as if he'd come up with the idea himself.

(6) Engage and inspire: To truly activate a vision within your organization, simply instructing team members isn't enough—inspire and engage them. Encourage active participation by involving everyone in discussions about the organization's direction. This not only deepens their commitment but also ensures that the vision resonates with their individual roles and values. Transforming vision from a directive to a dialogue cultivates a collective commitment that drives the organization forward effectively.

(7) Don't assume it's all clear: It's crucial to use diverse communication methods to ensure the message reaches everyone effectively. By consistently communicating the vision and integrating real-world examples of its implementation, leaders can help embed the vision deeply within the company culture, making it more likely to influence behavior and decision-making across all levels of the organization.

(8) Focus your experimentation: Promote projects that progressively align with your vision. Achieving a vision is rarely a linear process; often, the path forward isn't clear from the outset. This uncertainty is where strategic experimentation becomes valuable. By implementing small-scale tests, you can discover effective strategies and eliminate those that don't work, gradually steering your efforts toward your ultimate goal. To ensure these experiments contribute effectively to your long-term objectives, they must be carefully focused and aligned with your identity, intention, and imagined future.

(9) When selecting a partner, always think about their intentions: Intention is not just about what you want to change in the world. When we were starting our business, my father always advised us, "Ask yourself, what is the intention of this partner?" Considering that helped us find people who were aligned with our vision and avoid those whose ultimate intentions ran contrary to our own.

(10)Embrace sincerity: Sincerity is essential in developing your vision. It's not about chasing trends or outdoing competitors; it's about adhering to the core values that define who you are and focusing on the issues you aim to resolve. Larry Liu shared that his motivation stems from the value he creates and the problems he addresses, not merely the pursuit of business longevity. A sincere approach ensures that every decision and innovation aligns with your identity and goals, making your efforts more impactful and meaningful.

A Study through Homes

We live in imaginary countries

—*Etel Adnan*

When people ask where I'm from, where I'm *really*
from, I ready my permutations. My mélange of
autumnal streets, my obscure cities, the countries I
found built on a mound of papers
and tears, the pebble-sized universe occupying
my left shoe—I want to tell them everything.
I want to see how far we can go.

—

A Venezuelan couple moves into our neighborhood.
They share their story
with me, why they migrated to Peru: the
inflation, their hunger and fear, their love—they are
relieved they can send money back to their families.
They say they miss the soup their
grandmother used to make, the sleepiness after eating
it, the magic. When I ask what's home for them, they
say home is a fist that dreams.

—*Ae Hee Lee*

Courtesy of Ae Hee Lee.

6

Principle 3: Forge Connections Based on Identity and Authenticity

North Massapequa, New York, 2006

"Thank you for calling T-Mobile, you're speaking to Mary, how can I help you today?"

"Mary, my life is a disaster. I've been in this country for months already, and I still barely know anybody in this tiny town. Whole days drift by without me speaking to another soul, and most of the time, I just stare at the ceiling encircled by a fog of misery that I can't find my way out of. And I'd call home, but they'd all be asleep now, and I don't want to give them any more stress, having to add me to the list of their worries, so instead I'm calling you, Mary, to tell you my troubles and, more than anything, just to hear someone else's voice ..."

Or, at least, that's the sort of thing Saeju probably wanted to say. But, just a few months after leaving Korea, he was still struggling to string together the right words and be understood through his heavy accent. So instead, he started talking the woman in the call center through another imaginary problem with his cellphone, just to keep the faintest hint of connection with another person going for a minute or two more.

The last few years at home had been tough too. Worst, of course, had been watching his father, a doctor who had dedicated all his life to making other people better, being eaten away from the inside by the cancer that killed him at just 51. In their final month together, Saeju's dying father had shared his thoughts about how his profession had got it all wrong: "We treat illnesses after they show up, but we should prevent illness from happening in the first place."

Saeju's family was full of doctors, and he was supposed to follow them too, but he failed the required exam and found himself on a different lifepath—studying electrical engineering instead. After two melancholy years of compulsory national service, time spent still mourning his father, the 24-year-old decided to make a fresh start in the United States, moving to tiny North Massapequa on Long Island because rent there was relatively cheap and it was close to the college where he was signed up to study music. But at first, everything was just worse than ever, no friends and barely any human contact except when calling his cell phone provider to discuss imaginary connection problems.

But then, one day, came the phone call that, indirectly, changed his life.

It was from a relative he barely knew who had recently graduated from Princeton. Her alumni club, she explained, was always on the hunt for exotic new bars and restaurants for its socials, and she was keen to enlist the help of her distant relative who lived so far out of the city where everything was happening that he was sure to know some places that nobody else in the club had ever heard of.

Saeju wasn't actually being invited to join the club for the evening, but the little project briefly gave him something to do with his life, and he seized ownership of it with both hands. "I am going to take care of this," he told his relative. "You will be my guests. I am taking you out, and I know a great Korean bar nearby."

As the big night approached, Saeju was excited about the opportunity to finally create a social circle. But, as we all know, anticipation has a habit of setting you up for disappointment. And so it was for Saeju; as the heavily accented heavy-metal fan from Korea discovered he had very little in common with both his relative and all her Princeton friends.

But then he spotted someone who appeared to be another outcast, sitting in the corner by himself. And, unlike everyone else that evening, that young man listened to Saeju patiently, striving to understand him and never correcting him on any of his many English mistakes. Later that evening Saeju sent his new friend a carefully typed email thanking him for his patience, and he received an almost immediate reply that said, "I never received such a kind email, thank you."

It was the beginning of a beautiful, and extremely profitable, friendship. Artem, the other man in the bar that night, was a Ukrainian software engineer. "That is why he has so much empathy," thought Saeju after learning his new friend's story, "Because he is an immigrant just like me."

Eventually, the two went into business together, mixing their skills and a shared worldview about the importance of preventative healthcare to create a weight-loss app that focuses on behavior change and mental wellness. As of 2022, Noom, the company that Saeju and Artem co-founded in 2008, was valued at $3.7 billion. And the two friends still work closely together, with Artem Petakov serving as Noom's president and Saeju Jeong as its executive chairman.[1]

We will return to the story of Saeju and Artem throughout this chapter as it's a great illustration of how immigrant entrepreneurs forge the connections that create strong businesses. But first, we need to put the learning from the story into its proper context, and to do that, I need to take you away from a club in North Massapequa in the early 21st century to the chilly doorstep of a suburban British house one early morning in the 1930s …

Of Milk Bottles and Birds: What Titmice and Robins Can Teach Us About Immigrant Entrepreneurs

By the 1930s, the "milk round" was a well-established British tradition and a feature of the early morning in cities all over the country. Ever since the mid-19th century, milkmen had braved the early morning chill to drop bottles of fresh milk outside front doors, an invaluable service in the days before refrigeration was common.

But one cold morning in the 1930s, a very small but highly significant change was made to the tradition. For the first time ever, milkmen dropped off bottles with little red aluminum caps across the top. And this tiny innovation turned out to be a big disappointment for some of the milk round's keenest "customers." Before this lid was placed on it, the top of the bottle had been open, with its contents only covered by a rich layer of cream. For generations, early rising red robins and titmice had taken advantage of that, learning that if they nipped down to the doorsteps before householders collected their morning milk, they could enjoy a fine breakfast of their own, feasting on the cream on top.

So, you can imagine the disappointment of the first robin or titmouse to reach a bottle on that frosty 1930s morning to discover its route to the milk blocked not by a delicious layer of cream but rather by a cold, hard piece of aluminum. That shared moment turned, eventually, into a significant divergence in the birds' behavior. For while the robins never learned how to pierce the new barrier, the titmice eventually did and were able to return to their old habit of enjoying families' milk before they arose.

So, why were the titmice able to outsmart the milkmen but the robins never could? The answer comes from the work of the late Dr. Alan Wilson of the University of California, Berkeley.[2] From his studies of birds, he identified how a species improves its survival prospects through a specific pattern of behavior: flocking. He identified three essential conditions for this: mobility within the group, innovation from certain members, and a method of sharing these innovations across the community.

So, how does Wilson's theory explain why titmice were enjoying milk while robins went thirsty? It's simple: robins are territorial and solitary, whereas titmice are social, flocking birds who interact frequently and learn collectively.

Like the titmice, immigrant entrepreneurs often "flock" together with their kind, and such behavior can bring advantages beyond just strength in numbers; it can also be a driver of innovation that can help to lift a whole community up.

Academics use the term "homophilic ties" as a more esoteric way of describing the phenomenon commonly described as "birds of a feather flock together." It's a phenomenon that has been extensively commented on at least as far back as the great philosophers of ancient Greece. Aristotle noted that people "love those who are like themselves," and Plato similarly observed that "similarity begets friendship."[3]

Of course, you don't need to be a Greek philosopher to see the truth of those words. It seems obvious that people will form ties based on similarity, and my and others' research has consistently shown how important homophilic ties are for immigrant entrepreneurs. Using homophilic ties results in a higher level of trust, shared understanding, and interpersonal attraction than would be expected among less similar individuals. In the case of Saeju and Artem, their shared experience of being immigrants and navigating the challenges of adapting to a new country formed the basis of their friendship.

However, beyond the seemingly obvious benefits of homophilic ties, it is crucial to note that there are certain common misconceptions about how they work. And it's only when we have understood them, and learned about all the different ways in which entrepreneurs can use homophilic ties to their advantage, that we can truly see how anybody, whether immigrant or otherwise, can make use of this force to generate long-lasting impact.

But before turning to that, I want to briefly discuss the crucial importance of social capital, which sets the stage for understanding how immigrant entrepreneurs use homophilic ties to, once again, turn something that they appear to lack into one of their greatest advantages.

The Value of Social Capital

Every leader understands that smooth business operations hinge on personal connections both within and outside their organizations—contracts are executed more efficiently, teams deliver higher output, and individual learning and creativity thrive. Most will agree that strong interpersonal connections act as the organization's glue, facilitating smoother operations. Without these relationships, business may continue, but not as effectively or sustainably. These connections are one element of what is referred to as "social capital," i.e., the connections that enable people to work together effectively to achieve a common purpose, like the visions that we discussed in the previous chapter. Such connections are underpinned by shared values and cultural norms. As the term "social capital" itself suggests, an investment in your connections can yield tangible benefits in terms of increased organizational impact and improved financial outcomes.

When it comes to building and growing a business, it's universally acknowledged that social capital is crucial. To thrive on this journey, you need a network of connections, including friends, family, and colleagues. Despite many accounts of the heroic struggles of brilliant individuals to build businesses, entrepreneurship is never, in reality, a solo endeavor. Research extensively underscores the significance of social ties in business, especially during the initial stages of a venture. These early relationships are critical as they form the backbone of a company's growth and sustainability.

The process might seem straightforward—connect people and watch the benefits unfold. However, that is a misconception for a couple of reasons. Firstly, social capital faces challenges in many organizations due to the increased instability and volatility that is defining the business world today, coupled with a heavy reliance on remote interactions. Fostering relationships during uncertain times becomes even more challenging when team members are dispersed. Indeed, one of the most frequent questions I've had in recent years from the Oxford student startup founders whom I mentor is "How do I motivate my team when the majority of us are working remotely?"

Secondly, despite understanding the value of robust workplace relationships, many leaders struggle with how to cultivate this social capital. Recognizing the importance of good relationships is one thing; actively fostering them is another entirely. This task is made even harder in a modern world characterized by ever-increasing diversity both within and across cultures, where assumptions that people share the same sets of "traditional" values no longer hold water.

Perhaps the above challenges can be summed up by saying that people nowadays are not only more remote from each other in the literal terms of where they sit to work but also mentally more remote in the sense that they come from an increasingly diverse range of backgrounds and live at a time in which traditional cultures, characterized by relative homogeneity of values, are being splintered into a multiplicity of pieces that seem to drift ever further from each other.

Much is made of the many advantages of diversity—of which I am a great proponent—but even we advocates of diversity must be realistic about the social capital challenges that it brings. As workplaces and organizational partnerships become more diverse, does it become more difficult to forge the connections based on common ground that are at the heart of social capital? That is where, I believe, perhaps paradoxically, immigrant entrepreneurs come in. How they build, negotiate, and manage social capital is one of their greatest assets in helping them build businesses that last, and one of the keys to that is how they make use of homophilic ties.

Social Capital: Turning Weakness into Strength

We have seen in previous chapters how successful immigrant entrepreneurs are experts at turning seeming disadvantages to their favor. While some may see immigrants as being lost between different cultures, entrepreneurs see the opportunity to build a bridge between the two. Where others see immigrants as having fractured identities, entrepreneurs use the same as the foundations of businesses that last. So it is with social capital too, because it is precisely immigrants' lack of it that forces them to turn to powerful strategies that allow them to build and solidify it in ways that not only give their businesses strong foundations but also equip them to grow and develop through challenge and change.

Illustrations of immigrants' general lack of capital, in terms of their lack of access to connections, finance, and information, abound. Noubar Afeyan, the founder of Moderna, did not have the sort of knowledge that native-born people take for granted about something as simple as how to apply to university:

> The comedy of being an immigrant [is] that you actually don't know a lot of things because people don't tell you you're supposed to apply to five schools … So, I just applied to one school [MIT]; thank God they took me.[4]

Similarly, Calendly founder Tope Awotona reflected on how he left college without any job offers because neither he nor his mother understood the conventional ways to improve your prospects:

> I think being the child of immigrants maybe hurt my understanding of how to be successful in the business world in America … [because] I didn't do some of the things that my peers were doing, like internships … My parents … would've probably pushed me to do that if they were from here, but they didn't; my mom didn't know that herself.[5]

Such experiences strongly resonate with me; often, especially early in your immigrant experience, you feel like you're going along with the crowd, only to discover that they've all suddenly gone somewhere else without you knowing why. And then you have to work out why you're now no longer with the crowd but all alone in a dark forest.

Lacking information and a broad range of connections, immigrants have to make the most of what they do have. So, they rely on their kin: their families or the people who come from the same ethnic or cultural group. (It's important to emphasize here that ethnic identity is socially constructed rather than objectively determined. In other words, people belong to an ethnic group because they, and others, believe that they do.) At a time when you have nobody, no capital, and no access to information that is available to others, these ties can become your most valuable assets.

All the above is true. But it is also an overly simplistic view of homophily, which restricts the concept to just one type of tie and feeds misconceptions about its actual nature. As we shall see in the following section, there are actually three types of homophilic ties, and an understanding of each is essential if people, especially non-immigrants, are to enjoy the business benefits that such ties can create.

Heritage, Experience, and Value Homophily

The main misconception about homophilic ties is that they can *only* exist between people who come from the same ethnic or cultural background. Of course, such homophilic ties do exist and can be enormously important in some people's lives and entrepreneurial journeys. They are often crucial for immigrant entrepreneurs who have recently arrived in a country and lack social capital. Remember the young Isaac Larian getting his first job in LA because a kind chef recognized a fellow Iranian in need?

However, while such shared heritages may create a platform for connection, the existence of a platform does not guarantee that anything will take place on it. Think of Saeju Jeong's inability to connect with his Princeton-educated relative despite their shared cultural, ethnic, and even familial ties.

Furthermore, if we limit our thinking about homophily simply to ties based on a common heritage, we fail to recognize the other, perhaps even more beneficial, ties that can be forged on the basis of that which unites us. I'd go so far as to say that immigrant entrepreneurs who restrict themselves to ties based solely on common heritage may make some strong connections that help sustain a business, but by limiting themselves in that way, they make it less likely that their company will grow to become one of the success stories that I have been highlighting throughout this book. In other words, if an immigrant entrepreneur restricts themself to a narrow conception of their community, they limit the profit, growth, and impact that they can have.

A second level of homophilic ties are those that come not from our ethnic and cultural heritage but from the specific experiences that we have had during our lives. The distinction between the two may not seem clear, but we can understand it by considering our heritage to be those characteristics that would be common to most people born and brought up in the same time and place as we were. Whereas our experiences are the more unique aspects of our life journeys, which may have followed similar courses to the other people brought up around us but may also have diverged significantly.

In that context, a good example of an experience that lends itself to the forging of homophilic ties is the experience of emigration itself. The experience of leaving behind all you have known and moving to another place where you potentially find yourself feeling lost between different cultures is one that is common to people from a multiplicity of different heritages. We can see the power of homophilic ties formed on the basis of shared experiences through the story of Saeju and Artem, whose initial connection came from the fact that they were both immigrants. That experience alone was enough to start the formation of a bond; it didn't matter that their ethnic and cultural heritages (Korean and Ukrainian) were so very different.

So far, we have looked at two types of homophilic ties—shared heritage and shared experiences—and related both to immigrant entrepreneurs. The two types open up immigrants to a progressively broader range of different connections; there may be only a relatively limited number of people from your original home in your new home, but there will almost certainly be many more people there who share your experience of having emigrated from *somewhere* else.

But beyond those two levels, there is a third level of homophilic ties that, potentially, opens up connections to an even broader range of people, including those who have never had the experience of emigrating at all. And that is homophily on the basis of shared values. In some ways that can be the most powerful type of homophilic tie, and it by no means requires you to have emigrated to access it. We see the power of this type of tie in the story of Saeju and Artem, because while their initial connection did come from their common immigrant backgrounds, it only flourished into a highly successful, long-term collaboration because both had shared values, most significantly a commitment to preventative healthcare, which, in Saeju's case, came from his experience of seeing his father killed by cancer.

So, the three important types of homophilic ties—shared heritage, shared experiences, and shared values—and relationships based on these ties may use different ones at different times. All of which brings us to two other key misconceptions about homophilic ties: that they happen automatically and that when they have been established, they are static and unchanging.

Homophilic ties do not happen automatically even when the conditions seem to be right for a connection to be created based on significant commonalities. Further, for homophilic ties to be constructed and maintained at any level, they need to be actively worked on. One of the main ways in which immigrant entrepreneurs do this is through their use of narratives, storytelling that allows them to share elements of their own heritages, experiences, and values in ways that resonate with others and forge connections.

Immigrant entrepreneurs are typically blessed with rich and powerful stories, which they can use to their advantage when striving to create connections. The most successful immigrant entrepreneurs, as we shall see, are experts at using their stories to consciously create authentic connections with a diverse range of people, some of whom share their heritage, others their experiences, and others their values (and some all).

However, even when powerful stories have been thus employed and meaningful homophilic ties created, that is by no means the end of the story. My two decades of research on this subject shows that such connections are dynamic, evolve over time, and require continuous nurturing in order to thrive.

Finally, having had the experience of lacking connection, when immigrant entrepreneurs do make a new relationship, they cherish that asset and really lean into it, to make the most of it and compensate for their other disadvantages. And that is why immigrants are particularly strong at making connections that enable them to survive, learn, innovate, and, ultimately, thrive.

Essentially, what I am arguing here is that homophilic ties matter. And while the most successful immigrant entrepreneurs are particularly adept at creating and strengthening such ties on different levels, anyone can learn from them about how to do that. I'll give you my tips for creating and maintaining homophilic ties at the end of this chapter. But first, I want to turn in more detail to some examples of the benefits that homophilic ties produce for entrepreneurs, looking specifically at how they create deep connections between business partners based on the sort of trust that normally characterizes a well-functioning family.

Building Deep Trust and Family-Style Ties

Trust, truly, makes the world go round. People drop their children off at school trusting their teachers to take care of them. People go to work in the morning trusting drivers to obey traffic rules. People get married trusting the other person with all their heart when they say, "I do." Our society functions because we trust its institutions, laws, and systems. But despite the centrality of trust to our lives, and its importance in the world of business, there has been surprisingly little research on the subject in the context of entrepreneurship and very little said about how entrepreneurs create and maintain trust.

Again, the experience of immigrant entrepreneurs is instructive, and once again their strength in this area derives from how they compensate for their weaknesses. Immigrant entrepreneurs, being vulnerable members of society, are particularly required to trust others and to prove themselves trustworthy. Indeed, trust is one of the most essential forms of capital an immigrant entrepreneur has. And homophily plays a crucial role in the creation of trust. Homophily-based trust requires immigrant entrepreneurs, and others, to find deep and meaningful connections that will be strong enough to support them through serious situations in which a partner who lacked trust might just walk away, threatening to bring the whole business crashing down.

Shared heritage, shared experiences, and shared values can contribute significantly to the creation of trust. For example, when I interviewed Karan Bilimoria for this book, he offered the following reflections on the roots of the trusting relationships that have brought such strength to his business:

> My business partner was from Hyderabad. We knew each other from our childhood, our families [have] known each other well for four generations on his mother's side and his father's side. And there was a trust. So, there's that implicit trust, because the family, in your background … I would have trusted Arjun Reddy, my partner, with my life. I mean, that's how important trust is in life and in business. And that goes back again to our origins from Hyderabad and India where we were both born, and our family connections.

Here, Bilimoria draws upon a specific aspect of his heritage, his family's ties with another family from the same part of India, which contributed to the creation of his strong partnership with Arjun Reddy, the co-founder of Cobra Beer. Similarly, Larry Liu of Weee! told me that his business partner was a school friend who was basically family even before they worked together, and he used exactly the same words as Karan Bilimoria to describe the strength of that relationship: "I would trust him with my life."

Close ties are not restricted to the people you grew up with. In the following quote from our interview, Bilimoria shows how drawing on your broader heritage (in this case, the minority community that he belongs to and his mother tongue) can help form partnerships with people in other companies:

> The biggest wholesalers in the M25 area, the Greater London area, were of Indian origin as well. And I'm a Zoroastrian Parsi ... we're [a] very small, but very successful community ... we came from Persia over 1,000 years ago and settled in India. We left when the conversion to Islam took place. We went as refugees to India to keep the religion. So, we are a very, very close community; we landed on the western coast of India [and settled] in Gujarat ... And to this day, our mother tongue is Gujarati. So, the Gujarati community feels an affinity to us. So, the biggest wholesalers in the London area were Gujarati ... [and] what has strengthened the connection was the fact that I was Parsi, when they met my family, for example, there's that affinity because of that link of speaking the same language and for them having respect for us Parsis.

Similarly, when looking for funding in the crucial early days of his business, Bilimoria made use of homophilic ties rooted in his background and used them to grow trust and form relationships that became as strong as family ties, as he explained to me:

> The key challenge is, of course, raising finance for an unknown brand when you have no security. I had no money. I had no collateral. So, the owner of the brewery would tell his friends to lend me money for me to pay him. And that was all done on trust ... Three and a half years after we started, we had a business angel who put in £50,000 for 5% of the company, valuing it at a million pounds, which was a big deal in those days ... that was because it was through one of our advisors, again, a member of the Asian community, a Gujarati member of the Asian community, who then became one of my closest friends. He's godfather to one of my children ... And without his support, I would not have been able to get Cobra off the ground. So, it goes back to the relationship and trust.

What Bilimoria comes back to time and again is the building of trust and relationships based on a shared heritage that operates on the interrelated levels of locality, nationality, culture, and language. Sometimes these ties are based on family connections, but they can also develop into ties that are family-like in their strength.

From the outside, it might appear that people with a common heritage naturally flock together, but research shows that is not the case. What Bilimoria exemplifies is the active use of narratives to create a sense of shared identity, i.e., using homophily to create strong forms of trust. By sharing stories about aspects of his own identity—Parsi, Gujarati, Indian— Bilimoria is proactively creating connections through a process called narrative identity work. In other words, the benefits of homophilic ties are not produced by chance but rather by deliberate actions on the part of the immigrant entrepreneur. Immigrants may find it easier to find those connections with others who share their background or experiences, but what they do is something that any entrepreneur with an identity (i.e., anyone) can emulate.

I'll talk more about how to do that in the tips at the end of this chapter. But for now, let's stay with Karan Bilimoria. His ties with the Indian/ Gujarati community in London were clearly crucial, especially at the outset. But I would argue that one of the key reasons why Bilimoria has gone on to enjoy such success is because he has used the power of homophilic ties to establish powerful business connections with people who do not share his specific cultural heritage. Consider, for example, how he establishes commonality with people from different immigrant groups, which translates into trust and successful business relationships. Here, he is responding to a question about the potential for Turkish food to become more popular in the UK, and he starts by making connections between the experiences of other migrant communities (including the one to which he belongs):

> The wonderful thing ... [about] Britain's love of food ... now [is that you] get truly authentic food, the Indian food that you get here in the UK... is so authentic and high quality that anyone from India would say this is the best Indian food ... Similarly with Chinese restaurants, similarly with Turkish restaurants ... [6]

Bilimoria went on to explain how he observed the increasing popularity of Turkish food and thus started approaching restaurateurs to explain how he had created Cobra as a beer to go not only with Indian food but all food, which helped turn it into an instant hit in England's Turkish restaurants. No doubt, at least part of that success was Bilimoria's ability to create connections with the restaurants' owners based on the common experience of being immigrants trying to sell a product from their original home in a new country.

The power of the experience of immigration to forge ties between people, even when they come from countries with histories of antagonism, is evident in the connections between the Turkish immigrant founders of BioNTech and Albert Bourla, the Greek immigrant chief executive of Pfizer. "We realized that he is from Greece, and that I'm from Turkey," recounted Dr. Uğur Şahin of BioNTech, "[So] it was very personal from the start." That personal connection helped create such trust between the two companies that BioNTech did much of its work on the COVID-19 vaccine for Pfizer without having fully agreed the financial aspects of their partnership. "Trust and personal relationship [are] so important in such business, because everything is going so fast," said Dr. Şahin. "We still have a term sheet and not yet a final contract on many things." That trust contributed significantly to a partnership that saw BioNTech produce an enormously successful vaccine for Pfizer (a company founded, incidentally, by another immigrant, the German American Charles Pfizer).[7]

My own family's experience in business reiterates the power of the shared experience of immigration. Consider this quote from one of our employees talking about my father in an interview for an academic paper:

> I will work for [the company] day and night, vacations, weekends … without money even. I trust [Karra] very much, and I want him to be even more successful. After all, he is an immigrant too, and I would rather help an immigrant like me, than help a local.[8]

When we were building our own business and expanding it, we deliberately attempted to foster and leverage a sense of commonality and kinship that was based not only on shared heritage but also shared experience. Specifically, we focused on the experience of immigration, which linked most of our staff and our partners, and the experience of having lived under communism, which united us with distributors across the post-Soviet bloc.

That rhetoric helped create the foundation for those quasi-family ties, but rhetoric alone is not, of course, enough; those foundations only became strong because we backed up our words with actions. So, in addition to emphasizing what we had in common, we exhibited extraordinary levels of trust in the early stages of business relationships. For example, we advanced new partners significant levels of stock, without any contractual protection in the event of malfeasance—partners would be invited to repay after the stock had been sold, a highly unusual practice in Turkey and Eastern Europe, particularly during the 1990s, as those markets were riddled with uncertainty. This kind of apparently altruistic behavior, combined with an emphasis on shared ethnic, immigrant, or post-communist identity, fostered very high levels of trust among partners and resulted in a remarkably coherent network that operated ostensibly in the manner of a biological family but extended far beyond its traditional boundaries.

It's important to emphasize, however, that when I talk about using narrative to create identity, it is absolutely not about pretending to be someone who you are not. You may choose to emphasize some aspects of your identity more than others, but ultimately relationships, in business as in life, have to be based on authenticity if they are to be strong and survive. Frances Frei and Anne Morriss wrote in a *Harvard Business Review* article[9] about the crucial role of trust in business, and true trust can never exist in the long term when it is based on inauthentic behavior. Adapting their idea of the triangle of trust, I would argue that trust must be based on consistency, reliability, and honesty, i.e., you have to be the same person, stick to your word, and speak the truth in order to be trusted. So, emulate immigrant entrepreneurs by using your identities to forge connections, but if you truly want to create trust and achieve the success of the best of those entrepreneurs, then those identities must be authentically you.

A Caveat: The Danger of Overreliance on Family-Style Ties

I want to add one more final caveat here. As anyone who has ever been a member of a family knows, family ties are not *always* good things.[10] In the context of entrepreneurship, using homophilic connections to form family-style bonds with your staff and your partners can, of course, bring many advantages as I have shown above. But risks remain. Overreliance on these ties for too long can start to stifle innovation and, ultimately, impact business growth. Being mindful of that risk is the first step to mitigating it. And the way to do that is to recognize the value of venturing outside your comfort zone, which, in this context, can mean sometimes hiring people who are *not* like you, who could be classified as outsiders, but who bring valuable perspectives with them from the outside world. Tight-knit communities have many strengths, but they are particularly vulnerable to groupthink, and outside perspectives are the antidote against that. So, balance your tightness with enough looseness that will allow ideas to flow and fresh new thought streams to enter. Such freshness and the creativity it brings can become especially valuable as your business gets older and has to face and adapt to new challenges as it strives to remain relevant and grow in an ever-changing world.

Strategies for forging connections:

(1) **Focus on what unites us:** Not all communities are based on ethnicity or a shared heritage. In any situation during your entrepreneurship journey, you can strive to find some connection with the people you are dealing with and actively build on it through narrative identity work, always remembering that we have much more in common than what divides us.

(2) **Strengthen your ties by joining other networks:** Even if you're not an immigrant with strong homophilic ties with your community in your new home, you can find other ways to expand your network and make powerful connections with people who share your background, interests, and values; think about becoming an active member of an alumni network, a community group, or a sports team.

(3) **Show empathy:** Empathy is a cornerstone of effective partnership and collaboration as with Saeju Jeong and Artem Petakov. Empathy requires you to take the time to actively listen to others without prejudice, to understand where they are coming from, and to reflect on what they're telling you.

(4) **Be curious:** You can only truly forge and strengthen ties with someone when you really know who that person is. So, be curious and invest time in getting to know your staff, your suppliers, your partners, and your customers. It's crucial to know these people, what motivates them, and what they dream of. Be like Karan Bilimoria, who takes a hands-on approach by visiting the restaurants that will sell his products.

(5) **Take the attention away from yourself:** Charismatic leaders can achieve much in entrepreneurship, but you most effectively build and strengthen social capital when you shift the focus away from yourself. No single individual embodies the whole organization, and overemphasis on a leader's star qualities can undermine the essential elements of trust, collaboration, and fairness within a team.

(6) **Don't leave collaboration to chance:** Effective collaboration in the workplace doesn't happen by accident. Before any project, teams should engage in meaningful discussions about each member's strengths, preferred communication styles, and past experiences—both good and bad—in teamwork.

(7) **Plan for potential challenges:** Establishing protocols for addressing disagreements ensures that every team member feels respected and heard. This proactive approach strengthens trust and cohesiveness, making current and future collaborations more effective.

(8) **Cultivate trust through integrity:** As a leader, fostering trust is crucial, and this begins with a steadfast commitment to integrity. Ethical lapses, no matter how minor, must be addressed openly to build a culture of accountability. This approach prevents unethical behaviors from becoming normalized and strengthens trust across all levels of the organization.

(9) **Be proactive in sharing information:** To cultivate a "family-like" atmosphere in the workplace, where staff genuinely support one another, it's crucial to prioritize transparency. When information is freely shared, rather than hoarded or hidden, it prevents silos, reduces power struggles, and fosters inclusivity by making people feel valued. This not only builds trust but also sparks creativity and enhances performance.

(10) **Recognize the risks of creating too tight communities:** Avoid the risk of groupthink and remain open to innovation by hiring people who bring different styles and alternative perspectives.

Dear Immigrants

From the purses of immigrants roll out candies
like not-blessed eye balls, right in front of our feet.

And just about to say Well Come, we
rather remain silent
as if ripping off the tree roots from its soil
or sending the raindrops back where they came from
locking up our dear immigrants, outside
till we lock ourselves into cells,
shrinking more and more.

—*Elif Sezen*

"Dear Immigrants" was published in Elif Sezen's book
A Little Book of Unspoken History
(Puncher & Wattmann, 2018), page 46.

Courtesy of Elif Sezen.

7

Principle 4: Generate Profit the Right Way

Guatemala, 1980s

Luis was living every little kid's dream but in the middle of a nightmare.

First, the dream part: He was growing up in a candy factory. Or, at least, spending a lot of his childhood at the factory owned by his mom's family near their home in Guatemala City. While the young Luis was spending his time in the candy factory putting machines back together, the world outside around him was falling apart. When he was born at the end of the 1970s, Guatemala was halfway through what would ultimately become a 36-year civil war, characterized by coups, chaos, and genocidal campaigns against the country's indigenous population—the nightmare.

The conflict intensified in 1982, when Luis was three, when another military coup saw General Efrain Rios Montt briefly seize power and launch a vicious "scorched earth" crackdown on guerrilla forces and civilians alike that would later see him convicted of crimes against humanity. In 1983, Rios Montt was himself deposed, in yet another military coup. The conflict did not end until December 1996, meaning that, like millions of other Guatemalans, Luis had spent his entire childhood in the shadow of a war that had killed hundreds of thousands and led to the displacement of more than a million people.

In some ways, Luis had grown up in relative privilege throughout the chaos. Both his parents were doctors, and his mother, who raised him alone, could afford to send him to a private English-language school and had recourse to her family's candy factory as the boy's weekend playground. When not playing there, Luis was spending his spare time completing math textbooks for fun and teaching himself how to pirate video games for his cherished Commodore 64.

However, as he grew up, he did, of course, become increasingly conscious of the poverty and violence around him. And his family's wealth did not make them immune from the situation. Car theft was so common that every few months a member of his family would have a vehicle stolen, and when Luis was fifteen, one of his aunts was kidnapped and held for ransom for more than a week.

That was the tipping point that persuaded the young Luis that he did not want to live in Guatemala anymore. So, just before the official end of the civil war, he spent $1,200 flying to El Salvador to complete an English language test. With that expensive and inconvenient experience behind him, he was able to enroll to study math at Duke University in North Carolina before moving to do his PhD at Pittsburgh's Carnegie Mellon University (founded, incidentally, in 1900 by another migrant, the Scottish American entrepreneur and philanthropist Andrew Carnegie).

Luis's decision to change his life course then has had a direct impact on the life of you and every other computer user in the world. While working on his PhD at Carnegie Mellon, Luis took on one of Yahoo!'s biggest problems at the time—preventing fake email accounts from being created by bots. Luis and his advisor, Manuel Blum, devised a solution: CAPTCHA, a test to distinguish between humans and machines. This idea, though revolutionary and now ubiquitous, didn't earn Luis any immediate wealth. He gave the idea to Yahoo! for free, not realizing its commercial potential.

Though he didn't profit directly from CAPTCHA, Luis later developed reCAPTCHA, which helped digitize old texts as users completed CAPTCHA tests. This "side hustle" brought in a lucrative partnership with *The New York Times* and eventually led to a profitable sale of the technology to Google. Despite this success, Luis left Google early, walking away from substantial compensation, to focus on his true passion—education. He was motivated by the poverty he had witnessed in Guatemala, and his realization that the monetization of education meant that it was not curing poverty but rather exacerbating it:

> A lot of people … [think] education … brings equality to different social classes. But I always thought [of it] as the opposite, something that brings inequality … those who have money can buy themselves the best education in the world. And those who don't barely learn how to read and write.[1]

So, having made enough money to not have to worry about financial gain, Luis teamed up with one of his students, a Swiss immigrant called Severin Hacker, to try and come up with a way to offer improved education for free. Their experiences as immigrants had also made them realize the particular value of language education. And their vision of improved, free language learning eventually materialized as Duolingo, which has gone on to become the most downloaded educational app in the world. More than 800 million people have downloaded it to learn at least one of the 40 languages it offers. With around 40 million monthly active users, there are now more people learning languages in the United States through Duolingo than through the school system. And, although money was never its motivator, Duolingo currently has a net worth just more than $10 billion.[2]

I'm sure you've already noticed that the story of Luis von Ahn, Severin Hacker, and Duolingo is wonderfully illustrative of so many of the immigrant entrepreneurship themes that we've looked at in the previous three principles. For example, it's clear that shared experiences and values contributed to the homophilic ties between Luis and Severin (ties that created such trust that the only contract between them regarding their multibillion-dollar business is a few bullet points on a Word document).

It's also evident that Duolingo's vision was rooted in Luis's identity, and its imagined future clearly came from his intention to change the world in line with values that had been shaped by his experiences in Guatemala. That vision also helped attract the top-quality staff that any tech company needs to succeed, persuading people who shared it to turn their backs on attractive offers from top firms like Facebook in favor of joining Duolingo's Pennsylvania headquarters. In the early days, the team grew to around 60 or 70 employees, many of whom had received job offers from much larger companies. However, what drew them to Duolingo was a deep belief in the mission of providing free language education to the world. This shared sense of purpose created a dedicated team, focused not just on business growth but on a genuine commitment to the mission—something that still resonates with the company today.

But what I want to focus on in this chapter is another remarkable aspect of the story: It shows that commitment to a purpose beyond money can, ironically, be a direct route to financial success. Take, for instance, how Duolingo managed to surpass a giant like Rosetta Stone, which had dominated the online language learning market before Duolingo's launch. Despite being told that Duolingo would never be able to beat such a well-established company, the results proved otherwise. Duolingo now has many times more users, and its revenue far surpasses that of Rosetta Stone. The key to this success lies in Duolingo's mission of offering free language education, which has been not only good for society but also an excellent business strategy. Without spending heavily on marketing, Duolingo relies on its vast user base—97% of whom don't pay for the service—as its marketing engine, spreading the word and driving organic growth. This demonstrates that having a mission rooted in providing value rather than just making money can lead to an even greater level of financial achievement.

In the rest of this chapter, we'll look at why immigrant entrepreneurs are more likely to create a company with a higher purpose beyond profit and why that is better not only for the people they serve but also for their bottom line. But let's start by looking at how the modern context demands, and rewards, businesses that aim to do better, not just in terms of their financial performance but their social purpose.

The Rules of the Game Have Changed: Milton Friedman Is Outdated

Capitalism is facing increasing scrutiny, and many would say justly so. In recent years, the business sector has been criticized as a significant contributor to social, environmental, and economic issues. To take just the industry I know best as an example, the beautiful façade of fashion masks a reality in which the simple business of making clothes and accessories creates 10% of the carbon emissions that are tipping the planet toward climate catastrophe, 20% of all industrial water pollution, and a garbage truck full of discarded clothes every second. It's also estimated that more than $125 billion of fashion products are made using modern slavery practices.[3]

Fashion is far from an outlier here. Similar, or worse, charges could be laid against every essential sector, from the farming industry that puts food on our plates to the airlines that fly us and the energy companies that make the world go round. Most non-essential industries fall into the same category too—swilling down valuable resources at an ever-accelerating rate and spitting out ever-increasing quantities of trash.

As consumers become increasingly aware of the impact that industries have on the world around us, there is now a widespread perception that corporations thrive at the expense of communities, the environment, and their own employees. However, as companies have started to engage more with corporate social responsibility (CSR) initiatives, they paradoxically face more criticism for the failures of society. Companies are trying harder to highlight their sustainable credentials and their environmental, social, and governance (ESG) efforts, but they do so in the face of an increasingly skeptical public, who doubt the sincerity and effectiveness of these corporate initiatives, seeing them as little more than barely disguised marketing strategies. The term "greenwashing" was coined in 1986 by the environmentalist Jay Westerveld (who used it to describe the hotel industry's practice of asking people to reuse towels "to save the planet")[4]; both the word and the practice have become increasingly common since then.

Many of these challenges stem from a dated approach to value creation that prioritizes short-term financial gains without considering the long-term impacts on customers, natural resources, suppliers, and community welfare. Such approaches are summed up by the famous words of the highly influential 20th-century economist Milton Friedman, a Nobel Laureate and advisor of Ronald Reagan, who said:

> There is one and only one social responsibility of business—to use its resources and engage in activities designed to increase its profits so long as it stays within the rules of the game, which is to say, engages in open and free competition without deception or fraud.[5]

It's ironic that these words can be found in just a few seconds in the online version of a *New York Times* article written by Friedman in 1970. In other words, Friedman's statement is so readily available because it features in one of the many articles digitized by Luis von Ahn, a man whose career so completely contradicts the arguments Friedman was making here. Even the digitization itself was a spin-off from a project created entirely for social good. And the money that von Ahn earned from it was ultimately invested in Duolingo, a company that prioritizes its socially responsible mission to provide free language education all over the world, and it achieves that mission while also generating enormous profits.

As von Ahn's story illustrates, Friedman's view from 1970 is horribly outdated now. Perhaps we can attribute that to the fact that Friedman was ignorant of or impervious to the full impact that business has on the environment that sustains all human life. Also, as he was born in 1912, we can well understand that the business models of the internet age would be utterly alien to his thinking. But despite what Friedman would have thought, what von Ahn's story shows is that social responsibility in business is not just good for the people and the planet, it's also good for the bottom line.

It's an inescapable fact that if you want to create a self-sustaining business, it is essential to make a profit. Luis von Ahn saw that when he had to introduce advertising to Duolingo in order to keep the free app up and running. This recognition of the importance of balancing profit and purpose is neatly captured in the words that Colin Mayer, my colleague at Oxford, has added to the end of Friedman's famous dictum (I've underlined Colin's addition for emphasis):

> There is one and only one social responsibility of business—to use its resources and engage in activities designed to increase its profits so long as it stays within the rules of the game, which is to say, engages in open and free competition without deception or fraud <u>and not profit from producing problems for others</u>.[6]

That's an important addition, but it does not fully capture the essence of Colin's argument. It's one thing that our businesses make a profit and avoid creating problems, but it's even better if we can make a profit and actively solve problems, too. As Colin himself simply put it, "If [profit] comes from solving [the] problems of others that is all to the good, if it doesn't then it isn't."[7]

Agreeing with Colin Mayer's formulations, it's clear to me that businesses need to lead the way with what I term "inclusive purpose," i.e., an approach that recognizes that a company's success and the success of the communities in which it operates are inextricably intertwined and that its sustainability depends on how it contributes to the sustainability of the environment in which it exists. Inclusive purpose is the principle that both economic growth and social development should be pursued through value-oriented strategies. Here, "value" signifies a balance of benefits over costs, rather than merely focusing on benefits alone. While businesses have traditionally been adept at creating economic value—measuring profit as revenues minus expenses—they often considered social impact as a secondary concern. This perspective tended to obscure the potential synergies between a company's economic performance and social health.

Inclusive purpose is exemplified by how the immigrant entrepreneurs I have studied build and run their businesses. For them, inclusive purpose is not just a concept, or a marketing exercise, or a term that sits, ignored, in their companies' annual statements. Having inclusive purpose means that it is fully integrated into a strategy that aims to create economic value *and* societal improvement at the same time. This concept extends beyond CSR, ESG, and sustainability; it is about embedding societal needs into the core of business strategies, making them central elements of corporate operations and realigning success metrics with social progress.

Of course, anyone can say these things, and indeed everybody these days is talking about responsible business, but the crucial thing, obviously, is to make being a responsible business a reality and not just something that you're doing for the optics or to be awarded some sort of sustainability certification. So, what does that mean in practical terms? Again, much can be gleaned from looking at immigrant entrepreneurs; those whom I have studied have ingrained visions that come from their identities and their intention to change the world by solving issues that impact others.

Doing this requires them to have a detailed understanding of the problems that they aim to solve—it's not enough to just want to solve a problem; you have to be committed to learning about it so you can solve it properly without producing unintended negative consequences. Immigrant entrepreneurs often have an advantage in that regard because they are more likely to have personal experience of the problem that they are addressing or to have seen it all around them as they were growing up, as was the case with Luis von Ahn in Guatemala.

Equally importantly, immigrant entrepreneurs focus on the *means* by which they intend to achieve their ends, which is why they treat partners fairly, pay employees well, and support the communities to which they belong. Essentially, they understand that they are part of a broader ecosystem that consists of customers, employees, suppliers, communities, future generations, and the natural world, all of which must be valued. And they also understand that all their aims and actions impact that ecosystem, from the products they produce to the way they treat their workers.

Also, immigrant entrepreneurs show us that such socially responsible practices can, indeed must, be combined with profit-making. There are two key points related to that. The first is that, as is emphasized throughout this book, profit and purpose are not opposed. In fact, purpose can be, as the Duolingo example and many others show, a great source of competitive advantage. In other words, it's not purpose or profit but rather purpose = profit. Sometimes, when you pursue purpose, profit comes almost as a side effect of that.

The second key point is that not all profits are created equal. Profit with purpose is more likely to help a business grow and sustain itself over the long term. In other words, you can turn a quick buck dishonorably, but if you really want to generate a business, and an impact, that lasts, the best way to do it is to put it at the heart of a sustainable cycle of prosperity for yourself, your staff, your partners, and the communities you both rely on and serve. It reminds me of the often-cited proverb, "If you want to go fast, go alone; if you want to go far, go together." Applying that to a business context, we can say that a company with a conscience that places itself at the heart of a community is much more likely to remain vital for longer.

How Immigrant Entrepreneurs Make Profit with Purpose

The literature on entrepreneurship distinguishes between the values of the entrepreneur—such as growth and profit maximization—and the personal values of the social entrepreneur, who focuses on the welfare of others and producing societal benefits. However, my own research shows that these two sets of values should never be seen as incompatible. Immigrant entrepreneurs' values enable them to produce social and economic outcomes at the same time, never compromising on the former for the sake of the latter but also knowing that without profit, running a business is like trying to drive a car without refilling the gas—it won't go far. I'll add to that analogy by saying that putting the wrong gas in the tank will ultimately destroy the engine. When a business is based on inclusive purpose it generates profit in the right way; in other words, the company's commitment to its values puts the right gas in the tank and keeps the engine healthy in the long run.

We have seen in the previous chapter how immigrant entrepreneurs use value homophily to create links with those around them to achieve social and economic ends. In the following chapter, we'll focus on how they connect with and build broader communities, which again drive impact and profit. But here, we're going to look at how immigrant entrepreneurs put inclusive purpose and profit with honor at the heart of their enterprises by rethinking what growth means and focusing on altruism and philanthropy.

The old idea of business was growth for growth's sake alone; but ironically, over-committing to growth is, as discussed above, one of the reasons why so many companies die young: companies that are only interested in growth may burn brightly but quickly burn out.

I'm reminded here of an example from nature: the Great Basin bristlecone pine trees of California, Utah, and Nevada, which are famous as the longest-living trees in the world. Some have lived for more than 5,000 years. Their very slow growth rates produce dense wood that makes them resistant to the attacks of fungi, insects, rot, and erosion. Even the needles on the trees can live for up to 30 years, which allows the bristlecone pine to conserve valuable energy by not having to grow new ones. The analogy with companies that grow slowly and solidly and experience the benefits of hanging on to their staff for the long term is obvious.

In contrast to the old idea of rapid growth above all else, immigrant entrepreneurs tend to focus on growth strategies that generate true longevity by balancing their social commitments and their duties to their staff with their need for profit. Many seem to understand instinctively that the traditional economic model presents a false choice between profitability, on the one hand, and social benefits and treating staff right, on the other. In contrast to old-fashioned views, they think in the genuinely long term and recognize that what might be seen as a cost today is actually a benefit for tomorrow.

Consider the example of Hamdi Ulukaya, whom we met previously making yogurt in Upstate New York. Hamdi is a passionate advocate of doing business for a much greater purpose than profit, an ideal that he attributed to his background, growing up in a nomadic community in mountainous northeastern Turkey, a place where honor was much more important than money:

> Up in the mountains, you really don't have law … So, there are social norms [that] are extremely effective [in bringing] order … honor, dignity … trust … Really, wealth didn't matter much. What mattered the most is … [the] human qualities that you had that collectively [earned] … you that kind of respect.[8]

Because the personal accumulation of wealth was never his priority, Hamdi never made it the heart of his business. Instead, he committed himself, from the early days of Chobani, to sharing profit with his employees, an approach that he advocates as better not only for the employees but for the business as a whole and for the employer personally. The fact that Chobani has a 20% share of the American yogurt market is powerful evidence in support of Hamdi's argument.

Dominique Ansel of Cronut fame is another great example of an immigrant entrepreneur who has benefited from rejecting the old devotion to growth at all costs. Since that success, he has demonstrated on multiple occasions that he is motivated by much more than money. As Dominique explained in an interview with *Forbes* magazine when asked why he had resisted the countless offers he received to sell out and mass produce Cronuts:

> Looking back, I'm really glad I made all the choices I did—not to mass produce the Cronut, to keep it authentic, to keep the quality high ... to raise money for charity to fight against hunger ... I refused [all offers to cash out] because I love my craft too much.[9]

Dominique's commitment to fighting hunger comes from his own childhood experience of poverty, a theme that links many immigrant entrepreneurs. Also, by prioritizing quality over chasing cash, he has achieved the sort of steady and sustainable growth that sets a company up for long-term success and impact.

In the tips at the end of this chapter, I offer you some ideas on how you can take inspiration from the immigrant entrepreneurs we have been discussing to incorporate inclusive purpose into your own enterprise. But before turning to that, I'd like to just share some concluding thoughts about two closely related but distinct terms—*altruism* and *philanthropy*—highlighting how business is moving further and further away from the old Milton Friedman models and into a space where a commitment to making a difference is becoming a key component of competitive advantage.

Altruism and Philanthropy

In the last year of my PhD at Cambridge, I focused on the altruistic nature of doing business, and I remember presenting the results of my research to an audience at London Business School full of professors together with MBA and EMBA students. It did not go down well. In fact, it would be fair to say that the reaction was somewhere between skepticism and complete confusion; business, I was repeatedly assured by those who knew better, cannot be altruistic. I defended my findings, which used my company as a case study, and I detailed the altruistic motivations of my father as an immigrant entrepreneur who was motivated by a desire to give back to his family and community. The skepticism and criticism only intensified.

However, fast forward 20-odd years to today, and I see examples of altruism in business everywhere as part of the inclusive purpose that immigrant entrepreneurs employ when building their companies. Altruism is a concept that features prominently when we try to explain the characteristics of family firms, which makes sense because immigrant-founded businesses are more likely to be family-owned.

In religious studies and in some strands of philosophy, altruism refers to a moral value that leads individuals to act in the interests of others without the expectation of reward or positive reinforcement in return. In economics, on the other hand, altruism is considered to be a utility function that connects the welfare of one individual to that of others and, for the most part, it is this conception of altruism that has been applied in family business studies. When it comes to businesses with inclusive purpose, altruism is a defining characteristic. These are businesses that prioritize social value as their primary objective, rather than as a secondary outcome of profitability. These organizations are dedicated to serving their customers, suppliers, and communities through their fundamental business activities. They assess their success based on qualitative indicators such as customer satisfaction, supplier health, community well-being, and employee happiness. Laurent Marbacher and Isaac Getz of ESCP Business School in Paris (where I am an adjunct professor) highlight that "corporate altruism isn't business philanthropy. Altruistic companies focus unconditionally on the creation of social value, believing that the economic value will follow." Giving further evidence to support the arguments I have made throughout this chapter, their five-year study of such companies concluded, "In meeting the needs of their ecosystem's members, these altruistic companies were economically successful."[10]

Finally, a word on philanthropy because immigrant entrepreneurs place so much emphasis on it as one of their main priorities. That observation is supported by the research of Valeria Giacomin of Bocconi University and Geoffrey Jones of Harvard Business School, who wanted to understand the differing motivations behind philanthropic activities between emerging and established markets.[11] Their research examined foundations run by influential business leaders in these emerging regions, revealing a philanthropy that intertwines deep cultural, familial, and spiritual values with the practical needs of local communities. Unlike traditional philanthropic approaches observed in the developed world, which often focus on grand, overarching goals, foundations in emerging markets are deeply rooted in addressing immediate educational, health, and social challenges specific to their locales.

Significantly, the study found that a majority of business leaders in these regions are driven not just by the potential for financial returns but also by a profound commitment to societal progress—a commitment often shaped by personal experiences and the visible impact of poverty around them. This research suggests that the leaders in emerging markets often operate under a dual mandate: achieving business excellence and making significant social impacts. These findings propose a new narrative in the discourse on global philanthropy, emphasizing the unique role of personal values and cultural heritage in shaping business leaders' contributions to societal well-being.

My research on immigrant entrepreneurs shows that even when people leave such environments, they carry with them the same commitment to serving societal needs. Indeed, most of the immigrant entrepreneurs I interviewed for this book come from emerging markets, unstable regions, and places that they had to leave due to political reasons, poverty, or violence. Those backgrounds have a profound influence on how they create businesses with inclusive purpose and commit to philanthropy and community support (the subject of the next chapter). And that all brings us back to where we started, with the story of Luis von Ahn leaving war-torn Guatemala and going on to found a business with a purpose and a philanthropic foundation that is "committed to a future where all Guatemalans are equally valued, can thrive and are able to fully exercise their human rights."[12] When an immigrant entrepreneur creates a business with a purpose, that purpose often closely relates to the early experiences that shaped their life, and their philanthropic endeavors often align with that purpose and amplify its impact.

Strategies for building inclusive purpose:

(1) **Embrace a broader business purpose:** Recognize that true business success goes beyond mere profit. By aligning your business goals with societal improvements, you not only contribute positively to the community but also enhance your competitive edge. This symbiotic relationship fosters a cycle of mutual prosperity and sustainable profits.

(2) **Prioritize social and environmental considerations:** Integrate social and environmental factors into your business strategy. This isn't just about compliance or avoiding negative impacts like pollution—it's about actively seeking ways to benefit society and the environment. This approach not only mitigates risks but also opens up new opportunities for innovation and growth.

(3) **Reframe corporate responsibility:** Move beyond traditional corporate responsibility programs that are often seen as mere reputation management tools. Instead, view these initiatives as integral components of your core business strategy, essential for long-term success and genuine social impact.

(4) **Innovate for social impact:** Leverage innovation to address societal challenges. This could involve developing new products or services that meet unaddressed needs or enhance the well-being of communities. Such innovations not only drive market expansion but also build a loyal customer base that values your commitment to societal progress.

(5) **Beware of short-term compromises of your values and purpose:** When making any decision about your company, regardless of how small it may seem, always check that it is aligned with your values and the bigger purpose that your company aims to serve. You might be tempted to choose a path that appears attractive in terms of short-term profits, but if that requires you to undermine who you are as a company, then, in the long term, that decision will not be beneficial.

(6) **Cultivate an inclusive company culture:** Foster an inclusive workplace where every employee feels valued and empowered. This culture should celebrate diversity and encourage the sharing of unique perspectives, which can lead to enhanced creativity and problem-solving within your team.

(7) **Engage in meaningful collaboration:** Don't go it alone. Collaborate with other businesses, non-profits, and governments to address complex societal issues. By pooling resources and expertise, you can achieve greater impact than any single organization could on its own. Consistent engagement with stakeholders across your industry and the broader community can affirm your commitment to sustainability and position you as a leader in this dialogue.

(8) Take criticism on board: It's crucial to deal with external pressures constructively. Rather than ignoring or antagonizing critics, engage with them openly and honestly. Listen carefully and explain your stance on various sustainability issues, clarifying which are not currently central to your value creation, and be open about the limitations of what your company can realistically achieve regarding negative externalities. This transparency helps to manage expectations and mitigate conflicts.

(9) Try to make your products and services as accessible as possible: Depending on your industry, there can be great benefits in offering services that are very cheap, or free, because that allows you to impact a vast audience while creating a pool of users that can help you generate profit in other ways. Essentially, any attempts to make your services or products available at different price points can help to create equity.

(10) Don't force it: As I always emphasize, authenticity is key. None of this should be or feel forced. Align your company's purpose with the causes that you are passionate about and what you would like to change in the world. And explicitly link staying true to that purpose to your financial performance by emphasizing that following it is good for you, your community, the planet, and your bottom line.

The Tuft of Flowers

The mower in the dew had loved them thus,
By leaving them to flourish, not for us,

Nor yet to draw one thought of ours to him.
But from sheer morning gladness at the brim.

The butterfly and I had lit upon,
Nevertheless, a message from the dawn,

That made me hear the wakening birds around,
And hear his long scythe whispering to the ground,

And feel a spirit kindred to my own;
So that henceforth I worked no more alone;

But glad with him, I worked as with his aid,
And weary, sought at noon with him the shade;

And dreaming, as it were, held brotherly speech
With one whose thought I had not hoped to reach.

"Men work together." I told him from the heart,
"Whether they work together or apart."

—Robert Frost

8

Principle 5: Build Community

İliç, Northeastern Turkey, 1970s

Hamdi Ulukaya grew up in the heart of a nomadic community of shepherds whose way of life had scarcely changed since the time of the Bible.[1] "We are nomads," he says, still using the present tense despite, or perhaps because of, the fact that he's now settled in Upstate New York, "a Kurdish nomadic family of hundreds of hundreds of years caring for herds and shepherds and the fires and the stars."[2] In the mountains of northeastern Turkey, Hamdi's life followed a deeper rhythm than that dictated by clocks and calendars, to the extent that his family didn't even know the exact date of his birth, only that it was sometime in the autumn of 1972, at the time when the changing of the season would drive the community out of the high mountain pastures to the lowlands to escape the winter chill. There, the children went to school and were forced to follow a little the rhythm set by bells and teachers' watches. But when the spring broke through again, as it always did, it was time to return to the high mountain pastures where the children would learn the ways of the herds and the time-honored skills of making the feta cheese and yogurt that would sustain their community throughout the whole rest of the year.

Hamdi might be a billionaire now, but the values that he holds at his core still come from that other world where he grew up. "Money," he says, "meant nothing up there. You couldn't buy anything with it. What mattered more was your social reputation, the trust you earned. Whether you had a thousand sheep or a hundred, everyone ate the same—yogurt, cheese, and bread. There was no difference." Trust and respect come from treating the community with honor, and even though Hamdi now lives 6,000 miles from his original home, its values remain an essential part of him, as we shall see when looking at the crucial role that community has played in his incredible success with Chobani.

In Chapter 3, I told the story of how Hamdi came to the United States and ended up the owner of an abandoned Kraft yogurt production plant. Here, we'll look at how he, following the values instilled in him by his upbringing, not only bought the plant but also put working with and serving the community at the heart of his subsequent success.

When Hamdi visited South Edmeston it was not just the potential of the plant that impressed him but also that of the community. The closure had cut at the heart of the little hamlet and its population of 150 people, but Hamdi was straight away struck by their individual and communal strength.

> They were just heads-up and doing their best to close this factory. And there was no screaming, there was no deep cursing or anything. They were just sad and quiet and supporting each other.

Fresh from the relative failure of his feta cheese business, Hamdi had little cash to invest, and he was originally only able to employ five members of the 55-strong workforce that Kraft had laid off. But as the saying goes, "From little things big things grow," especially when they have the required soil, nutrients, and water, which in this case meant the determination and talent of the community that Hamdi, the Kurdish shepherd boy, suddenly found himself at the heart of. Focusing on yogurt, Hamdi and the team perfected a recipe that was based on those he had grown up with, which provided a refreshing alternative to the typically sugar-heavy options that filled fridges in American stores. Sales started in the shops that served the community, and it wasn't long before Hamdi received a call from the owner of a local store telling him that his yogurt was flying off the shelf. It was the moment, Hamdi recalls, when he realized that he'd be spending the next few years in his factory, cultivating his business.

Chobani's rise to the stars had begun, but Hamdi reaffirmed his commitment to the local community by continuing to hire from it, strengthening the bonds within the team. At the same time, he led from the front, using as a CEO in America the skills he'd learned as a child in Turkey to work alongside his staff. He never asked anyone to do anything without doing it himself first, a policy that saw him packing products, driving forklifts, and fitting trucks, deeply integrating himself with the plant's workflow and fostering a deep sense of unity and co-ownership.

As Chobani's success escalated, Hamdi looked to extend his community-focused approach to nearby Utica, a city home to a significant number of refugees struggling to find employment and integrate. Seeing parallels with his own experiences as an immigrant, he was determined to make a difference and moved to act. Hamdi initiated programs to help these new community members overcome barriers, including organizing transportation, providing language training, and opening up job opportunities at Chobani. But throughout he always called it not refugee work but community work, emphasizing the inclusive nature of his efforts.

This philosophy not only elevated the spirit of the town but also propelled Chobani to achieve massive scales of production and revenue growth without outside capital, going from $25 million to a billion. The tendency in Western culture, when we hear such dramatic success stories, is to attribute them to the heroic leadership of an individual and to look to them to see what lessons we can learn from their personal qualities. But Hamdi Ulukaya, like many of the immigrant entrepreneurs featured in this book, comes from a culture that celebrates communal effort over individualism, which explains why he, accurately, attributes his success not to himself but to the people around him:

> No one can do this alone ... [I] created my community within the company. I really didn't have much of a network. When I settled in

Upstate New York, I didn't know many other people who have done this. I didn't know people who wrote books about this or studies … I did not have a board. I did not have people who have done this before. So, my support system was in that community in Upstate New York, and the people that I work with. And I would ask them to warn me if they see me going in the wrong direction.[3]

Of course, it's common for CEOs to talk about the importance of their staff and the community in which they are based. What is rare is to see them putting their money where their mouths are. But Hamdi has done just that, by not only creating jobs for the community but also sharing the results of the labor with it; in 2016, he gave 10% of the shares in Chobani, a company valued at billions, to his employees. Hamdi's model of community integration and co-ownership not only reshaped a hamlet in Upstate New York but also set a new standard for how businesses around the world can profoundly impact and uplift the communities they inhabit.

Hamdi's journey from a small-scale yogurt plant to a global business exemplifies the impact of integrating community values into business practices. His efforts in South Edmeston (and subsequently in Twin Falls, Idaho) show how businesses can serve as catalysts for community revitalization, proving that the right approach to business can indeed lead to what Hamdi describes as "miracles" in local development and social cohesion. His story is a powerful example of how a community can be rebuilt, integrated, and expanded (by including local refugees within its definition) by a business that can enjoy astounding success powered by that same community.

However, Hamdi's story, as we shall see in the rest of this chapter, is far from the only example of how an immigrant entrepreneur, almost by definition an outsider, has tapped into the power of community to achieve long-term success and impact. In this chapter, we will see how they have done it and reflect on the lessons that any entrepreneur can learn about the importance of intertwining their endeavors with communities both near and far. But first, I'd like to start with some general reflections on community and why it is that immigrant entrepreneurs are so adept at creating it and connecting it with their companies.

The Essence of Community: From Breaking Bread to Sharing Roots

When thinking about the importance of community for companies, it's instructive to think about where the words come from. The word "company" derives ultimately from the Latin *companio*, a term used to describe someone you would share bread (*panis*) with. By medieval times, the word *compagnie* was being used in Old French to describe a society or a group of friends, and from there the word ended up in Middle English meaning "a number of persons united to perform or carry out anything jointly."[4] Eventually, the word ended up developing the sense of a business association, but we can see how the roots, etymologically speaking, of the businesses we call companies extend deep into the soils of collaboration and friendship. And, just as the word "company" shares roots with "community," so should any company actually be rooted in its community if it wishes to survive and thrive.

But where do immigrant entrepreneurs fit into that picture? After all, as we have seen, much of the literature on immigrant entrepreneurship focuses only on how they draw strength from and serve what is perceived to be their *own* community, i.e., the people with whom they share an ethnic/cultural heritage. Of course, as we saw in Chapter 6, immigrant entrepreneurs do draw on such homophilic ties as sources of strength. But, as we also saw, they do not limit such ties to people from the same ethnic/cultural backgrounds, using value homophily to forge strong connections with people who share the same worldviews and follow the same moral compasses. In this chapter, we'll look at how they situate themselves within the broader communities in which they operate and create communities within their companies to achieve the sort of long-term success that lifts everyone up together.

In the modern business world, community is often spoken about in the context of online communities or the creation of networks to sell more products. But the sort of community that I am talking about here goes much deeper and extends far beyond that. When trying to understand the real nature of community, I find, once again, that an example drawn from the natural world is instructive because it shows us how we are all much more deeply intertwined than we ever realize. And it's an example that I only learned about thanks to a question from my young son.

In the garden of our family home just outside Paris, we are blessed to have four mighty trees—two chestnut and two sycamore—each more than 150 years old. I like to sit in their cool shade with my son, chatting and playing together. For me, the trees were the silent and solitary sentinels of the garden. But then one lazy afternoon as I was explaining to my son, who was four at the time, how the trees took their food from the sun above and the soil beneath, he turned to me and asked whether the trees' roots "touch each other underground."

As is often the case with children's questions, his words sent me off on a journey to learn about something I'd never really considered before. And that journey led me to Rachel Sussman's beautiful book *The Oldest Living Things in the World,*[5] which brings to life the incredible interconnections of the forests that sustain ancient trees. Her description of the sprawling Pando in Utah shows us how what appears to be a forest made up of around 47,000 separate trees is, in fact, a one-tree forest interconnected through an intricate web of roots covering an area the size of 86 football fields.

In its scale, Pando is exceptional, but in another way, it is illustrative of the interconnections that all forests depend upon for their survival. Suzanne Simard's astounding PhD research on the "wood-wide web" showed how trees use the fungal networks that connect their roots to trade and share food, supporting each other through tough times. As Simard puts it:

> Plants are attuned to one another's strengths and weaknesses, elegantly giving and taking to attain exquisite balance. There is grace in complexity, in actions cohering, in sum totals.[6]

All of which sounds like a perfect description of the complex power of community. These revelations about Pando and the wood-wide web reshape our understanding of individualism. Each tree, despite appearing solitary, is actually part of a vast network of communication and support. Drawing on that natural metaphor, we can see the profound significance of community for entrepreneurship. But what my research has shown is that immigrant entrepreneurs, who have been uprooted and lost many connections, are particularly likely to make community a vital part of their existence and their success.

Throughout the rest of this chapter, I want to discuss community on two levels: external and internal. External is the larger ecosystem, the community, the geographic region, and the environment where you exist. It is also where your philanthropic activities typically take place. The internal ecosystem is the community within the company and its immediate partners, which consists of your employees, suppliers, and agents.

The two levels are, of course, deeply intertwined, and immigrant entrepreneurs, as we shall see, are particularly skilled at tying external and internal communities together in ways that produce great strength. Nevertheless, I have chosen to separate them for the purpose of this analysis to encourage people to think about the importance of cultivating community on both levels and the different actions that are required to do that.

External Community

External community in the case of a business refers to the larger ecosystem in which you exist. Of course, on one level, such communities can exist virtually these days and link people from all over the world. But, while not disregarding the importance of such connections, here I want to focus on the more traditional notion of community in the sense of your geographic environment and the people within that region with whom you have connections. I do that because the evidence from studying immigrant entrepreneurs suggests that the strongest community connections are those rooted in real, rather than virtual, relationships.

Sometimes, such external communities constitute particularly powerful economic clusters and ecosystems that are capable of birthing and sustaining entire industries. An obvious modern example would be California's Silicon Valley for tech or, if we look just a little further back in time, Michigan's Detroit (Motown) for the automotive industry. Such ecosystems eventually generate their own momentum, continually attracting new innovators in their particular space to join the community and benefit from the support and resources it offers. We have already looked at the example of how Eren Bali, of Udemy fame, moved from

Turkey to Silicon Valley because he realized his vision for his firm could not be achieved without access to the resources that proliferate around the Bay Area.

However, it's important to remember that these ecosystems did not emerge out of nowhere; they result from the endeavors of a small group of pioneering entrepreneurs. For example, at the start of the 20th century, there were lots of American cities that could potentially have emerged as the whirring heart of the automobile industry. The reason Detroit ended up becoming Motor City is because of the pioneers who kickstarted the industry there and, ultimately, filled the city with the talent and networks necessary to run successful car manufacturing, thus attracting many other firms that wished to become established in the industry.

More recently, Michigan has become home to an immigrant entrepreneur whose career exemplifies the value of both being a pioneer and plugging into your local external community. Dug Song was born just outside Washington D.C. to parents who had emigrated from Korea. In 2010, Dug founded Duo Security alongside Jon Oberheide, with the vision of building "an organization that tries to do right by others and to do the right things in security." That vision stemmed from the three core values that have guided the company since its foundation: simplicity, empathy, and integrity. Explaining how those values and that vision distinguished the company from its competitors, Dug emphasizes its focus on collaboration to solve people's real problems:

> We have always partnered very closely with customers … Every decision starts with asking: What's the right thing for the customer? Then, what's the right thing for our company? Then, what's the right thing for our community? If those things align, then we go and do it.[7]

But despite having grown up on the East Coast and working in an industry synonymous with the West Coast (tech) he decided to set up his own firm in the heart of the Midwest. Nevertheless, despite what some might have considered its unpromising location, Duo Security, the company that he founded in Ann Arbor, 40 miles west of Detroit, has gone on to become Michigan's first tech unicorn.

But why did Dug start in Michigan? And why did he become so attached to the place that when he sold Duo to Cisco for $2.35 billion he insisted that it stayed in the state? The answer to both questions, fundamentally, is community. Dug was impressed by Michigan's business-friendly environment, high-quality universities, and low cost of living. But, even more than that ecosystem, he was impressed by the people he found there. According to Karim Faris, a general partner with Google Ventures and one of Dug's early funders, "Sometimes when you look at companies, there is the cult of the entrepreneur, one person who drives things, but for Dug, there's no such thing. It's the cult of his team and the community. It's very rewarding to see success being driven by someone with that kind of mindset." We are reminded here, of course, of Hamdi Ulukaya with his constant stress on the importance of the collective. As Dug himself puts it, when praising the team that comes from Ann Arbor's "freaks, geeks, and jocks" cultural mix:

> I don't think we could have built this company anywhere else, at least … not in the way I would have wanted, which is not just to do really well, but to do good, to have successes larger than ourselves. I'm really proud of the fact that we've done it here.[8]

As the quote implies, Dug fully understands that community is not just a resource upon which you can draw but also a living force that you must support. That's why he has focused his philanthropic efforts on the region where he is based. As well as Dug being a trustee of the Ann Arbor Summer Festival, his wife, Linh, is the executive director of the Ann Arbor Public Schools Educational Foundation. Dug is also the co-founder of the Ann Arbor Entrepreneurs Fund, and his foundation also donated $1 million to support local businesses through the pandemic. But instead of seeing himself as a benefactor of Michigan, Dug is always grateful to the state for what it has given to him, hence his insistence to Cisco that it couldn't move Duo Security out of the state even when they were paying billions for it. The community has given so much to Dug and continues to do so; so, it's only right that he reciprocates.

We can see the same spirit with other immigrant entrepreneurs like the brother-and-sister team behind Numi Tea, Ahmed Rahim and Reem Hassani, whom we met in Chapter 4. When explaining the origins of their business, Ahmed and Reem relate it to the understanding of community that comes from their Iraqi heritage and their experience as immigrants in the United States. Ahmed describes it thus, with details that show a close connection to the sort of experiences I had growing up in a close-knit and supportive community in Istanbul.

> We were born in Baghdad and raised in the Iraqi culture of hospitality. It's a tribal culture. Four or five generations live together and take care of each other from beginning to end. Serving tea is a way to get people together. Our parents would always take in Iraqi refugees from the wars, although they didn't know them. My sister and I learned how important it is to take care of people, surround yourself with love, and be thoughtful.[9]

The ethos that inspired their company has continued to drive their philanthropic activities within the various communities that they work with and belong to around the world—from Oakland, California, to Iraq, to China. When describing Numi Tea's community support efforts in our interview, Reem explicitly linked them to her family's heritage and background as immigrants:

> When COVID happened, we did a COVID relief program for the city of Oakland, for folks who couldn't get food. We delivered produce to families in need. We've done a school curriculum program for inner city kids in Oakland. I think that comes from being exposed to—we used to go to Iraq and my parents used to take us traveling. When you see people from other cultures or you see people who don't have what you have and you know how privileged you are to grow up in the States and have what you have, I think you naturally—that was instilled in us from an early age, that you want to give back to those who don't, and especially if you're working directly with them and you see how poor they are, you feel compelled to do something.

As part of their efforts to help, Reem and Ahmed established the Numi Foundation in 2012 with a mission to nurture and empower thriving communities. In 2016, as part of its Together for H2OPE initiative, the foundation built 23 wells to bring clean, safe drinking water to more than 4,000 turmeric-farming villagers in Madagascar. Through the foundation, they also run educational initiatives in Oakland and Iraq. Echoing the sentiments of so many of the immigrant entrepreneurs whom we have met on this journey, Ahmed sets out how chasing money is far less important to Numi than growing community:

> Community is how you get inspiration, share resources, and learn. I have been to a lot of business conferences where the focus is only on how to make a bigger dollar, and I just don't understand that. I want to focus on how business can improve the health of the planet. I think there's a common denominator beyond business that drives people to do good.[10]

Some cynical views of companies' community-building efforts focus on the notion that businesspeople try to generate prosperity in the communities around them as a means of generating extra customers with more money to spend. However, the immigrant entrepreneurs that we have studied could hardly be accused of such non-altruistic motivations when they are trying to build basic community infrastructure in parts of the world that are unlikely to become markets for their products.

Other critics of entrepreneurs' community-building efforts argue that startups are not big enough to effect change. But we have seen how companies can have a very significant impact even as they are developing (as was the case with Chobani in South Edmeston). Immigrant entrepreneurs have successfully pioneered community transformation by focusing from the outset not just on developing products, boosting sales, and driving growth but also on their broader civic responsibilities. Through such efforts, immigrant entrepreneurs are pioneering the path to what I believe will be seen as the new American dream, where the dream aligns with the reality that success is not an individual but rather a community endeavor.

Internal Community

As the above stories emphasize, the external and internal community of a business should be interwoven and work together in unison; there really is no such thing as building one and ignoring the other. As we have already seen, one crucial way to build your internal community is to establish a vision that inspires your staff and acts as their guiding star, aligning every employee's efforts toward a common goal. Having covered in Chapter 5 how to create such a vision, here I want to focus on some of the more specific details of how you build a community within an organization by hiring the right staff and creating a culture in which such people can thrive. I also want to stress the importance of leadership when it comes to creating internal culture, an issue that we can see exemplified in the styles of some of the immigrant entrepreneurs discussed in this chapter.

Let's start with the crucial first step: hiring the right people. Take Fadi Ghandour of Aramex (Arab American Express, a logistics company) as an example. When he first started Aramex in the Middle East, he strategically focused on hiring and empowering local talent. He wanted people who understood the local culture to develop and build the business, but he also wanted them to help grow the community and empower people from the region who were usually excluded from the usual talent pool. Reflecting his commitment to his community, many people who started in entry-level jobs in Aramex have ended up in top executive positions today. His investment in his employees and the broader community exemplifies the ethos of the one-tree forest—a cohesive, thriving network that enhances the resilience and sustainability of the business ecosystem.

When a company knows its vision and mission, it can look for individuals who not only have the necessary skills but also share its core beliefs and values. This alignment is essential for building an internal community where each member is motivated by similar goals and driven by the same overarching purpose. Employees who resonate with a company's vision are more likely to invest themselves fully, contributing to a collaborative and supportive workplace culture. This synergy enhances teamwork and encourages a collective approach to problem-solving and innovation. Articulating the importance of hiring staff who are aligned with your vision and values, Reem Hassani told me:

> You're not looking for just a skill set; you're looking for all kinds of things. You want to be able to sit around and have dinner with them and joke around with them. So, their values are really important in that sense. And some folks haven't worked out for that reason; they don't carry those values. You have to have a team spirit, and … when you're in an entrepreneurial company, you have to have a can-do spirit where you're going to help your neighbor, take on other work. It's always a work in progress … When we interview people, I always make sure that person's really kind. I want to be able to spend time with them … [I don't want someone] if I find them to be too hard-edged or cut-throat or whatever you want to call it … You want somebody who's kind and nice and a good person.

Once the right team is in place, the focus shifts to cultivating a sense of responsibility and inclusivity. Every employee should feel not only responsible for their contributions but also secure in the knowledge that they are a valued part of the company. Inclusivity is particularly significant as it addresses the human need to feel accepted and valued. Immigrant entrepreneurs' lives have often shown them what it feels like to not be included, which might explain why they are so particularly focused on encouraging and embodying inclusivity within their own companies. This means creating an environment where open communication is encouraged and diversity is celebrated. Sharing—setbacks and success alike—becomes a central theme, fostering transparency and trust. As we have seen with Chobani, this openness extends to sharing profits, reinforcing the principle that everyone benefits from the company's success, thereby enhancing their commitment and loyalty.

However, as one startup founder I consult for pointed out, managing people and building a community is more challenging than managing the business itself, especially in an increasingly digital world; it's harder to motivate a team and nurture a sense of community when interactions are mediated through screens. We think of the benefits of remote working but we don't notice the intangible things we lose (like community connection). So, either insist on people working together (at least some of the time) or make sure you proactively manage this challenge. Companies like Numi Tea exemplify how embedding the values of community, creativity, and collaboration into the corporate culture can contribute to success. Ahmed Rahim and Reem Hassani have not only promoted these values within their company but also across their network of growers and business leaders, initiating sustainability projects to address global challenges.

This approach exemplifies the "we are in this together" mentality, viewing customers, suppliers, and partners as integral parts of a whole. Such a perspective is prevalent in immigrant-led businesses where community and collective effort drive success. It's not just about what one founder or business can achieve alone but about leveraging the power of community to effect significant, lasting change. This holistic view fosters a culture of solidarity and togetherness, where the success of the business is seen as a shared achievement, benefiting all involved and contributing to a resilient, enduring enterprise.

Cultivating a true community culture requires you to continually prioritize it and embody it, as Reem Hassani described it in my interview with her for this book:

> We've had people for 20 years ... probably a good seven or eight of [our employees] have been around for over 15 years. I think that aspect of the culture, that sort of family connection and that loyalty, the employee isn't just a commodity, in a sense, they're human beings with a family and a livelihood. That connection, it's just sort of family. It's maybe because we were brother and sister who started it, but it's a family business and it's a family environment. We prioritize that. For example, one of my employees, her sister was sick last year. She was out a lot ... and I said, "Take care of your sister. If you need to take time off, whatever you need, go do it." And just recently she said, "I know you're busy with your niece and everything. I'll be there for you if you need any support, if you need me to do anything." So, it was very sweet for that feeling to be the top—it's the first thing that prioritizes the company values, versus produce, produce, produce kind of thing.

Finally, strong leadership is the glue that holds the vision, the mission, and the people together. Leaders who embody their company's core values and demonstrate a commitment to its vision inspire their teams to do the same. They play a critical role in nurturing an environment where shared goals are pursued with passion and determination. By setting an example through their decisions and actions, leaders reinforce the importance of the shared mission and vision, ensuring that these principles permeate every level of the organization. This type of leadership cultivates a robust internal community, united by a common purpose, where every member is empowered to contribute to the company's overall success and growth. Through this integrated approach, companies can create a powerful internal ecosystem that drives both individual fulfillment and corporate achievements.

Strategies for cultivating one-tree forests:

(1) **Start with hiring the right people:** When recruiting, prioritize candidates who demonstrate a commitment to your organization's vision and mission. Use structured behavioral interviews to gauge how potential hires have engaged with similar values in past roles. Also, clearly communicate your company's mission and what it stands for right from the first point of contact to attract candidates who are in harmony with your ethos and set clear expectations about your organizational culture.

(2) **Ensure that your hiring process is transparent and reflects your company values:** This could include involving various team members in the recruitment process to assess cultural fit from multiple perspectives. By prioritizing fit and alignment from the outset, you lay a foundational stone for a cohesive and committed internal community.

(3) **Cultivate community trust:** Embedding your organization deeply within the community hinges on building trust-based relationships. Start by actively listening to stakeholders to understand their unique perspectives and skills. This engagement goes beyond surface interactions, requiring a sincere commitment to valuing and incorporating local insights and experiences into your business practices.

(4) **Transition your networking from transactional to relational:** Consistently engage in meaningful ways that affirm your commitment to the community, such as supporting local initiatives or

participating in governance. These efforts should integrate seamlessly into your business strategy, fostering a durable network of advocates and enhancing your competitive edge.

(5) **Foster a solidarity-driven culture:** Creating a workplace culture centered on solidarity and shared purpose is essential for building a cohesive team. This culture ensures that every team member feels valued and that their contributions are recognized, which in turn boosts morale and aligns efforts toward a common goal. Emphasize the importance of each voice in the organization by implementing inclusive decision-making processes and open communication channels that invite input from all levels.

(6) **Celebrate successes collectively:** Recognizing achievements as collective efforts rather than individual victories enhances team spirit and reinforces the idea that every member plays a critical role in the organization's success. Regular team-building activities and community service projects can also strengthen bonds and reinforce shared values, helping to embed these principles deeper into your company's culture.

(7) **Redefine success metrics:** Implement performance indicators that recognize contributions enhancing your internal and external community connections. This might include employee initiatives that promote diversity and inclusion, leadership in community outreach programs, or innovative projects that align with your organization's long-term sustainability goals.

(8) **Enhance empathy and collaborative innovation:** An empathetic culture should permeate all aspects of your business, from daily interactions to strategic decision-making. Encourage employees to practice empathy by actively listening to their colleagues, role-swapping or shadowing, and considering diverse perspectives. This approach not only improves team dynamics but also enhances individual understanding of different roles and challenges within the company.

(9) **Commit to collaborative problem-solving:** Work together across teams to solve company problems and with stakeholders from your external community to try to address broader problems

affecting that community. Such approaches will improve team integration and facilitate deeper connections with the broader community upon which your company depends.

(10)Promote transparent and inclusive communication: Promoting transparent and inclusive communication within your organization is vital to building a culture of trust and belonging. To achieve this, create safe spaces where employees can freely express their ideas and concerns by implementing town hall meetings, anonymous suggestion boxes, and open-door policies. Such communication practices help to identify and address issues early, enhance organizational resilience, and ensure that all team members feel they are an integral part of the company's community.

Borderbus

.....

No somos nada y venimos de la nada
pero esa nada lo es todo si la nutres de amor
por eso venceremos

We are nothing and we come from nothing
but that nothing is everything, if you feed it with love
that is why we will triumph

We are everything hermana
Because we come from everything
                    —*Juan Felipe Herrera*

Juan Felipe Herrera, "Borderbus" from
Notes on the Assemblage. Published with permission of
City Lights Books, www.citylights.com

9

Principle 6: Reframe Rejection

Atlanta, Georgia, 2013

The well-known English expression "there's plenty more fish in the sea" is used as a consolation to someone whose relationship has just ended unhappily. It encourages the jilted lover to rethink their situation so that instead of focusing on the unique qualities of the person they just lost, they focus instead on the many more equal, or maybe better, possibilities that they have in a world of billions. The phrase inspired the title of the world's biggest dating site, and that site's success was itself the inspiration for the first plunge into entrepreneurship of a young Nigerian immigrant in the United States who soon discovered that the startup world can be just as challenging to navigate as the search for true love. But in keeping with the spirit of the phrase, that immigrant entrepreneur never let the repeated rejection and failure of his business ideas blind him to the infinite possibilities that still existed. And, in fact, as we shall see, he was able to reconceptualize rejection in ways that eventually propelled him to success on a scale he could scarcely have ever imagined.

That immigrant was Tope Awotona, whom we first met in Chapter 5. He relocated to Georgia as a teenager with his mother and three brothers after witnessing the murder of his father in a carjacking in Lagos. Nigeria is a country with an extreme disparity between rich and poor, and Tope's parents came from both sides of that divide; his mother grew up in a wealthy family, and his father came from a poverty-stricken, broken home. But both enjoyed successful careers: His mother worked as a pharmacist for Nigeria's Central Bank, and his father was a microbiologist at Unilever. But Tope's father always retained an entrepreneurial streak and dabbled in dreams of building his own successful business until those dreams died in a hail of bullets on a Lagos roadside.

When asked how he'd dealt with the death of his father, Tope reflected on a theme that is common to the experience of many immigrant entrepreneurs, the importance of "family ties" with people beyond one's blood relatives:

> One of the things I really appreciate about the Nigerian culture is really everybody's your family, right? Even your family friends essentially think of themselves as your family.[1]

Tope also turned his father's death into the fuel that drove him to seek success that would allow him to fulfill the dreams he had left behind:

> I felt like he didn't get a chance to complete his work. There was a part of me, from a very early age, that wanted to redeem him.[2]

The road to that redemption, as we have already seen, was a rocky one. As mentioned in Chapter 6, Tope's career in the United States got off to a slow start because he didn't know you were expected to apply for internships while still at university. His career thus began doing cold call sales from call centers and then selling alarm systems door-to-door. Further, as described in Chapter 5, his first steps into startups were not just faltering but outright failures; his dating website suffered rejection (in fact, he never ended up launching it), next his company selling projectors crashed, and then he got his fingers burned in the grill business.

We've already looked at how Tope turned things around by turning away from just chasing money to focusing on solving a practical problem that would improve people's lives, which led to him creating Calendly, a tool that simplifies meeting scheduling so effectively that it is now worth more than $3 billion. But here, we don't want to focus on how he built that, but rather how he did something equally important: Get over being a three-times failure and find a way to use experiences that would have crushed someone else to turn himself into a wildly successful entrepreneur who has proudly fulfilled his father's dream.

Overcoming the fear of failure and being able to deal with it when that fear becomes real are essential steps on the path to success in business and in life. And immigrant entrepreneurs tend to be highly skilled at reframing painful experiences, rejection, and failure, turning them into the fuel that powers their success. But why are they so good at it? And what can everyone learn from the experiences of immigrant entrepreneurs like Tope, who have the mindsets and skills required to reimagine failings and turn apparent disaster into triumph? We'll explore those questions in this chapter, but first let's get to the root of the problem by trying to understand why failure exerts such a detrimental influence on our lives, to the extent that many of us don't achieve our full potential simply because we fear it so much. And I'd like to start my exploration of the hold that dark power has over us by sharing my own experience of failure.

Cambridge, England, 1996

In 1996, I was 18 years old and in Cambridge, England, waiting for the phone call that would confirm that the dream I had had as a little refugee girl was about to come true. I've told the story of how I had sworn to myself that I would get a good education. And now that vision was about to become a reality, and all the hard work that I put in to turn myself from a child who could barely speak Turkish to a straight-A student was about to be rewarded. So sure was I that I would be accepted to study business management at the school of my dreams, Istanbul's highly prestigious Koç University, that I had gone to Cambridge to complete the preparations for the Test of English as a Foreign Language (TOEFL) that would follow my acceptance; my chosen degree was taught in English, and passing the TOEFL would allow me to skip the first year and get straight into the main course, which was exactly where I was hungry to be. All I was waiting for was one phone call to confirm that I was in, and that would be the moment my life would take off.

It was the mid–1990s, just at the end of the BC (before cellphones) era. Being reliant on a landline for my connection home, I spent more time than I would normally in my room, waiting for that call. It was a particularly moody August morning when the phone rang unusually early, and I rushed to answer it. I remember what happened next like it was yesterday. It was my mother on the phone, and straight away I heard that her voice was unusually distant and cold. I first thought she would tell me someone had died. Someone hadn't but something did; my dream of joining Turkey's top school ended with these seven words: "You failed to get into the university."

The first big failure of your life hits you hard. I felt like I'd been punched in the gut and then had a door slammed in my face, a door that would never be opened again. And all the hard work that had led me to that doorstep, what was the point of all that? How stupid I had been to believe that I'd ever amount to anything. I felt like I'd let myself down and worst of all let my family down, after they had supported me so much. As a teenager, away from home again, I felt like my whole world was collapsing.

Why do failure and rejection hurt us so badly? It's a question that fascinates me, and if I'd known then as an 18-year-old in Cambridge what I know now, then I'd have realized that the tracks of my tears could be traced back hundreds of thousands of years into our evolutionary history as a species. Let's take a look at what I mean because I'm convinced that we need first to understand the hold that failure has on us before we can reframe it in ways that allow us to escape that hold and turn failure into a friend.

The Roots of Fearing Failure: From the Savannah to Social Media

Fear is one of the most fundamental human emotions. Anyone can understand why the fear of physical attack is so acute, but why is the fear of failure and rejection such a powerful force? As with so many of the problems we face in our "modern" minds, the answer to the question lies deep in our evolutionary history, when we depended on our tribe for survival and rejection from it would almost certainly equal death.

I had a recent visceral experience of the fear of failure when I returned to Cambridge, the scene of my earlier rejection from Koç University. This time I was returning as an alumna of the University of Cambridge itself to deliver a keynote speech at a reunion dinner. But, despite all the successes that separated my first experience of failure in Cambridge and the speech I'd been invited to give, I still had to deal with intense nerves; my hands shook, my heart raced, and my face flushed as my body overreacted to a sense of imminent danger while simply sitting at dinner with friends. Meanwhile, my thoughts raced with worry: "This is a small room. What if they think I'm inadequate? There's no escape. What will they think of me?" Essentially, a survival mechanism honed over millions of years of evolution on the African savannah was taking control of my body and mind in a Cambridge hall on a late summer's evening in 2024.

Reflecting on that experience, I was reminded of the work of Harvard professor Amy Edmondson, one of the world's leading experts on failure. Her book *Right Kind of Wrong: The Science of Failing Well*[3] dives bravely into an uncomfortable topic—our aversion to failure—and shows just how deep it runs. Rationally, we know that failure and rejection are part of life and provide valuable, indeed essential, lessons. But, as can often be the case, the rationality of the brain's front is overridden by the emotions that live deep in its back, such as shame and fear. Fear activates the amygdala, triggering a fight-or-flight response. Essentially, our intense fear of rejection and failure is ingrained in our DNA, and our brains still struggle to differentiate between fears that are ultimately irrational, like appearing foolish, and genuine life-threatening dangers, like a bear attack.

That's why the pain of failing, even in relatively trivial ways, is felt much more acutely than the joy of success and why a single negative remark stands out even when it's surrounded by gushes of praise. Research shows that we remember our failures much more vividly and longer than our triumphs. But the bitter irony of all this is that aversion to failure makes actual failure more likely because it either prevents us from trying in the first place or encourages us to bury the painful memories of past failures, thus limiting our abilities to extract their necessary lessons. According to Amy

Edmondson, addressing failures and extracting lessons require a high cognitive effort, which fear directly impedes. In her book *Bold Move*, the psychologist Luana Marques of Harvard Medical School identifies that pattern as avoidance.[4] She argues that by dodging the smaller, more manageable challenges of our lives, we hinder our capacity to live boldly and embrace the full spectrum of our experiences. Moreover, in today's social media-driven society, the pressure to appear successful and flawless is overwhelmingly intense, often deterring us from openly discussing our failures and vulnerabilities. Ironically, the pressure to appear perfect is itself a massive stumbling block on the road to self-improvement.

What Is Reframing and Why Are Immigrant Entrepreneurs So Good at It?

So, how can we deal with our fear of failure when it is so deeply wired into us? And how can we turn an apparently crushing rejection into a springboard for success? We can find answers to these questions by looking to the experiences of immigrant entrepreneurs and their expertise in reframing.

To explain the concept and practice of reframing, I'd like to start with an example from the world of sport. As I'm writing this book, the Olympics and Paralympics are taking place in Paris where I live. I've been struck by the resilience and dedication of the athletes who have pushed themselves to such limits for so many years for the chance to compete and win gold. Watching their inspiring efforts, I was reminded of a remarkable story that took place during the 2004 Summer Olympics in Athens when Vanderlei Cordeiro de Lima, a Brazilian marathon runner, reframed and transformed a challenging moment into a testament to resilience and sportsmanship.

While leading the race and on course to win gold, Vanderlei was abruptly assaulted by a spectator named Neil Horan, a former Irish priest who was seeking to publicize his belief that the end of the world was nigh. Horan's attack cost Vanderlei crucial seconds and, ultimately, the gold medal. Yet, as Vanderlei entered the stadium, set to secure a bronze instead, his demeanor was not of defeat but of joy and gratitude, and his smile when crossing the finishing line was as broad as that of any gold medal winner.

When asked about his positive attitude despite having been robbed of the success he had sought, Vanderlei famously said, "It's bronze, but it means gold." He explained further, "When I entered the stadium, I was so happy just to compete, to be there, that I had already forgotten the incident."[5]

The circumstances of Vanderlei's story are obviously exceptional, but they point in the direction of a general truth. Studies show that athletes who finish third tend to be happier and feel less of a failure than those who finish second. Psychologists explain this phenomenon as an example of "counterfactual thinking"—the human tendency to frame events in terms of "what if" or "if only." According to researchers, silver medalists who placed second frame their performance as a failure because they did not get the gold medal, whereas those who came in third feel happy to have avoided fourth and won a medal at all. In other words, the silver medalists reframe their gain as a loss, the bronze medalists reframe their loss as a gain.

As this example shows, reframing can be both negative and positive, but my own study shows that immigrant entrepreneurs are experts in the latter. They powerfully reconceptualize the painful experiences and failures of their past as life lessons, see the word "no" as an opportunity, and reframe the closing of a door as an invitation to find another, better, one. But before we look at how immigrant entrepreneurs reframe past negative experiences, rejection, and failure, let's first try to understand why they are so good at it. I believe there are three main reasons.

The first is related to their pasts and the process of immigration itself. Immigrants either tend to have had painful experiences that caused them to leave home, or they have experienced the pain of moving into a new place. Those who do succeed have normally found ways to come to terms with those experiences so they can turn them from sources of pain to sources of power. Further, the very act of immigration involves risk and uncertainty, regardless of your circumstances, and therefore immigrants tend to be more comfortable with risk and uncertainty. Max Levchin, the co-founder of PayPal, emigrated with his family from the Soviet Union to Chicago in 1991 as a 16-year-old. When talking about his subsequent success, he attributes a significant role to the hardship he encountered as a result of immigration and the economic, cultural, and linguistic challenges it presented:

> I think the backdrop of coming to the U.S. with nothing, just trying to survive as a multi-time startup failure. Once you get some good-life barnacles on you, that's when you get scared. Until you have something to lose, it's not that scary to be in this permanent concern state.[6]

Second, immigrant entrepreneurs tend to have an intense motivation to succeed, which runs so deep that it can even overcome setbacks that would permanently stall others. Diana Verde Nieto, an Argentinian immigrant in the U.K. who has pioneered sustainable fashion through her influential firm Positive Luxury, argues that immigrant entrepreneurs have "a different kind of hunger." As she put it when I interviewed her for this book, "When we're faced with challenges we just keep going until we find a way." Typically, if someone has given up their home and the security that typically comes with it in favor of chasing better opportunities in another place, they are not going to allow themselves to be thrown off track by the simple facts of failure or rejection.

Third, immigrant entrepreneurs derive significant strength from their support networks. As discussed in Chapters 7 and 8, homophilic ties—connections between individuals with similar backgrounds—and kinship or familial bonds play crucial roles, as does the broader community. When confronted with rejection or failure, immigrant entrepreneurs are adept at turning to these networks for insights and alternative approaches. Each setback is thus not merely an obstacle but an opportunity to engage with their community and refine their strategies. The adversity is not experienced as a profound setback but is instead reframed as a valuable learning experience.

Let's look in more detail at how reframing works, and how immigrant entrepreneurs do it.

How to Reframe Past and Present Failures

Everyone carries the burden of their past, consisting of all their regrets and perceived missteps, the roads and actions not taken. Immigrant entrepreneurs tend to recount their pasts not merely as a series of events but rather as foundational lessons that shaped their resilience and outlook. Instead of lamenting past hardships, they view them as crucial steppingstones on the path to success. In other words, they don't regret the past because they reframe it as the force that has made them who they are today. For example, consider these words from Tope Awotona whose story is characterized by multiple mistakes, struggles, and failures:

> Everything I did along the way helped me get here. No part could be omitted and have me still end up where I am today.[7]

An extreme example of the power of reframing the past comes from the story of Diane von Fürstenberg. Just 18 months before von Fürstenberg was born in Belgium, her mother was in Auschwitz, her weight down to 49 pounds. When she was liberated, she was, in von Fürstenberg's words, "a bag of bones in a field of ashes." She was barely expected to live, let alone to have a child. "I was born so close to being liberated that I consider myself a survivor, too ... My birth was a triumph of love over misery. That is my flag. My mother used to call me her torch of freedom, and she wanted me to have a big life."[8] Here, the reframing occurs by focusing on the positive thing that emerged from the horror, the birth of a baby who would go on to fulfill all her mother's dreams.

This capacity to reframe is not just about seeing the silver lining but involves a deep, rigorous cognitive process known as cognitive reappraisal. Cognitive reappraisal involves two key strategies: positive reframing and examining the evidence. Positive reframing encourages individuals to find the good or the lessons in adverse situations, while examining the evidence challenges one's initial interpretations of events, fostering a more balanced perspective. For instance, an entrepreneur might use positive reframing to see a failed business venture as a rich educational opportunity rather than a career-ending setback. Similarly, by examining the evidence, an entrepreneur could reassess their initial belief that a single failure will ruin their career by recalling past recoveries and successes.

This discussion focuses primarily on dealing with the failures of your past which can, if not reframed, come to restrict your present and shrink your future possibilities. But what about how to deal with the immediate experience of failure and rejection in the present? How can such negative experiences be prevented from festering and instead turned into opportunities for positive growth? Once again, the stories of immigrant entrepreneurs give powerful examples of how failure can be handled through reframing. Consider this from Tope Awotona describing his early career in sales:

> Cold calling people requesting donations, which is one of the most difficult things that you can do. After you get [over] the initial shock of people saying no to you, you actually fall in love with being able to persuade people to give you their money … And then after that I [sold] alarm systems door to door … [It] was the first job I ever had that was … all commission … And I think it ultimately gave me the understanding that there's a hit rate, right? So, if you knock on X amount of doors, you will ultimately make X amount of dollars. So, to me, it was a very predictable thing and in between, there's a lot of rejection. You know, people weren't happy that I interrupted their dinner. That part was tough. But the rejection of people not really wanting to buy, that didn't really faze me. The other thing I really liked was it was the first time like I could really influence how much money I made. I could work harder. I could improve my skill and … I could make more money the next day, the next week.[9]

Awotona reframes rejection as a necessary part of the process of making money from sales. In other words, the more rejection, the higher the probability of making money.

So, what happens in the minds of people like Tope who see failure as research and lessons? And what strategies can we use to reframe and learn from failure? What I have seen with immigrant entrepreneurs is that the strategies they employ when it comes to learning from failure start with their mindset and the language they use. When discussing failure, they never use terminology that frames it as an unmitigated disaster equivalent to death. In their minds, there are always solutions and other paths to find.

Central to this adaptive approach is the language used to discuss and digest failure. Immigrant entrepreneurs tend to frame their setbacks not as irreversible losses but as formative experiences rich with potential insights. This linguistic shift is not merely rhetorical; it fosters a culture where failure is seen as a resourceful guide rather than a grim verdict. By verbalizing failure in constructive terms, even to themselves, these entrepreneurs cultivate an environment where setbacks are openly discussed and analyzed, rather than being shrouded in blame or shame.

This reframing extends beyond individual attitudes to influence organizational culture. When leaders speak about failures as stepping-stones rather than stumbling blocks, they embed a powerful narrative within their teams that encourages resilience and creativity. This narrative empowers employees to explore innovative solutions without the paralyzing fear of making mistakes. It promotes an explorative approach to problem-solving, where various paths are considered and reconsidered, underscoring the belief that there is always another way, another solution to be uncovered.

Immigrant entrepreneurs' approaches to reframing failure align closely with what Amy Edmondson describes as a spectrum of reasons for failure, which ranges from deliberate deviation to thoughtful experimentation. By understanding this spectrum, leaders can better discern which failures warrant corrective actions and which should be celebrated as valuable learning opportunities. This nuanced understanding helps to ensure that the lessons embedded in each failure are not lost but are leveraged to propel the organization forward.

The mindset and language surrounding failure are crucial in determining how an organization navigates challenges and harnesses the full potential of setbacks. By embracing a constructive dialogue around failure, these leaders enable their teams and their ventures to thrive in uncertainty, turning potential failures into enduring successes. I am reminded of the Japanese manufacturing company YKK whose corporate values state: "Do not fear failure; experience builds success/creates opportunities for employees."[10]

I have also observed that immigrant entrepreneurs are experts in what Professor Sim Sitkin at Duke University calls intelligent failures. Usually, these types of failures happen when you need to experiment, but you do not know if something will work or not, such as a new business idea, preparing a new course, designing a new product or service, or entering a new market with an established product. In all these instances an element of failure is almost inevitable, perhaps necessary, but it is important that they should be intelligent failures. Or, perhaps better, we should use the terminology that Tope Awotona uses, where he describes such things not as failures but as experimentations.

In these cases, it is not about actively trying to fail or adopting an "anything goes" mentality but rather establishing the conditions in which failure can, like a fire, be contained in a small space so that you can benefit from it without having it destroy your entire organization. Following such contained failures, it is essential, as it is with any other experiment, to take time to consider what you learned from the experience and how you will apply that learning next time, which is what Tope Awotona did with his three failed startups before eventually achieving billion-dollar success with Calendly.

Another great example of how to reframe rejection comes from the immigrant entrepreneur Haim Saban. Born in 1944 in Alexandria, Egypt, Haim was raised in a cosmopolitan melting pot of cultures and religions. But tragically, that pot boiled over during the Suez War of 1956, and Haim and his family were forced to flee their home and move to Israel, living in a rough Tel Aviv neighborhood where his father, the joy sapped from his life, made a living trudging the streets selling pencils and erasers.

Haim's subsequent life involved multiple emigrations and rejections. In the aftermath of the Yom Kippur War in 1973, he moved to Paris carrying with him the burden of $600,000 worth of debt. And after enjoying some success there in the music industry, he moved to the United States where he found a lucrative niche producing music for cartoons. But his attempts to break out of that niche were rebuffed with multiple rejections for the children's TV show he planned to import from Japan. Undeterred, Haim took strength from his own sense of what would be a success and reframed those rejections as proof that he was actually right:

> It's called in Yiddish *kishke*, meaning "in my gut" … the biggest hits that I had … have been always as a result of significant rejections and repeated rejections. So, every time I have an idea that people tell me, "No, don't do that," I say, "Oops, I'm onto something."[11]

Haim maintained his dogged backing for the show despite multiple rejections, and his instincts were eventually rewarded when the Mighty Morphin Power Rangers went from being an obscure Japanese series to a global cultural phenomenon, the zenith of Haim's multibillion-dollar career.

Immigrant Entrepreneurs' Reframing Superpower: The Community

All the points about mindset, language, experimentation, and intelligent failure are crucial elements of reframing failure in ways that extract the positive elements from an ostensibly negative experience. Immigrant entrepreneurs do tend to be experts in each of those elements; however, they also tend to possess an extra resource that has not been discussed extensively in the literature on failure and reframing: their communities. As we have already seen, the creation, nurturing, and usage of homophilic ties and community connections play very significant roles in the success of immigrant entrepreneurs. What we have not yet discussed is how those same connections strongly influence their abilities to reframe failure. In other words, reframing, as practiced by immigrant entrepreneurs, is not just dependent on an individual's mindset but rather on a community's collective strength.

The help of others plays a crucial, but understudied, role in reframing failure and rejection. Through my interviews and observations, it became evident that immigrant entrepreneurs often leverage their emergent networks—comprising kin, fellow immigrants, and local community members—to a significant extent. These networks do more than provide moral support; they provide frameworks within which these entrepreneurs can reframe setbacks not as definitive failures but as learning opportunities.

In other words, resilience stems not just from an individual's internal fortitude but also the strength of their community connections that buffer against the harsh realities of business failures. This communal dimension of resilience is vividly manifest in the lives of immigrant entrepreneurs, which offer a compelling narrative about the power of drawing on collective wisdom, shared resources, and mutual encouragement to reinterpret and overcome business setbacks. Essentially, social networks contribute to collective sensemaking, which is crucial after experiencing setbacks. Through interactions within these networks, individuals can access diverse perspectives and insights, which can challenge and often alter their initial negative perceptions of failure. This collective process not only aids in developing a more balanced understanding of the event but also diminishes the personal blame that one might feel, framing the experience in a broader, often less personal, context.

Social support also acts as a critical buffer against the negative impacts of stress and failure. This phenomenon, known as "social buffering," indicates that the presence and active engagement of supportive relationships can mitigate psychological and physiological stress responses. When individuals face rejection or failure, the knowledge that they have a supportive network can significantly reduce the intensity of their stress reactions.

Emotional support from others also provides a safe space for expressing the distress associated with failures. This support goes beyond mere sympathy, offering emotional scaffolding where individuals can lean on the emotional strength of others, which in turn can fortify their own resilience. Such interactions help lessen feelings of isolation, making the recovery process more manageable and less daunting.

Networks also facilitate modeling and vicarious learning, where individuals can learn resilience by observing how others in their network handle similar rejections or failures. This modeling can demonstrate that setbacks are both common and surmountable, normalizing the experience and providing practical strategies for coping.

Finally, the tangible resources that networks can provide—be it financial assistance, strategic advice, or other forms of direct help—can significantly impact one's ability to address and move past failures. These resources can alter one's trajectory of recovery by providing not just moral but substantial material support.

By incorporating the role of social support into our understanding of resilience, the literature can offer a more comprehensive view of how individuals not only survive but also thrive after experiencing significant setbacks. Recognizing the integral role of others in this process highlights the interconnectedness of human experiences and the collective nature of resilience.

As we have already seen, immigrant entrepreneurs are experts at nurturing supportive communities. And such communities play key roles in the establishment of a sense of psychological safety, which is an important element of learning from failure. One needs to have psychological safety to reframe the situations, and diverse teams in particular will only perform well when there is psychological safety in place. My research has shown me that immigrant entrepreneurs offer such safety because they have typically been exposed to discrimination and know what it feels like to be an outsider. Therefore, as we saw in the previous chapter with the example of Hamdi Ulukaya, immigrant entrepreneurs use community to create the psychological safety that allows failure to be reframed.

Strategies to turn apparent failure into a springboard for success:

(1) **See "no" as a steppingstone:** Instead of seeking affirmations and yeses, aim to embrace "no" as part of your journey. Reframe your perception of "no" from a setback to a vital step closer to your goal. Entrepreneurs view each "no" as an exciting opportunity that brings them nearer to success, reframing rejections into milestones of progress, indicating that you are on the right path and pushing the boundaries toward your objectives.

(2) **Be genuinely curious and listen:** If you want an environment in which your staff will feel comfortable with and benefit from failure, you need to create a sense of psychological safety. That sense can be cultivated by making genuine inquiries that draw out others' ideas and listening thoughtfully to what they have to say in response. The willingness to listen—*really* listen—to what others are saying is not a given, particularly in diverse teams. It takes practice and involves asking the right kinds of questions.

(3) **Frame differences as a source of value:** All of us are prone to being frustrated by differences in opinion or perspective. Even if we recognize differences as sources of potential value and opportunities for learning, overcoming our instinctive preference for agreement takes effort. Being explicit in framing differences as a source of value can help. For instance, you could say, "We are likely to have different perspectives going into this meeting, which will help us arrive at a fuller understanding of the issues on this project."

(4) **Frame meetings as opportunities for information-sharing:** Most team meetings are implicitly framed as updating and decision-making encounters—a framing associated with judgment and

evaluation. This frame makes people less willing to speak up and raise questions or concerns and offer novel ideas. To override this default frame, it helps to open a meeting by making the sharing of information and ideas an explicit goal. And in those meetings, you can ask "What did you fail at, and what did you learn? What do you think we can learn?"

(5) **Focus on learning:** The chips aren't always going to fall where you want them to—but if you understand that reality going in, you can be prepared to wring the most value out of the experience, no matter the outcome. But avoiding challenges that make you anxious isn't going to help you grow. To overcome your fear of failure, redefine what the concept means to you. For example, instead of thinking about failure (or success) in terms of what you *achieve*, reframe it in terms of what you *learn*.

(6) **Focus on what you want to do rather than what you want to avoid:** When you're dreading a tough task, you may unconsciously set goals around what you don't want to happen. Creating a "fear list" can help; write down the challenge's worst-case scenario, how you can prevent it, and how you'll respond if it comes true. Creating a plan for a bad outcome can give you the courage to move forward.

(7) **Move beyond the blame culture:** Replace the pervasive fear of blame with a paradigm that acknowledges the inevitability of failures in today's intricate work environments. Organizations that rapidly identify, correct, and learn from failures gain a competitive edge. Cultivating an environment that looks past blame to understand the root and systemic causes of failures fosters a culture of continuous improvement and innovation. Recognize that those entrenched in blame dynamics stagnate while those who use failure as a springboard for growth will thrive.

(8) **Reframe failure as a learning opportunity:** Redefine failure as a valuable component of the learning process and treat every "no" as an opening to refine and advance. This perspective shifts the focus from fearing failure to leveraging it as a critical tool for knowledge and development. Encourage teams to perceive each failure and "no" as a question to be explored, not a verdict to be feared.

(9) **Cultivate transparency in communication:** Foster an organizational culture that prioritizes openness and transparency in communication. Encourage team members to share their thoughts, concerns, and ideas without fear of negative repercussions. Transparent communication helps demystify failures and rejections, allowing everyone to understand their context and contribute to solutions.

(10) **Be honest about your own failings:** Leaders should model behavior that encourages staff to take positive attitudes toward failure. For example, you can share stories about your own rejections, challenges, and learning experiences, thereby reinforcing that openness is valued and vital for collective growth and success.

A Day Without an Immigrant, Dallas, Texas

At Pearl Street station,
two brown-skinned men

in painter's pants stand
out in a sea of white

I am just one more face
sticking out in a crowd

& it is my privilege

that prevents me from
understanding why

the workers want to know
how to buy one-way trips

the automated machine
sells only one roundtrip fee,

back to where you came from

he isn't asking me for change
says it clear enough so that

there can be no mistake
Sí. Yo sé.

But a dollar fifty is a lot of money.

—*Shin Yu Pai*

10

Principle 7: "Fry in Your Own Oil"

Cali, Colombia, 1985

In 1985, the southwestern Colombian city of Cali was the second-most dangerous place in the world outside of countries at war.[1] And the gangs on the city's streets actually made Cali more deadly than several of the world's worst war zones. Its murder rate was three times as high as the number of deaths in Iran that year,[2] a country in a major conflict with neighboring Iraq. The only city outside a country at war that was more dangerous than Cali was Medellin, also in Colombia, which was partly so deadly because the gangs of Cali were doing battle there for control of the lucrative cocaine trafficking trade.

But in among all the chaos and death in Cali in that dark year, there was a 15-year-old boy whose focus was only ever on his great passion in life: dancing. Even ignoring the danger on the streets around him, Beto did not have an easy life. Raised by a single mother, he was already working three jobs at 14 to try to help make ends meet for his family. But whenever he had spare time, he would dance and, even though he was too poor to afford lessons, his talent helped him win a national lambada tournament, which led to him winning a place at one of Cali's premier dance schools. But he had to teach aerobics classes to cover the cost of his own tuition.

169

Happily, it turned out that the teenage Beto was as good a teacher as he was a dancer. People loved his classes because he was an entertainer and a storyteller who focused on making them happy, turning exercise from a chore into a pleasure. And then one day, a happy accident made his classes even better: He forgot the cassette with his music for class and was forced to play the only other tape he had with him, a collection of Latin music; Beto improvised some new moves to go with the beats, and that went down a storm with his students and turned the whole class into a *rumba* (Spanish for "party").

Throughout the 1990s, Beto's studio was a different world from the violent streets outside, a constant, life-affirming party. Beto's dance and aerobics fusion classes had become wildly popular in Cali, to such an extent that he decided it was time to take on the world, and in 1999, he booked himself a ticket and headed to Miami, in pursuit of the American Dream.

Beto actually moved back and forth between Colombia's capital Bogota and Miami several times as he struggled to find a gym in the U.S. that had any interest in his class. He struggled partly because he didn't speak English, but eventually he was able to get an audition for a class in North Miami and was able to invest a few hundred dollars in buying a cheap car and renting a basic apartment in Little Havana.

By this time, he had teamed up with Alberto Perlman, a young Jewish Colombian businessman whose family had originally emigrated there from Jerusalem. Alberto himself had moved to the United States to study in 1994, and then subsequently made, and lost, millions of dollars when the dot-com bubble burst at the turn of the new millennium. Scrambling to find a way out of the wreckage of his previous company, Alberto followed a recommendation from his mother, who had taken Beto's classes in Colombia, and teamed up with the fitness instructor, and another Colombian friend, Alberto Aghion, to try to launch a new Latin-inspired fusion dance and aerobics class. As Alberto Perlman put it when I asked him about meeting Beto Perez for the first time:

> [It] was a pivotal moment. I was inspired by Beto's passion and unique approach to fitness, using Latin-inspired dance movements and music. Beto's authenticity and deep understanding of how to get people moving in a way that was joyful and engaging stood out. The partnership made sense because of our shared vision to disrupt the fitness industry by making workouts feel like a party.

But in the post-dot-com and 9/11 world, lots of businesses were discovering that the party was over, and fundraising for Beto and Alberto's new venture did not go so well. Each of the company's founders was required to work day jobs while investing all their spare time and money trying to get the new business off the ground. According to Beto, the little team would often be up past midnight packing DVDs to send out or doing whatever other work was required. But their experience of relying on themselves to do basically every job that the company required was ultimately very valuable because it meant that when they were eventually in a position to hire people, they knew exactly what qualities were required for each post.

Being self-funded was teaching the three co-founders valuable lessons, but it was stretching their resources to breaking point, to the extent that they eventually only had $14,000 left in the bank between them. Pooling their money, they decided to stake everything on a new strategy, as Alberto Perlman described it in our interview for this book:

> Limited funding forced the team to be resourceful and selective about where we invested. We had to be creative with marketing, often relying on word of mouth and grassroots efforts rather than expensive ad campaigns. It pushed us to focus on building a loyal community of instructors and participants rather than spending heavily on initial promotions.

Creating that community of instructors was the new strategy that the three friends spent their last $14,000 on, and after they sent the email inviting people to join what they called the Zumba Instructor Network, they set a target of 200 sign-ups to keep the business going. It was an approach that, according to Alberto Perlman, became the company's big turning point:

> The creation of the Zumba Instructor Network changed everything. We empowered instructors to become brand ambassadors, growing the brand organically. This allowed us to scale the business while maintaining tight control over expenses. Leveraging social media and partnerships were other key strategies for stretching our budget ... The growth was managed by focusing on scalability. By empowering instructors and

creating a community-driven business model, Zumba expanded quickly without the need for external funding. This was intentional: building a strong, loyal following and reinvesting profits back into the company to fuel further expansion.

Zumba, a company built by immigrants out of $14,000 and a network of enthusiasts, is now a global brand worth more than half a billion dollars. And although the movement grew out of a violent environment, it has helped to bring people together even in conflict-affected countries, showing, at the same time, that the very borders that immigrants have to cross are, in one sense, irrelevant, as Beto puts it:

Music and dance are a universal language. We have classes in luxury neighborhoods. We have [free] classes in the inner cities … We have classes in Russia with Ukrainians and Russians … We have classes in Israel with Arabs and Jews taking classes together. Dance brings people together.[3]

The Importance of Frying in Your Own Oil

Many lessons can be learned from the story of Beto Perez and Zumba, but there is one in particular that stands out for me. But before discussing that, I want to set it in the context of a little piece of wisdom that comes from deep in my own family's history and continues to guide my life today.

That wisdom came to me from my grandfather, but who knows how many generations of struggle it had been passed down through before it came to him? My grandfather was born in 1923 into a world that seems scarcely imaginable now, just one year after the fall of the Ottoman Empire. As a member of the Turkish ethnic minority in Bulgaria, he spoke not one word of the Bulgarian language and lived on the fringes of society in a hut in the mountains. Orphaned at the age of 15, he never went to school and supported himself, and later our family, through any self-taught trades that could bring in a little money.

He looked after the horses and cows that the family depended on for transport and milk. He grew his own fruit and vegetables on the harsh soils around his home, which also had space for a few tobacco plants. And the meager income that came from selling their leaves was supplemented by the few extra cents that came from my grandmother's work from home as a self-taught tailor and sales from the bread she baked before dawn every morning.

My grandfather might never have spent a minute at school, but his life of struggle equipped him with a certain homespun wisdom that has stood me and my family in good stead through all our subsequent challenges in life and in business. And there is one phrase of his that I always return to when I'm looking for advice about how to lead my life or run my business: "You have to fry in your own oil."

Essentially, his advice was a call for self-reliance, on every level. From a financial perspective, he meant you should make the most of what you already have rather than taking on debt, which can rapidly escalate to the extent that what you have borrowed has crushed you.

But when my grandfather encouraged us to rely on our own resources, he did not only mean financial ones. He was a man who never had much money, but he was highly skilled at turning whatever he did have, from his meager possessions to his many talents, to good use, getting as much as possible out of his own resources so that he, and his family, could survive and, ultimately, thrive.

Frying in your own oil also requires you to reduce the amount of money you spend on things from outside, to reuse what you already have, and to recycle that which can be employed again for different purposes. In other words, the essence of the modern sustainability movement is captured in my grandfather's simple saying.

I've increasingly come to reflect on the fact that his wisdom is, at its deepest level, a reminder to us all that the answers that we seek are always inside ourselves: "All you need is within you" as Nisargadatta Maharaj put it.[4] In those senses, my grandfather's advice to fry in your own oil can be interpreted on financial, environmental, and even spiritual levels, and it continues to guide me long after his passing.

So, how does that all relate to the story of Beto Perez, the two Albertos, and Zumba? Throughout the story we can see how they fried in their own oil. When Beto forgot the tape for his class in Cali, he improvised and used what he had to create something new, which was the very start of the Zumba movement. When he first came to America, Beto and his partners initially failed to raise the outside funding that they thought they required. But instead of giving up they turned to themselves and did all the jobs required to get the business moving. And that turned out to be a great platform for growth because they came to understand every aspect of their operations, which helped them to later hire the right people to do those jobs.

The failure of their fundraising also forced them to make creative use of the limited resources that they did have, and that led to them turning their network of instructors into the force that supercharged their growth. In other words, the answer was within, and the creation of their own network allowed them to grow sustainably, on their own terms, without taking on the excessive, and often crippling, levels of debt that many startups think is the fast track to success. And that's why the creation and global success of the Zumba brand is a great example of frying in your own oil.

Immigrant entrepreneurs generally typically start with fewer resources than their native-born peers, which forces them to use what they have creatively. And the art of making more from less, which they learn from necessity, becomes a skill that they can use throughout their entire careers to continue driving sustainable growth. Even when they do have access to more, the most successful immigrant entrepreneurs tend to continue frying in their own oil because that is the most efficient, effective, and sustainable way to run a business. And that leads us to a key point: It is not just about how you get a business started; it is also the best approach at all stages of turning a startup into an established firm. So, let's look at and learn from how immigrant entrepreneurs apply that principle when starting and growing a company.

Frying in Your Own Oil When First Starting a Business

Entrepreneurship is often celebrated as a liberating escape from the nine-to-five grind, offering the independence of being one's own boss. But beneath that appealing veneer lies a challenging reality—it takes three to five years to see your first profit, and that is if you are lucky enough to last that long; as we have already seen, 90% of startups fail, 10% of them in the first year. At the foundation of every entrepreneurial venture is the critical need for capital. Starting a business is hardly a trivial financial endeavor. Obviously, the natural inclination of many entrepreneurs is to immediately start looking for investors and borrowing the money that they think they require to get their startup off the ground, but in my opinion, that is a mistake.

One reason for that is when you are dealing with other people's money, you are less careful and more liable to make mistakes. Of course, as discussed in the previous chapter, mistakes are okay and can be extremely valuable, even essential, sources of learning. But we have to remember the concept of intelligent failure, and your failures are more likely to be intelligent ones when you are dealing with your own money. Further, you won't have the opportunity to learn from your mistakes if you are so saddled with debt that the whole company sinks as a result of some early errors.

If you do succeed in borrowing lots of funds, there is also a risk that money might curtail your creativity by making you think you can simply buy a solution rather than make one. As we saw with the Zumba story, necessity really can be the mother of invention, and often what you invent is better than what you would have bought. Relying on your own resources and creativity also helps create a business that is less dependent on constant cash injections for growth, meaning you're better positioned to grow sustainably in the long term.

In the case of my own company, we looked to see what resources we could access without needing major cash injections, and the offcut scraps of leather that we took from Italian factories and transformed into accessories became the basis of our whole business. At that time, *sustainability* was not such a buzzword, and the whole concepts of upcycling and the circular economy were barely discussed. And we were certainly not consciously applying those concepts; we were just using our creativity to make the best of what we had. And in the process of, intentionally, frying in our own oil, we, unintentionally, turned ourselves into sustainability pioneers, creating a business model that has served as the foundation for all our future expansion.

Immigrant entrepreneurs face particular challenges as they often have limited financial and social capital and have to try to find ways to acquire them in unfamiliar business environments. Yet, it is precisely their ability to fry in their own oil by maximizing limited resources that helps them create businesses that can grow sustainably, be resilient, and last longer. Dominique Ansel, who also struggled to find outside financing for his bakery in New York and was, therefore, forced to fry in his own oil. Or, rather, the mixture of his limited savings and those of his girl-friend, which they used to jointly start the bakery with a 10-year lease on a property that desperately needed renovation. And, with such limited financial resources, they set about doing all the work that was required, from rewiring the building to cleaning the toilets and mopping the floors at the end of each day.

Reflecting on how those early days of struggle shaped his attitude to business and discouraged over-spending, Dominique says:

> You know when you start with so little, every dollar off feels like, like so much money … Like I remember my first check I wrote [when] my vendor for one month was $10,000 and I took a deep breath like "Oh, my God, $10,000 for one month."[5]

As we can see, not being able to borrow money actually became the foundation of Dominique Ansel's success. Relying on his own talents showed him what he was capable of, and financing the business with his girlfriend gave them the independence to develop the business on their own terms.

Similarly, Jane Wurwand of Dermalogica, the multi-billion-dollar skincare brand, started her company with an investment of $14,000 of her own money and was working 16 hours a day, seven days a week, operating without external funding and refusing to be bought out as the company grew.

Emphasizing the dangers of bringing in outside investment and borrowing money in the early stages of a company, Fadi Ghandour of Aramex argues:

> Entrepreneurs that raise money without revenue are delusional … It's partly their failure too, because they need to listen and know when the warning signs are there. Because of this, many companies will cease to exist. You need to sell products to people, and people have to want to buy your product. Just someone investing in you, giving you money. It's endless.[6]

Unfortunately, I have recent experience of the very issue that Fadi is discussing here. One startup that I was indirectly advising was continually borrowing money in its early days in an attempt to kickstart growth. I explained to the concerned chief financial officer that the company should not be asking, "Where can we get money from" but rather "Why is our business struggling and what should we be doing differently?" Despite my warnings, they continued down the path of constantly seeking outside investment, leading eventually to bankruptcy.

The principle of frying in your own oil reflects a commitment to growing within one's means, emphasizing sustainability and the wise use of available resources. It teaches us that growth should be pursued only as fast as a company's existing capabilities allow. This approach ensures that expansion never compromises the quality or the culture that made the company successful in the first place. In Chapter 5, I wrote about the importance of vision for immigrant entrepreneurs, and here we see how frying in your own oil helps you to remain free to pursue that vision in whatever way seems best to you, without having to compromise to the caution of investors who may not share your vision but are only interested in the potential to turn it into money. Therefore, businesses that adhere to the fry in your own oil principle can achieve sustainable growth without surrendering their identity or core values, leading to the achievement of impact that transcends profit.

Frying in Your Own Oil as Your Business Grows

The advantages of relying on your own resources in the early stages of a business are clear, but what do you do when your company is starting to experience levels of growth that stretch your resources beyond the breaking point? Typically, as businesses move beyond their initial phases, they face a host of new challenges and often make unforced errors that can derail their entire operations.

It's easy to understand why businesses make such mistakes. After all, not many even get to experience the heady rush of growth; indeed, after adjusting for inflation, most businesses barely grow at all.[7] So, when your business is suddenly taking off and you are seen as a rising star, it's easy to get caught up in the buzz that comes from having a desirable new product and always attracting new customers. At such times, the temptation is to think, "Finally, after all my hard work, everything's going great." And in such a mood, you may find yourself using the results of an exceptional boom period to forecast your future growth. And based on that highly optimistic outlook, further bolstered by the personal sense of achievement derived from your success, you might commit to over-ambitious borrowing, extensive hiring, and aggressive business growth plans that are no longer grounded in reality, forgetting about the virtues of prudence, self-reliance, and sustainability.

Entrepreneurs caught up in their own star moment might find themselves wooed by investors who smell the chance to make money, but whose desire to do everything to get it might end up undermining the very things that made the business special and unique in the first place. It's easily forgotten when high on soaring sales figures that while strategic borrowing can facilitate growth, debt also poses substantial risks if not carefully managed or if sudden market changes blow the conditions that underlay your success away. After all, the received wisdom on this subject states that you should try to grow as swiftly as the market allows. However, a considered strategy requires aligning growth ambitions with a firm's actual ability to manage and capitalize on such expansion effectively. In other words, growth is not merely a number to chase; it demands thoughtful integration with a company's operational capabilities, financial health, workforce dynamics, and overall organizational ethos.

As we shall see, companies aiming to achieve and maintain profitable growth must strategically balance seizing market opportunities with the cultivation of necessary capabilities and resources. This involves a calculated approach to growth that includes making deliberate decisions about the pace of growth (how fast to grow), identifying new opportunities (where to grow), and systematically developing the financial, human, and organizational assets required for expansion (how to grow). By adhering to this disciplined growth strategy, companies can ensure they utilize their resources wisely and sustainably, embodying the principle of frying in their own oil—maximizing their current assets without overreaching, thereby fostering a resilient and enduring business.

So, in the remaining two sections of this chapter, we'll look at how to use the fry in your own oil principle to manage the two main challenges that come with growth: how to secure the increased financing you need without sinking your whole ship and how to recruit and nurture all the extra staff you will require so they can deliver your original vision with the quality that made your name in the first place. And, once again, we shall see how immigrant entrepreneurs often have special expertise in achieving sustainable growth, balancing prudence and the cultivation of their resources in ways that lay stable foundations upon which further success can be built.

Balancing Financing Needs with Sustainable Growth

Let's look at the financial side first. Immigrant entrepreneurs often adopt conservative growth strategies, informed by their early experiences with resource constraints, thus avoiding the risks associated with heavy debt loads. When they raise money, they do it at the right time with the right intentions. But avoiding overdependence on external funding is only one aspect of sustainable growth. Other facets like employee expertise, organizational wisdom, and internal processes are equally critical and often become the limiting factors in a firm's expansion. A prudent leader monitors these resources to prevent growth from outpacing the company's ability to deliver quality and maintain operational stability.

So, instead of narrowly focusing on financials, a broader view that considers the readiness of all company resources—people, processes, and systems—is essential. Companies that don't align their growth and operational capacity often find themselves in a bind, with the rush to expand leading to mistakes that can have long-term impact on employee well-being and market reputation.

The right strategy for many firms, therefore, is to say no to faster growth, just like Dominique Ansel, who rejected eye-watering offers to mass produce the Cronut because he realized that would ultimately undermine the very quality that made it so desirable, thus destroying its long-term sustainability.

Of course, outsider investment is normally required to help your business grow, but the key is always to ask are the initial benefits worth the long-term costs? I repeatedly ask that question of the startups I advise for the British Fashion Council. Some of these highly creative, young designers experience incredible growth trajectories that take them from operating out of a tiny East London studio to enjoying overnight success after, say, Beyoncé is pictured wearing their coat. Of course, it's natural to try to maximize your resources to ride a wave like that; but I always tell the designers, whenever a new investor wants to get on board, you must ask how fast they want you to grow and how much you will have to sacrifice to achieve their plan. And if that sacrifice will threaten your long-term sustainability and impact, I would advise against it.

Maintaining Quality as the Workforce Grows

The final area of growth challenges that I would like to discuss relates to the increase in staff numbers that are required when a business really starts to take off. Achieving long-term, sustainable growth is complex and challenging; without a dedicated and capable team, it's virtually unachievable. To face that challenge, immigrant entrepreneurs fry in their own oil. By investing in their teams and promoting a culture of autonomy, immigrant entrepreneurs create self-sustaining workforces capable of propelling the business forward without constant external input, enhancing efficiency and resilience.

Deloitte refers to this approach as "human sustainability," emphasizing the strong link between employees' well-being, their sense of purpose, and organizational performance.[8] Researchers from Oxford and Harvard at the Wellbeing Research Centre also found a strong correlation between employee well-being and firm performance.[9] When employees are healthy, engaged, and motivated, they not only excel at their work but also strengthen their interpersonal relationships and drive meaningful change within their organizations.

Despite widespread recognition of the importance of human sustainability—with 76% of global organizations acknowledging its role in their success—Deloitte's 2024 report reveals that only a small fraction, about 10%, have established effective strategies to harness its benefits.[10] This gap highlights a critical oversight in many growth strategies that fail to prioritize employee well-being, leading to issues like persistent disengagement, burnout, and stagnation in innovation. As businesses plan for future growth, it's vital to consider a strategy that places employee well-being at its core. Before embarking on new initiatives, leaders should reflect on how their decisions will impact their workforce. After all, you can't fry in your own oil if that oil's already burned out.

Zeynep Ton of the MIT Sloan School of Management is a staunch advocate of quality leadership and the creation of enriching job environments.[11] She argues that sustainable growth is both an economic target and a human-centric endeavor. Ton's analysis emphasizes the pivotal role of frontline managers as key to a company's growth and health. Her findings suggest that experienced managers greatly enhance performance metrics, such as profitability and customer satisfaction, due to their deep understanding of company operations and employee well-being.

This ties back to the concept of frying in your own oil, where nurturing internal talent and fostering a supportive work environment are as crucial as financial investments in achieving long-term growth. Specifically, Ton's approach aligns with the principle that businesses should grow within their means and capabilities, particularly those of their human resources. In her view, growth should not just meet short-term financial goals but also enhance the workforce's collective capability and satisfaction. She offers the example of Costco, where sustainable growth has been achieved through a steadfast focus on the welfare of its employees and customers. Given everything we've learned about how immigrant entrepreneurs operate, it may not be surprising to discover that one of Costco's two founders, Jeffrey Brotman, was from an immigrant family.

As we have seen, sustainable and self-sufficient business practices are necessities that redefine the metrics of business success. In that context, frying in your own oil is a holistic approach to entrepreneurship that values careful planning, moderation, and a profound respect for resources. Immigrant entrepreneurs' journeys illustrate how businesses can achieve longevity and influence broader industry practices toward more sustainable models. By embodying these principles, immigrant entrepreneurs offer powerful lessons on building durable businesses that prioritize long-term impact over short-term gains.

Those lessons are perhaps best summed up in the words of Yvon Chouinard, the rock climber, surfer, environmentalist, and one-time billionaire founder of the clothing company Patagonia (he stopped being a billionaire after giving his company away to a not-for-profit trust). In an interview with McKinsey, he connected business longevity with a cautious and resource-conscious vision of sustainable growth:

> We have to be cautious about growing too big. A company doesn't last 100 years by chasing endless growth. There's an ideal size for every business and, when companies outgrow that, they die. We know we have to be intentional in our growth to be around for another 50 years, so we're focused on longevity, not expansion.[12]

Strategies for achieving sustainable growth in business:
(1) **Prioritize strategic self-funding:** Consider internal financing to fuel initial growth phases, which enhances understanding of the business's fundamental strengths and minimizes dilution of the founders' vision. By relying on generated profits or existing capital, companies can maintain strategic autonomy and foster a culture of resourcefulness.

(2) **Take a hands-on approach to business building:** Frying in your own oil often requires you to be prepared to "get your hands dirty" during the early stages of getting a company off the ground. But doing all the jobs yourself doesn't just save you money, it also teaches you every aspect of your own business, which helps you recruit the right people later and manage them more effectively as the company grows.

(3) **Innovate within constraints:** Limitations should be viewed as a framework within which creativity can flourish. Encourage teams to innovate by maximizing their current resources. This approach not only encourages ingenuity and problem-solving but also aligns with sustainable business practices by minimizing waste. Companies that fry in their own oil innovate in ways that are both cost-effective and resource-efficient.

(4) **Grow at a sustainable pace:** Growth should be aligned with the actual capacity of the organization and the external market environment. Rapid expansion that outpaces the company's ability to deliver consistent quality and service can harm the brand in the long term.

(5) **Develop new metrics to prevent overdevelopment:** Gauge the true impact of growth on your business by using a balanced scorecard that includes both traditional financial metrics and new measures such as employee workload, system reliability, and customer satisfaction.

(6) **Cultivate a strong company culture:** A robust company culture that mirrors core values and mission is critical for sustainable growth. Such a culture attracts and retains top talent, encourages engagement, and enhances overall performance. Initiatives like transparent communication, recognizing and rewarding behaviors that align with company values, and regular engagement surveys can strengthen culture and enhance employee loyalty.

(7) **Maintain focus on core values and mission:** Every strategic decision should reinforce the company's core mission, ensuring that the business remains focused on its long-term goals and does not deviate into ventures that dilute its brand or alienate its base.

(8) **Emphasize quality over quantity:** Quality should never be compromised for the sake of expansion. High standards in product and service offerings build brand reputation and customer loyalty. Implement quality assurance processes that identify potential issues before they reach the customer, ensuring that scaling efforts do not compromise the quality that established the brand.

(9) **Encourage resourcefulness and self-reliance:** Promoting a culture of resourcefulness can lead to significant innovations and cost savings. Reward employees and teams who deliver results by optimizing existing resources rather than through increased spending or expansion. This not only improves the bottom line but also encourages a deeper understanding of the business's capabilities and limitations.

(10) **Plan for long-term resilience:** Future-proofing a business involves anticipating changes in the market and adapting strategies accordingly without compromising the company's core values. Regular strategic reviews that consider potential market disruptions can help a company pivot quickly and effectively, minimizing risk and leveraging new opportunities.

Kismet

Dice tossed at the wall.
Isn't it a miracle, your geography?
The whispered prayers. I watch my father
count his blessings under a broken streetlamp—
Mashallah, because the night swallows so much.
I watch my father, and the watching is reverence,
so I guard my gaze. The wind hums like an old friend.
What is fate but a pattern in the chaos?

There's a lover who kisses a locket each night,
fearing the envy that shadows good fortune.
Mashallah.

I dream I am a tree, ancient and upright.
I dream I rewrite histories, this time
I don't lower my eyes when they challenge.
I don't bless them for leaving me be.
Later, my mother whispers, they couldn't touch
your spirit.
But you know that, don't you?

I don't know what they could take.

I only know that shimmering hope.

Only that whisper of kismet,

as tender and uncertain as a promise.
                                        —*Neri Karra Sillaman*

11

Principle 8: Dare to Play Your Hand

Trying to trace a story to its start is an impossible task. The further back you go in search of its origins, the more you discover that the depth of any story is effectively infinite. And whenever you think you've reached the point at which it begins, you realize there is always somewhere further and deeper back you could go, tracing the seeds of the seeds of the seeds of the story that ultimately flowered in so many different ways.

I chose to start this book with the story of my early struggles at the University of Miami, my second experience of emigration. But I could have gone back deeper and started it in many other places and times. And now that I'm coming toward the end of this book, and focusing on the final principle, I'd like to go back to one of those other times and places, a windswept beach on Bulgaria's Black Sea coast in the early summer of 1987, and start with the sound of a girl singing as she plays on the sand because there is a direct line between that moment and the book that you are reading now. The song she was singing was an ancient folk tune the girl had learned from her mother, stemming from the land where their roots lay but where neither had ever been, and the melody was both sprightly and melancholy as it told a story of love, travel, and the unexpected things that happen on the road: "*Üsküdar'a gideriken* (On the way to Üsküdar)," the girl sang,

"*Bir mendil buldum* (I found a handkerchief). *Mendilimin içine de lokum doldur-dum* (I filled the handkerchief with Turkish delight)." Her song disappearing, it seemed, into the sound of the winds and the waves.

But every song carries its own significance and also has the power to assume new meanings when it is heard. And the significance of that song at that particular moment on that particular beach was that it was sung in Turkish. Or, more specifically, the significance of the song was that it was heard by a businessman from Turkey on vacation who was surprised to hear his own language being sung on a beach in another country and decided to approach the girl's family, my family, to say hello and find out why.

It's easy to understand why he was surprised. A visitor to Bulgaria in the 1980s might well have never noticed that there were any Turkish people living there at all. After all, the government was doing everything in its power to erase all traces of our Turkishness from the land; they were forcibly changing our names to Bulgarian equivalents, prohibiting us from express-ing our culture, and banning us from using our language. So, even singing the song I'd learned from my mother in our native language on the beach was an innocent, and unconscious, act of resistance. And although it was nothing more than the tiniest drop in the ocean of resistance to Bulgarian communism, from that drop flowed consequences that changed my family's life in unimaginable ways.

Because during the course of the conversation, the curious Turkish vacationer mentioned to my father that he had a business in Istanbul manu-facturing leather accessories. And he even gave my father his business card and an invitation to look him up if we ever found ourselves in the Turkish metropolis, which was only a few hours, drive away, but on the other side of a seemingly uncrossable border. Of course, it was just luck that we met this man at all, pure random chance that he had decided to travel to Bulgaria and happened to be within earshot of me rather than a few meters farther away when I decided to start singing in Turkish on the beach. Luck too that over the next three years, my father never misplaced that tiny slip of paper that would eventually prove, quite unexpectedly, to be our ticket to another world.

But it was a ticket that was worthless while we were at home, and it was only luck that got us to a place where that ticket could become of value. Luck that, when the time came for us to flee Bulgaria in June 1989, my father happened to be friends with a policeman who agreed to help us get to the border. Luck too that the border itself was in such chaos that we were able to cross despite my mother not having the right papers. Luck too that the fall of the Berlin Wall in November 1989 and the subsequent complete collapse of Eastern European communism opened up new markets. Luck too that all my family had been forced by communism to learn Russian at school, so we were able to access many of those opportunities. And luck too, I guess, that when my father went to Russia in search of a job and noticed that the people were carrying their belongings in plastic bags that he had in his wallet the business card of a man who had heard a Turkish song on a beach three years before and who could help him with his new business idea.

And it was only as a result of all those chances colliding that my father came to be walking down a particular road in Istanbul, consulting the business card gripped in his hand like it was a star he was following, until he found the place and exchanged handshakes: "Remember me? We met on the beach in Bulgaria years ago when my daughter was singing that song?" And then eventually, he pitched the businessman the idea that ultimately made our family and led to everything else that was to follow, right up to the writing of these words now: "There is a lot of opportunity there, let me sell your leather bags in Russia ..."

My father had no experience in sales to trade on (in Bulgaria he worked in construction) nor did he have any contacts in Russia. But his pitch was somehow successful, and although our business was not exactly born that day (we didn't start selling our own "Neri Karra"–branded products until after I'd graduated from the University of Miami in 1999), it was a major step toward the creation of our own family firm and label.

Rewinding my family's story to that beach reminds us of the role of an extremely potent factor that is often ignored in the literature on business success: luck. It's understandable why luck doesn't feature so heavily in that literature. After all, the protagonists of the stories, i.e., the builders of the business, are naturally more inclined to emphasize the importance of their own actions rather than acknowledging the massive role that chance played in their success. And, even if they were to acknowledge it, the writers of the stories, i.e., the authors with books to sell, are unlikely to emphasize the importance of a factor that may appear to be utterly uncontrollable. You might accept that so much of success is down to good fortune, but that realization doesn't readily translate into the sorts of action plans and blueprints that business books typically try to peddle.

I wonder sometimes about the role that luck might have played in the successes, and subsequent failures, of some of the firms lionized in the sort of bestselling business books that I mentioned in Chapter 1. As I discussed there, iconic classics like *In Search of Excellence*, *Good to Great*, and *Built to Last* attempted to distill the lessons learned from the triumphs of a selection of very high-performing firms into blueprints that anyone could copy to create a booming business. However, as also pointed out in Chapter 1, following the books' publications, many of the firms celebrated in them turned out to be not lions but rather little cats, with many struggling, failing, or even going fully out of business, which begs some questions. If those companies weren't the privileged holders of special secrets, what role did good luck (a factor that cannot be worked into any blueprint) play in their success? If they were doing everything right, what was the role of bad fortune in their downturns and downfalls? And is there anything we can actively do to attract and maximize good luck and mitigate the effects of misfortunes?

As luck isn't something that you can readily sell or buy; it doesn't feature in most of the bestselling business books. But it is certainly something that immigrant entrepreneurs are happy to acknowledge in their accounts of their successes. The very nature of immigration is that it is filled with uncertainty; you are thrown into chaos and every aspect of your life as you knew it is disrupted. That might explain why one of the things that I was most struck by when working on this book was the extent to which luck was cited as a major factor in almost all the interviews that I conducted or listened to during my research. As a business researcher, I did not expect luck to be so readily discussed, but it was to such an extent that I had no choice but to make it one of the main principles.

Consider, for example, this quote from one of Andrew Grove's interviews:

> I was extraordinarily lucky ... [straight after university] my first assignment was ... [analyzing the] device structure out of which modern integrator services are made ... Weeks out of school I was one of the world's experts in a nascent, emerging field; and there were no experts, so ... I became one of the experts.[1]

Or this from Dominique Ansel:

> Yeah, I was lucky. I was lucky I thought of the idea. I was lucky I tried.
> I was lucky I worked hard for it. I was lucky I met my wife. I was lucky
> for all of things. I also worked very hard for it. Luck is a part of it, but
> yes, but I think if you are a good person in life, you attract good people
> to you and good things happen to you.[2]

Or this from Tope Awotona:

> Growing a company is exciting AND humbling every single day. I've
> made a lot of deliberate decisions, but I've also had luck in the process.[3]

Or this from Haim Saban, when reflecting on his success:

> I'm a lucky guy, on multiple levels.[4]

Such quotes might suggest that the experiences of immigrant entrepreneurs support those academics who do stress the importance of luck over skill and other factors. While management strives to minimize uncertainty and standardize outcomes through strategic planning and control, the reality often involves a blend of both predictable and unforeseen elements. In organizational theory, there is a dichotomy between viewing businesses as carefully designed entities where every outcome is the result of deliberate planning and seeing them as organic constructs where chance plays a significant role. The most extreme version of that position attributes so much of success to luck that it takes, in the words of Alex Coad and David J. Storey, "the entrepreneur out of entrepreneurship" altogether,[5] leaving only a ship constantly buffeted on the waves and winds of chance. The counter to that argument is the very well-established entrepreneurship literature that focuses almost exclusively on the background, experience, characteristics, and skills of the entrepreneur. And the truth, as usual, is somewhere in between the two poles. The journey of entrepreneurship can be compared to that of a boat crossing an ocean where it can be driven or struck by winds, waves, storms, and rocks that appear to be the utterly random consequences of blind chance. But at the same time, as Aracely

Soto-Simeone, Charlotta Sirén, and Torben Antretter pointed out in their response to Coad and Storey, the role that the captain and crew play in navigating those seemingly random examples of good and bad luck cannot be ignored.[6] And a skilled and experienced captain and crew are far more likely to appear lucky than novices without knowledge.

The experiences and attitudes of immigrant entrepreneurs show us that while luck may play a huge role in the success or otherwise of any entrepreneurial gamble, there is still much to be said for the importance of how one maximizes the opportunities that luck presents. And while there is not much we can learn about how we can just be luckier, we can also redefine our notion of luck to recognize it for what it really is: an interaction between good fortune and people with the ability to spot and maximize the opportunities that chance presents. Therefore, there is very much that we can learn from immigrant entrepreneurs about how to recognize and take advantage of luck when it does appear. With that in mind, I've divided the following sections as follows: The first is about how you recognize luck, the next is about how you maximize it, which requires both bravery and, often, good timing, and the final section is about how grit is the essential ingredient that helps you to persevere through inevitable times of bad luck.

Recognizing Luck: Serendipity Is a Capability, Not an Event

When I was completing my PhD at Cambridge's Judge Business School, I was fortunate that one of the professors there was Mark de Rond, an inspiring thinker about management science who tends to throw himself into unorthodox activities for his research, from living with surgeons in Afghanistan to rowing the whole length of the Amazon. One of Mark's most interesting insights concerns luck: He describes serendipity as not an event but a capability, the point being that fortune only becomes good when you have the ability to recognize it as such and act accordingly. According to Mark, serendipity does not result from a single event that happens to us but rather from the active process of making connections between events, which may appear unrelated to most. His perspective is shared by many of the immigrant entrepreneurs studied for this book. Karan

Bilimoria actually referenced Mark de Rond when describing his own attitude to luck in our interview for this book:

> Mark de Rond describes serendipity as seeing what everyone else sees but thinking what no one else has thought ... And linked to that is luck. And the best definition of luck that I've ever heard is luck is when determination meets opportunity. If you're not determined, you won't even see the opportunity. If you're determined, you'll see that opportunity. And I visualize it like waves that go past you in life. If you're determined, you might catch one of those waves. If you're not determined, the waves will just go past you all your life. So, I think it's that combination of determination and opportunity that is luck. And I think there is no running away from it. We've all had some luck from time to time.

There's a lot to unpack in that quote, but one of the key points is that you must be able to recognize good fortune when it occurs, a task that requires awareness and insight. And I would argue that immigrant entrepreneurs are particularly well-equipped to see that which others have missed because they are blessed with the sort of cross-cultural expertise and multiple perspectives discussed in Chapter 4.

Recognizing luck also requires the wisdom to determine the extent to which it should influence our actions. In other words, it's about discerning whether a stroke of luck is a fleeting distraction or a long-term opportunity that aligns well with our overall objectives and vision. Making this call requires a blend of intuition and rationality, ensuring that our plans remain resilient against the randomness of chance. Understanding the extent to which we should allow luck to alter our strategic direction is as crucial as recognizing it. To navigate that complexity, we must engage both our intuition, which taps into our experiences and gut feelings, and our analytical skills, which assess the tangible benefits and alignment with long-term plans. This translates to a disciplined approach where leaders must discern the potential impacts of unexpected opportunities on their long-term vision. It involves a careful analysis of risk and reward, considering the sustainability and potential integration of this new path into the existing strategy. Therefore, the art of handling luck effectively in business lies in this dual capacity to detect it and then judiciously decide if and how it should influence our journey toward our goals.

As the quote from Karan Bilimoria also suggests, luck is not just about recognizing what is in front of you but also being able to take the action required to maximize your good fortune, which is the subject of the following section.

Maximizing Luck: Timing, Location, and Daring

According to Haim Saban, "The definition of luck is having the skill to grab the luck when it is presented,"[7] which chimes with the views of Karan Bilimoria expressed above; luck may be a chance occurrence, but it only really becomes good fortune when the occurrence happens to someone who can spot the opportunity and who has the capabilities and characteristics required to capitalize on it. A similar view was expressed by Dominique Ansel, who identifies several of the key characteristics that are required to turn a fortunate occurrence into a fortune:

> Luck is part of it, but it's not the main thing ... You have to dare. Someone asked me if I would have done this if [I was] still in France. I told them probably not. New York is a very open-minded city that will let you explore.[8]

This quote touches on three of the key aspects of maximizing luck I'd want to stress in this chapter: daring, effort, and location. The final aspect, not covered in the quote but also important, is timing. In my research interviewing immigrant entrepreneurs, it became evident that while they recognized the role of luck in their success, they also consistently emphasized the importance of timing, the right location, and their own hard work. These entrepreneurs shared insights on how strategic decisions aligned with specific cultural and economic contexts significantly influenced their trajectories. For instance, launching a business in a city known for its openness and opportunity could yield different results compared to other locations less conducive to entrepreneurial ventures. Another example of this is the decision taken by Udemy's founders Eren Bali and Oktay Caglar to move from Turkey to Silicon Valley to kickstart their startup's growth. In the case of my own family, Istanbul turned out to be the perfect location to produce quality products that could meet the emerging needs of the post-communist eastern bloc.

The stories of pioneering immigrant entrepreneurs also underline the critical impact of timing—entering the market when conditions were ripe for innovation or when a particular consumer trend was on the rise, which again was the case for my family's efforts to bring new products to markets in the former Soviet countries. In the immigrant entrepreneurs' stories, optimal timing, coupled with proactive efforts and resilience, not only amplified their success but also helped them capitalize on opportunities that might otherwise be seen as mere luck. For example, when I asked Alberto Perlman from Zumba about the role that luck had played in the company's success, he actually spoke about timing instead, a factor that has elements of luck, but which can also be controlled by analysis and strategic decision-making:

> Timing is everything; we launched when there was a growing appetite for fitness trends that were fun, and social media was beginning to amplify niche fitness movements. Latin music was just starting to become mainstream, and we were one of the only places to engage with this music. This helped Zumba gain traction at a critical time, positioning it to become a global movement.

The importance of maximizing luck through hard work comes across in many of the immigrant entrepreneurs' accounts of their success. For example, consider this from Andrew Grove:

> The way I see it is that for the most part you can create opportunity; but when life provides you with opportunity, it's up to you to make the most of that opportunity. I tried to do that, but I'm very mindful that had I not had that one or several of those opportunities, the same characteristics, the same perseverance, the same hard work wouldn't have led to the same results.[9]

This synthesis of diligence, skill, location, and timing shapes what many perceive as serendipity in business success, showing that while luck may open doors, it's the entrepreneur's readiness and strategic actions that ultimately define their success.

Persevering Through Bad Luck: The Crucial Importance of Grit

Any consideration of the role of luck in success has to focus not only on recognizing and maximizing good fortune but also on how to deal with bad luck. Whether the winds of fortune are fair or foul, the goal is to leverage them in a way that propels us forward. In other words, it's about maximizing the benefits from good luck and mitigating the setbacks from bad luck, ensuring that each random event adds value to our journey. In that regard, preparation plays a pivotal role, too. Just as sailors prepare for storms, we must equip ourselves to withstand periods of bad luck. This resilience ensures that when misfortune strikes, it finds us ready, not resigned, turning setbacks into setups for future successes. The immigrant entrepreneurs I interviewed had "unlucky" moments ranging from recessions to the impact of wars and many nearly lost their businesses on multiple occasions. But as I described in the previous chapter about reframing, they also had the resources and the mental agility that enabled them to make comebacks.

Examples of such misfortunes include the collapse of Haim Saban's concert promoting business in Israel during the economic downturn that came in the wake of the Yom Kippur War, a disaster that left the future billionaire floundering under the weight of debts worth several hundred thousand dollars. Dominique Ansel may not have faced misfortune on the same scale, but he still identified in my interview with him the importance of being able to persevere through failures that could be attributed to bad luck:

> For me, it's never about luck, but about the effort made in trying. I can't tell you the number of pastries we launched that didn't have the same viral popularity of the Cronut. The success came not in a moment but in 20-something years of trying new things.

My research into immigrant entrepreneurs has left me convinced that the essential ingredient that allows them to persevere through bad luck and periods of failure is grit, the quality of being able to push through adversity and continue striving even when all the odds seem against them. Fadi Ghandour describes grit as the relentless drive that turns passion into tangible impact. In other words, it's not just having a strong feeling about something but being able to turn that feeling into actions, even in the face of strong challenges.

Commenting on immigrant entrepreneurs' grit, Diana Verde Nieto, the co-founder of Positive Luxury, told me, "We have fire in the belly, and we work extra hard and persevere no matter what. We have one chance!" Because of such characteristics, immigrant entrepreneurs embody an exceptional level of perseverance. Despite the challenges of navigating new cultural and economic landscapes, their dedication to creating a better life in a new country remains unyielding. They persist in refining their businesses and innovations, constantly pushing the boundaries of what is possible. Even when simpler, more familiar routes might exist, their commitment to their goals is unwavering. In other words, they excel in that unique blend of resilience and tenacity called grit.

Angela Duckworth's book *Grit: The Power of Passion and Perseverance* describes the extraordinary stamina of high achievers who continually strive to improve, even if they are already on top of their game.[10] Grit, according to Duckworth, is a greater predictor of achieving challenging goals than either academic talent or athletic ability, and it is the key component that propels people to the highest levels of leadership in demanding roles. It is my belief that if luck is about having the talent to recognize the hand that chance has dealt you and the daring to play it, then grit is the element that lets you stick with your winning hand even when doubts might creep into your mind about how strong it really is.

However, despite, or perhaps because of, its importance, there are still several common misconceptions about grit that are important to clear up. The first relates to the source of grit. Some believe that it is an innate characteristic that cannot be learned or think that it comes only from having been through extraordinary circumstances or dramatic experiences that don't happen to most. While I was writing this book and discussing it with friends and people I met, I lost count of the number of times I was told something like, "Oh, but I'm not an immigrant so I didn't have those experiences that would have made me more resilient." In fact, although grit may seem to come more naturally to the immigrant, its component elements, such as hard work and perseverance, are not the preserves of a select few. In other words, grit can be cultivated, and it does not exclusively belong to any one demographic or personality type. Grit involves everyday determination and the consistent application of effort toward long-term objectives, regardless of one's starting point. Ultimately, anyone can display the necessary grit to weather bad fortune and take maximum advantage of the good.

A second misconception is that grit is simply sheer persistence against all odds. In reality, there's a strategic element to grit that involves knowing when to pivot or let go of unattainable goals, which can be as important as perseverance itself. This strategic flexibility is crucial to preventing the potential downside of grit: the stubborn pursuit of unfeasible goals that can lead to significant personal or professional costs. It's important to understand that misdirected or excessive grit can lead to burnout and an unhealthy disregard for one's well-being when pursuing goals. Relatedly, there is an idea that grit is a constant characteristic that remains a consistent part of one's personality, but in reality, grit can ebb and flow depending on one's circumstances or mental state.

Finally, and very significantly, there is a misconception that grit is a solitary endeavor, the preserve of a powerful individual who undertakes a lonely journey propelled only by their own convictions and strength of will. Again, the reality is quite different. Grit tends to be nurtured and sustained by networks, communities, and mentors. Indeed, the doctoral research of Christian Tekwe on grit and immigrant entrepreneurs has shown how their communities place positive pressure on them to succeed and act as sources of strength that they can tap into during difficult times.[11] Relatedly, organizations can also develop what we could call "organizational grit." This is achieved by creating cultures that praise perseverance, encourage resilience in the face of setbacks, and provide support networks that help individuals rebound from failures.

Leadership plays a crucial role here, demonstrating a commitment to goals and a willingness to navigate through challenges rather than seeking quick exits. Traditionally, some might perceive leadership with grit as being something tough and harsh. But actually, leading in a gentle way with compassion and kindness can help to create the sort of communities that nurture grit and help people to stick together through hard times.

Understanding grit in its full complexity allows us to foster it more effectively both in ourselves and within our organizations. By debunking these myths and embracing a more nuanced view of grit, we can promote a healthier, more balanced approach to achieving our goals. This approach recognizes the importance of adaptability, the need for support, and the wisdom of sometimes resetting our paths in response to new insights and circumstances.

The Role of Luck in Business Longevity: Passivity Versus Action

Acknowledging the role of luck and serendipity does not imply a passive acceptance of fate. Instead, it suggests that while entrepreneurs and managers can steer their ventures through strategic decisions and robust design, they also need to remain flexible, adaptable, and open to unanticipated possibilities. This dual approach—strategizing for the expected while remaining agile enough to capitalize on the unexpected—is crucial for sustaining business success.

In my research on business longevity, it's clear that those who last aren't just lucky; they're adept at making the most of whatever luck they encounter. They attribute their successes to both their efforts and the serendipity that aided them, yet they never blame their failures on misfortune alone. This balanced perspective keeps them grounded and focused, ready to capitalize on positive turns and to learn from the adverse ones. Embracing luck in this way transforms it from mere chance into a catalyst for sustained achievement. The key issue is not waiting for the stars to align but rather aligning ourselves in such a way that the stars, when they do appear, guide us rather than govern us and lead us to achieve long-term impact.

Strategies for recognizing and maximizing luck:
(1) **Embrace uncertainty with open arms:** Understand that entrepreneurship involves navigating through unpredictable waters. Accept that luck and chance play significant roles and prepare to pivot strategies on the fly. This acceptance will prevent rigidity and enable you to respond to opportunities and challenges more creatively.

(2) Cultivate a prepared mindset: Louis Pasteur famously said, "Chance favors the prepared mind." Consistently educate yourself, stay aware of industry trends, and maintain a network of contacts. A well-prepared mind is more likely to recognize and seize serendipitous opportunities when they arise.

(3) Build resilience against misfortune: Develop strategies that help your business stay afloat during tough times. This includes maintaining a healthy cash flow, diversifying your client base, or having a crisis management plan in place. Resilience turns potential disasters into mere setbacks.

(4) Consciously develop your own grit: Anyone, regardless of their background and previous experiences, can foster grit through intentional practice, such as setting long-term goals and challenging oneself to step outside of comfort zones. Also, remember the influence of community on grit and seek support from mentors and others to help you weather storms and persevere through periods of misfortune.

(5) Create organizational grit: Increase grit across your company by showing leadership and creating support networks that help others overcome individual failings by encouraging reframing and maintaining a focus on long-term objectives.

(6) Harness the power of reflection: Regularly take time to reflect on your business journey. This practice can help you recognize the role of luck and serendipity in your success. Reflection also aids in understanding which strategies worked, which didn't, and how random events shaped your path.

(7) Foster an environment of gratitude and recognition: Encourage a culture where team members acknowledge each other's contributions and luck's role in their success. This can enhance morale and promote a positive and supportive work environment.

(8) Stay open to serendipity: Encourage curiosity and experimentation within your organization. Allow employees to explore side projects or new ideas that might seem unrelated to your core business. These can lead to unexpected and profitable innovations. Fostering an environment where employees can experiment and pursue curiosity-driven projects may lead to innovative ideas that structured research and development efforts might miss, which is what happened with Google's creation of Gmail.

(9) **Strategically plan for luck:** While you cannot control luck, you can strategically place your business in situations where the probability of encountering luck increases. This could mean entering new markets, leveraging new technologies, or networking in different industries.

(10) **Practice humility and adaptability:** Recognize that despite all your planning and hard work, luck will often play a part in your success. Maintain humility and be ready to adapt your plans based on new opportunities or information that may come your way unexpectedly.

Pioneers! O Pioneers!

All the past we leave behind,
We debouch upon a newer mightier world, varied world,
Fresh and strong the world we seize, world of labor
and the march,
Pioneers! O pioneers!

—Walt Whitman

Conclusion: Our Future, Together as One

Immigration is, of course, a journey. So is creating a book. And while both journeys may appear to have clear end points—arrival in the new country and publication—in reality, the points at which they stop are very difficult to determine. Arriving in the new country is only really the start of the immigrant's journey, and the consequences of that unfolding expedition extend far beyond even the lifespan of an individual, continuing to flower in new ways on and on into the future. Similarly, publishing a book is only the start of its journey, as it goes on to assume a life of its own through all its interactions with its readers and whatever influence, however small, it may have on their ideas and actions, which also each have consequences of their own.

Nevertheless, approaching the end of the writing process, it is only natural to look back and reflect on what you have learned and try to put those reflections into a format that will help the book on its way by making it as useful as possible to as many readers as you can. Therefore, in this conclusion, I aim to summarize the key messages of the book and also point out some of the main lessons that can be applied as you endeavor to build businesses and achieve an impact that lasts.

Whenever I think of how to summarize something complex into its compressed essence, I am reminded of the famous story of Hillel the Elder, a Jewish scholar and contemporary of Jesus, who was born in Babylon but who moved, emigrated we could say, to Palestine. Hillel was once challenged by a man who said he would convert to Judaism if the rabbi could recite the whole Torah while standing on one leg. Hillel accepted the challenge, and his response entered the annals of legend: "That which is hateful to you, do not do to your fellow. That is the whole Torah, all the rest is commentary. Now, go and learn."[1]

In that spirit, what is the "stood-on-one-foot" version of this book? Perhaps surprisingly for a business book, it exists in the same spirit as Hillel's famous reply; when I was trying to think of how to summarize the key message I've learned from studying successful immigrant entrepreneurs, the best I could come up with was: "If you want to build a business that has long-term impact, prioritize kindness and community over chasing every last dollar."

It's immediately clear that such advice runs contrary to the spirit of almost all books about building a business that lasts, tied up as they are in focusing on doing everything to keep shareholders satisfied and financial growth constant. It may also be a surprise even to readers of this book given that the word *kindness* has not featured prominently in any of the eight principles that I have identified and elucidated based on my research into immigrant entrepreneurship. But if you read the book carefully, it's not difficult to determine that kindness is the principle that underlies and connects all the others; we could even say it is the one leg on which all the principles stand.

It's there even in the preface, with its assertion that real longevity does not come from the money you take but from the difference you make, a challenge to the normal definitions of business longevity, which focus on keeping a company alive irrespective of whether it's having a positive impact on the world at all. It's there in the first chapters of the book, too, where the story of Charles Worth, the creator of the modern fashion industry, is a reminder that real longevity comes from making changes that last long after your last balance sheet has been filed. Because if all you did was take money and never make a change, then all you did was worthless. It's there in the same chapter again when I summarize the results of my research on business longevity, which shows that treating staff and stakeholders well and focusing on communities, all elements of kindness, are key ingredients of real longevity and characteristics that are particularly common in the businesses of immigrant entrepreneurs.

And when we turn to the eight principles of success from immigrant entrepreneurs, we can see how the thread of kindness and community building runs through them all. Its presence may not be immediately obvious in Principle 1—be a bridge across cultures—but it is there. After all, you'll notice that the advice is not about exploiting connections in poorer countries to produce cheap products that can be sold for high profits in richer markets. Instead, it's about creating products and services that form bridges between cultures and that are mutually beneficial for people from both countries, creating trade links, jobs, and, in some cases, ultimately improved understanding between some of the many cultures on our crowded little planet. The advice in that chapter also focuses on the importance of your partnerships with people from different cultures in different countries, and both my research and my career have given me a deep conviction that such partnerships will flourish best when you cultivate them with kindness and turn business links into a basis for community.

Kindness and community are there in Principle 2—build from the past forward and the future back—in which the 3-I framework encourages anyone thinking about creating a business to look deep inside themselves and see what they want to change about the world in order to imagine the better future that their company will help to create. The example of Jan Koum and WhatsApp shows how the core values that derive from an individual entrepreneur's past can drive a vision of the future that becomes a reality for billions of people worldwide. Principle 2 also highlights how an inspiring vision is a powerful means of bringing a community of people together to deliver it.

Principle 3—forge connections based on identity and authenticity— shows how immigrant entrepreneurs achieve impact by making connections and forming communities. However, it also demonstrates how they go beyond ethnic and cultural ties to forge links based on shared values, where a common commitment to doing good binds people together into powerful partnerships, as we saw with the stories of Saeju Jeong, Artem Petakov, and Noom. Similarly, in Principle 4—generate profit the right way—the remarkable story of Luis von Ahn and Duolingo shows how many immigrant entrepreneurs find success by eschewing profit in favor of purpose, generating income almost as a side effect of doing what they would have done anyway even if money was no object. Rather than thinking about how to find financial success, many of the leading immigrant entrepreneurs have focused on what problems they can solve for people, an inherently kind act that, when done right, can lead to both positive social impact and significant profit.

Principle 5—build community—focuses explicitly on the power of community and shows how immigrant entrepreneurs such as Hamdi Ulukaya of Chobani tap into the power of new and existing communities to achieve remarkable results that lift everybody up together. That same power is evident in my analysis of Principle 6—reframe rejection—where I argue that immigrant entrepreneurs' abilities to reframe failure and rejection, turning negatives into positives, are greatly enhanced by the way in which they draw on the collective strength of their communities, a force that I describe as their "reframing superpower."

The importance of community and kindness is again clear in my discussion of Principle 7—frying in your own oil—which draws from my grandfather's wise advice about relying on your own resources to achieve success. Frying in your own oil requires you to draw on the resources you have, including the people in your community, and necessitates taking a sensible and sustainable attitude toward growth to avoid overstretching those resources, making it a philosophy rooted in kindness to yourself, other people, and the planet. Frying in your own oil also frees you to follow your own vision and your heart rather than being forced to do things that are against your ethics to satisfy the demands of funders and shareholders. Finally, Principle 8—daring to play your hand—shows how immigrant entrepreneurs maximize good fortune and endure bad luck by balancing grit with compassion and kindness.

Immigrant entrepreneurs come from a great diversity of backgrounds but what seems to unite the highly successful ones featured in *Pioneers* is their great determination to achieve. Many of them seem to derive that determination from their commitment to a purpose greater than themselves, i.e., to create impact through businesses that solve real-world problems and generate positive change that will resonate into the future, maybe even long after their firms have finally folded. Of course, I don't pretend that these entrepreneurs are disinterested in profit; after all, without money their businesses would not exist to achieve any impact at all, but what they do tend to exemplify is seeking profit the right way; they do what they do not just to put extra zeros at the end of their bank balances but to add something to the world, leaving it a better place than they found it.

Because many of them have faced discrimination or know what it means to be an outsider or to struggle in an unfamiliar place, seemingly cut adrift from community, they deeply value treating their employees and stakeholders well, and they strive to create communities in which everyone is included, pulling together toward the achievement of a greater purpose. From my research, I can clearly identify the common threads of decency, respect, generosity, compassion, and gratitude that run through the careers of the immigrant entrepreneurs I have studied. Sometimes they focus on employing people from disadvantaged backgrounds, like refugees; they always seem to prioritize creating close bonds with the people they work with. On a foundation of trust, they build great businesses that pioneer positive, tangible change.

I'm aware that what I'm arguing here may seem to some naïve. Aren't quick wins that satisfy shareholders essential to get a firm off the ground? How can we build a business that lasts in the long term without focusing on profit? I'm also aware that some of my conclusions fly in the face of conventional business wisdom; I know very well what the orthodoxy teaches, but in response to it, I can only share what I have found through my own career and my research, and my conviction that true longevity comes not from the money you take but the positive contribution you make.

The world is changing; fresh challenges, some of them dishearteningly familiar and others apparently unprecedented, seem to rear up every day. And each challenge provides ever more compelling evidence for the inter-connectedness of everything on our little planet because what appears just a small tremor in one place becomes a giant tsunami elsewhere. We are no longer living in the world of Milton Friedman where we can say that companies have no responsibilities to anyone other than their shareholders. Colin Mayer had it right when he said that companies also have the respon-sibility to not do anyone any harm. But we are passing even that stage; now companies have the responsibility to actively be doing good, and it's my conviction that only those who do that will survive. Kindness is, and must be, the way forward; indeed, it's the only way. As humanity we must realize that we are part of this earth, all connected, like the roots of the tree, and ultimately, we will stand or fall together.

My beliefs are starting to be backed up by an increasing body of research beyond my own. Wharton professor Adam Grant shows in his book *Give and Take: A Revolutionary Approach to Success* that individuals who are "givers"—those who provide support to others without expecting anything in return—often achieve greater long-term success.[2] I believe that we can increasingly apply the same to firms, and the immigrant entrepreneurs highlighted in this book who pursue positive impact and prioritize kindness to communities are lighting the way toward a better future for all.

I would like to finish this book with a few expressions of gratitude and some further reflections that start from the personal and spread to the global level. First the gratitude: I owe an enormous debt of thanks to all the pioneering immigrant entrepreneurs who generously gave of their time, shared their experiences of crossing borders, and helped me to unlearn what I thought I already knew about business longevity. Their insights and experiences were enormously inspiring to me and taught me how we can balance creative journeys focused on our singular passions in ways that actually create and bond together powerful communities. The sharpness of their minds and the warmth of their hearts will continue to inspire me on my ongoing entrepreneurial and academic journey after this book is finished. I hope that I have done their life stories, insights, and lessons justice.

Next, I wanted to share a little about how the journey of writing this book has affected me personally. I don't think I fully appreciated at the start how emotional it would be to dive so deep into the waters of my own history and share stories of some of the most painful and the most positive moments of my past. Doing so has shown to me once again how the roots of the positive are often deep in the pain, and the opposite can also apply. Going through old photographs and memories was an enormously emotional process, sometimes tears would roll for hours, and I even found myself having to take a day off writing sometimes to allow myself to recover from the emotions evoked. The extent of the emotion was not the only surprise for me on this journey. At its beginning, I felt confident as an immigrant entrepreneur and a professor teaching business that I knew what I would write, but along the way, I discovered much that challenged my thinking and showed me new directions. It's often said that one teaches what one has to learn oneself; I now know this to be true, and I can add to it that one writes what one needs to read.

I also want to reiterate that my motivation for writing this book has never been political. But at the same time, I can't ignore the fact that I am writing during some of the most heated political divisions and debates around immigration, not only in America but across the world. Everywhere there is division and fear over immigration, and in that context, I do hope to point toward the fact that what unites us is much bigger than what divides us. It is my sincere wish that we can show understanding and compassion to one another—and this goes for both sides—show compassion to someone who feels fearful and show compassion to someone who has lost their home because, as I also said in "Kismet," the poem I wrote for this book, our geography is dice tossed at the wall.

Despite all the turmoil of our times and the dread predictions for the future, I know a new earth is possible, and it begins with each of us recognizing that beneath the surface roles we play and the labels that society imposes upon us—immigrant, native, refugee, citizen—there lies a deeper identity that connects us all: a spark of awareness inherent in every being. It is the very spark that created this earth on which we live. By fostering this awareness within ourselves, we cultivate a presence that transcends our differences and dissolves the barriers of fear and separation. It is through this inner transformation that we can truly embrace compassion and understanding, not as concepts but as the very basis of our actions. In this awakened state, we see not strangers or threats but expressions of our shared humanity, each person a vital thread in the tapestry of life on our planet. This is the foundation of the new earth: a world built not on conflict and division, but on the bedrock of collective consciousness and interconnectedness.

Finally, I'd like to reemphasize a point that I made at the very start: This book is not intended to be a blueprint or a guarantee of success for anyone. But it is an invitation to learn from successful and impactful entrepreneurs and a call to action: I encourage you to take the ideas in this book, try them out, and see what works for you. And if you still feel reticent about starting out, I recommend to you the inspiring words of Teddy Roosevelt, who said:

> It is not the critic who counts; not the man who points out how the strong man stumbles, or where the doer of deeds could have done them better. The credit belongs to the man who is actually in the arena, whose

face is marred by dust and sweat and blood; who strives valiantly; who errs, who comes short again and again, because there is no effort without error and shortcoming; but who does actually strive to do the deeds; who knows great enthusiasms, the great devotions; who spends himself in a worthy cause; who at the best knows in the end the triumph of high achievement, and who at the worst, if he fails, at least fails while daring greatly, so that his place shall never be with those cold and timid souls who neither know victory nor defeat.[3]

All the immigrant entrepreneurs in this book dared greatly. And this is your moment now, whether immigrant or not, to try to follow their path in your own way and join them—businesses that create impact are the future of the world. No company can live forever but anyone can have an impact that resonates through the ages. The challenge, therefore, is to accept the fact of your end but to make the most difference you can with the time you have, and the impact you make is what will endure. On which note, I'd like to finish with two questions that come from the poetry of Mary Oliver, which I encourage you to reflect on long after you close this book:

Doesn't everything die at last, and too soon?
Tell me, what is it you plan to do
with your one wild and precious life?[4]

Notes

Preface: Entrepreneurs Will Change Your Life

1. Cesar Maximiliano Estrada, "How Immigrants Positively Affect the Business Community and the U.S. Economy," American Progress, June 22, 2016, accessed November 7, 2024, https://www.americanprogress .org/article/how-immigrants-positively-affect-the-business-community- and-the-u-s-economy/.
2. American Immigration Council, "New American Fortune 500 in 2023," https://www.americanimmigrationcouncil.org/research/new- american-fortune-500-2023 (American Immigration Council, August 29, 2023), accessed November 7, 2024.
3. Stuart Anderson, "Most Billion-Dollar Startups in the U.S. Founded by Immigrants," *Forbes*, July 27, 2022, https://www.forbes.com/sites/ stuartanderson/2022/07/26/most-us-billion-dollar-startups-have-an- immigrant-founder/?sh=392311086f3a.
4. Sari Pekkala Kerr and William Kerr, "Immigrant Entrepreneurship," *Harvard Business School*, June 2016, https://www.hbs.edu/ris/Publication %20Files/17-011_da2c1cf4-a999-4159-ab95-457c783e3fff.pdf.
5. Bernhard Schroeder, "How to Avoid Being in the 90% of Entrepre- neurial Startups Who Fail. Six Insights on How to Find Real Problems," *Forbes*, June 20, 2023, https://www.forbes.com/sites/bernhardschroeder/ 2023/06/15/how-to-avoid-being-in-the-90-of-entrepreneurial- startups-who-fail-six-insights-on-how-to-find-real-problems/.

Chapter 1: The Myths and Reality of Business Longevity

1. The details and quotes regarding Andrew Grove's life in this chapter were sourced from Andrew S. Grove, *Swimming Across: A Memoir* (Warner Books, 2001).

2. "Refugee Heading Engineers' Class," *New York Times*, June 15, 1960.

3. Joshua Cooper Ramo, "Andrew Grove: A Survivor's Tale," *Time*, December 29, 1997, http://time.com/andrew-grove-survivors-tale/.

4. Mike Sager, "Andy Grove: What I've Learned," *Esquire*, January 29, 2007.

5. Tom Peters and Robert H. Waterman Jr., In *Search of Excellence: Lessons from America's Best-Run Companies* (Harper & Row, 1982).

6. James C. Collins and Jerry I. Porras, *Built to Last: Successful Habits of Visionary Companies* (HarperBusiness, 1994).

7. James Collins, *Good to Great: Why Some Companies Make the Leap ... And Others Don't* (HarperBusiness, 2001).

8. L. P. Hartley, *The Go-Between* (New York Review Books, 1953).

9. Nick Forster, "Exposing the Contradictory Claims, Myths and Illusions of the 'Secrets of Business Success and Company Longevity' Genre," *The Journal of Business Perspective* 14, nos. 1–2 (January–June 2010): 21.

10. The information in this and the following sentence was sourced from "What Happened to the World's 'Greatest' Companies?," McKinsey & Company, September 7, 2017, https://www.mckinsey.com/capabilities/strategy-and-corporate-finance/our-insights/the-strategy-and-corporate-finance-blog/what-happened-to-the-worlds-greatest-companies.

11. "Whatever Happened to Jim Collins' 'Good to Great' Companies?," Exit Planning Exchange, April 10, 2023, https://www.exitplanningexchange.com/kx/whatever-happened-to-jim-collins-good-to-great-companies/.

12. American Immigration Council, "New American Fortune 500 in 2023"; Estrada, "How Immigrants Positively Affect the Business Community and the U.S. Economy"; Anderson, "Most Billion-Dollar Startups in the U.S. Founded by Immigrants."

13. Pauline de Metternich, *Je ne Suis pas Jolie, Je Suis Pire, Souvenirs, 1859–1871* (Tallandier, 2008), 111–114.

14. Quoted in E. A. Coleman, *The Opulent Era, Fashions of Worth, Pingat and Doucet* (Thames & Hudson, 1989), 90–91.

15. For more details on Charles Frederick Worth and the creation of the global fashion industry see Neri Karra, *Fashion Entrepreneurship: The Creation of the Global Fashion Business* (Routledge, 2021).

16. IMD Business School, "Why You Will Probably Live Longer Than Most Big Companies," IMD Business School for Management and Leadership Courses, July 15, 2024, https://www.imd.org/research-knowledge/disruption/articles/why-you-will-probably-live-longer-than-most-big-companies/.

Chapter 2: Immigrant Entrepreneurship and the American Dream

1. Alejandro Portes and Rubén G. Rumbaut, *Immigrant America: A Portrait*, 5th ed. (University of California Press, 2024).

2. Niccolo Conte, "Ranked: The Most Innovative Countries in 2023," Visual Capitalist, November 14, 2023, accessed November 7, 2024, https://www.visualcapitalist.com/most-innovative-countries-in-2023/.

3. Gloria Steinem, *My Life on the Road* (Random House, 2015).

4. Noah Webster, *An American Dictionary of the English Language* (S. Converse, 1828).

5. Samuel Johnson, *A Dictionary of the English Language* (W. Strahan, 1755).

6. Neil Larry Shumsky, "Noah Webster and the Invention of Immigration," *The New England Quarterly* 81, no. 1 (March 2008): 126–135.

7. Bridget Anderson and Scott Blinder, *Who Counts as a Migrant? Definitions and Their Consequences. Migration Observatory Briefing* (COMPAS, University of Oxford, 2024).

8. I have accessed the definition from *Glossary on Migration*, International Organization for Migration, https://publications.iom.int/system/files/pdf/iml_34_glossary.pdf, and *Who is a Migrant?*, International Organization for Migration, https://www.iom.int/who-migrant-0.

9. International Organization for Migration. *World Migration Report 2024*, accessed October 8, 2024, https://worldmigrationreport.iom.int/msite/wmr-2024-interactive/.

10. Merriam-Webster.com Dictionary, s.v. "entrepreneur," accessed November 7, 2024, https://www.merriam-webster.com/dictionary/entrepreneur.

11. Mawlānā Jalāl Al-Dīn Rūmī et al., *The Essential Rumi* Harper San Francisco eBooks, 2004, http://ci.nii.ac.jp/ncid/BA74847838.

12. Migration Policy Institute. "Second-Generation from the Last Great Wave of Immigration: Setting the Record Straight," accessed October 8, 2024, https://www.migrationpolicy.org/article/second-generation-last-great-wave-immigration-setting-record-straight.

13. Quotes and details are from Johan Nordstrom, *The Immigrant*, 2nd ed. (Dogwood Press, 1971).

14. Mohamad Ali, "Immigration Is at the Heart of U.S. Competitiveness," *Harvard Business Review*, May 15, 2017.

15. Sandra Sequeira, Nathan Nunn, and Nancy Qian, "Immigrants and the Making of America," September 13, 2018, accessed August 3, 2024, https://scholar.harvard.edu/files/nunn/files/migrants_v28.pdf.

16. Ran Abramitzky and Leah Boustan, *Streets of Gold: America's Untold Story of Immigrant Success* (PublicAffairs, 2022).

Chapter 3: Who Are Immigrant Entrepreneurs?

1. The story of Isaac Larian, including quotes, details, and insights, has been compiled using information from a variety of sources. These include interviews, such as his conversation on *The Founder Hour* podcast (December 10, 2023), his appearance on *WellBuilt* (December 21, 2023), and his interview with Guy Raz on *How I Built This* (March 25, 2024). Additional information was gathered from *The New York Times* article by Katherine Rosman (April 16, 2020) and Parija Kavilanz's feature for *CNN Business* (November 21, 2018).

2. For a more comprehensive review on the immigrant entrepreneurship literature, you can refer to Marina Dabić, Bozidar Vlačić, Justin Paul, Leo-Paul Dana, Sreevas Sahasranamam, and Beata Glinka, "Immigrant Entrepreneurship: A Review and Research Agenda," *Journal of Business Research* 113 (2020): 25–38.

3. Warsan Shire, *Teaching My Mother How to Give Birth* (Flipped Eye Publishing, 2011).

4. Carson Duan, Bernice Kotey, and Kamaljeet Sandhu. "A Systematic Literature Review of Determinants of Immigrant Entrepreneurship Motivations." *Journal of Small Business & Entrepreneurship* 35 (2021), doi:10.1080/08276331.2021.1997490.

5. William R. Kerr and Martin Mandorff, "Social Networks, Ethnicity, and Entrepreneurship," *Journal of Human Resources* 58, no. 1 (January 2023): 183–220.

6. Andrew Leon Hanna, *25 Million Sparks: The Untold Story of Refugee Entrepreneurs* (Cambridge University Press, 2022).

7. In addition to current research done for this book, my previous research on ethnic entrepreneurship, kinship, and homophilic ties began with my PhD thesis and has since been explored through multiple publications, including two books: *Family Business in Emerging Markets* (Routledge, 2017) and *Understanding the Born Global Firm* (Routledge, 2016). In addition to these works, I have co-authored several peer-reviewed academic papers that delve deeper into these themes, such as "Building Entrepreneurial Tie Portfolios Through Strategic Homophily: The Role of Narrative Identity Work in Venture Creation and Early Growth," published in *Journal of Business Venturing* (2013) and "Rethinking Institutional Distance: Strengthening the Tie Between New Institutional Theory and International Management," featured in *Strategic Organization* (2009). Other relevant works include "Building the Born Global Firm: Developing Entrepreneurial Capabilities for International New Venture Success" (*Long Range Planning*, 2008) and "Altruism and Agency in the Family Firm: Exploring the Role of Family, Kinship and Ethnicity" (*Entrepreneurship: Theory and Practice*, 2006). These studies collectively offer a comprehensive examination of the intersections between entrepreneurial ventures and familial, cultural, and social networks.

8. Asian Hustle Network, "Weee! Co-founder and CEO Larry Liu Reflects on His Underdog Journey," May 30, 2024, https://www.linkedin.com/pulse/weee-co-founder-ceo-larry-liu-reflects-his-underdog-mybkf/.

Chapter 4: Principle 1: Be a Bridge Across Cultures

1. ABC News. "Dominique Ansel's Cronut Recipe Revealed on 'GMA,'" October 6, 2014, https://www.abcnews.com/article/dominique-ansels-cronut-recipe-revealed-on-gma.

2. Greg Morabito, "Cronut Sorcerer Dominique Ansel Casts His Spell on Fallon," *Eater New York*, August 1, 2013, https://ny.eater.com/2013/8/1/6392857/cronut-sorcerer-dominique-ansel-casts-his-spell-on-fallon.

3. TIME Staff, "The 25 Best Inventions of the Year 2013: The Cronut," *TIME*, November 13, 2013, https://techland.time.com/2013/11/14/the-25-best-inventions-of-the-year-2013/slide/the-cronut/.

4. Hailey Eber, "Meet Dominique Ansel, the Willy Wonka of NYC!" *New York Post*, July 31, 2013, https://nypost.com/2013/07/31/meet-dominique-ansel-the-willy-wonka-of-nyc/.

5. William Drew, "The World's Best Pastry Chef Dominique Ansel on Boulud, Veal Brains and Moving Beyond Bakery," *World's 50 Best*, April 21, 2017, https://www.theworlds50best.com/stories/News/pastry-chef-dominique-ansel-boulud-veal-brains-beyond-bakery.html.

6. Rupi Kaur, Facebook post, January 14, 2019, https://www.facebook.com/photo.php?fbid=2117692428325022&id=513614775399470&set=a.523823527711928.

7. The narrative and details about Jane Wurwand, including insights and quotations, have been derived from multiple sources to ensure a comprehensive portrayal. Key interviews include her discussion on *BBC Worklife* with Jacqueline Schneider (January 18, 2024), her conversation with Felicia C. Sullivan for *HuffPost* (July 30, 2009, updated December 6, 2017), and her appearances on NPR's *How I Built This* with Guy Raz (October 24, 2016). Further insights were gathered from her feature on the *Breaking Beauty Podcast*, titled "'The Great Reset' With Dermalogica Founder Jane Wurwand, LIVE from Los Angeles! Extended Cut" (March 11, 2021).

8. This quotation and the previous one are both from Karan Bilimoria, "Cobra's Chairman on Turning an Indian Beer into a Global Brand," *Harvard Business Review*, November–December 2018.

9. Andrew S. Grove, *Only the Paranoid Survive* (Currency Doubleday, 1996).

10. Karra, *Fashion Entrepreneurship*.

11. The quotes from Hernan Lopez in this section are taken from Wondery: Hernan Lopez, "How I Built This with Guy Raz," Episode 578, December 11, 2023, accessed August 3, 2024, https://podcasts.apple.com/us/podcast/wondery-hernan-lopez/id1150510297?i=1000637227126.

Chapter 5: Principle 2: Build from the Past Forward and the Future Back

1. The insights and quotes from Jan Koum, co-founder of WhatsApp, have been compiled from a diverse array of interviews and discussions. These include his fireside chat at "4Years From Now" with Martin Varsavsky, viewable on YouTube (https://www.youtube.com/watch?v= 4QRx0RsnmmU) and his conversation with David Rowan at DLD14 (https://www.youtube.com/watch?v=U4iY1CJvF8k). Additional perspectives were drawn from his interview with RBC on September 8, 2015 (https://www.rbc.ru/interview/technology_and_media/08/09/ 2015/55e84f0d9a79477a4bb3e516), Parmy Olson's *Forbes* article titled "Exclusive: The Rags-to-Riches Tale of How Jan Koum Built WhatsApp into Facebook's New $19 Billion Baby," published on February 19, 2014 (https://www.forbes.com/sites/parmyolson/2014/02/19/exclusive- inside-story-how-jan-koum-built-whatsapp-into-facebooks-new-19- billion-baby/), and his lecture at Stanford's CS183F: Startup School, "How to Build a Product IV" (https://www.youtube.com/watch?v= s1Rd4UShDxQ).

2. "Interview with Noubar Afeyan of Flagship Pioneering, Full Interview," Harvard Online, accessed July 27, 2024, https://www.youtube .com/watch?v=V5TrUzA30Yo&t=7s.

3. Alex Keown, "Flagship's Noubar Afeyan Aims to Answer Science's 'What if' Questions," BioSpace, November 15, 2021, https://www .biospace.com/flagship-pioneering-s-noubar-afeyan-aims-to-answer- science-s-what-if-questions.

4. Grove, *Swimming Across: A Memoir.*

5. Mel Cornford, "Dermalogica Founder Jane Wurwand's Skincare Success," *Vogue Australia*, May 11, 2010, https://www.vogue.com.au/beauty/ vogue-loves/dermalogica-founder-jane-wurwands-skincare-success/ news-story/c2e073b1b4cc0febcb95f794c11859ec.

6. "The Ideas That Inspire Us," *Harvard Business Review*, November– December 2022.

Chapter 6: Principle 3: Forge Connections Based on Identity and Authenticity

1. Public.com, "Noom IPO: What You Need to Know About a 2022 IPO," accessed August 12, 2024, https://public.com/learn/noom-ipo-what-you-need-to-know-about-a-2022-ipo?wpsrc=Organic+Search &wpsn=www.google.com.

2. Jeff S. Wyles, Joseph G. Kunkel, and Allan C. Wilson, "Birds, Behavior and Anatomical Evolution," *Proceedings of the National Academy of Sciences, USA,* July 1983.

3. In Aristotle's *Rhetoric* and *Nichomachean Ethics*, he noted that people "love those who are like themselves." Plato observed in *Phaedrus* that "similarity begets friendship." Aristotle. *Rhetoric*. Translated by J. H. Freese (Harvard University Press, 1934). Plato. *Phaedrus.* Translated by Harold North Fowler (Harvard University Press, 1968).

4. Noubar Afeyan, "Noubar Afeyan, Co-Founder of Moderna," *How I Built This with Guy Raz*, NPR, March 25, 2024, audio, 50:43, https://www.npr.org/2024/03/25/noubar-afeyan-modena.

5. Tope Awotona," Tope Awotona, Founder of Calendly," *How I Built This with Guy Raz*, NPR, June 14, 2021, audio, 60:17, https://www.npr.org/2021/06/14/tope-awotona-calendly.

6. Greenlanes London, "Lord Karan Bilimoria," Greenlanes London, accessed August 12, 2024, https://www.greenlanes.london/blog/lord-karan-bilimoria.

7. All quotes in the paragraph are from: David Gelles and Melissa Eddy, "The Husband-and-Wife Team Behind the Leading Vaccine to Solve Covid-19," *The New York Times*, November 10, 2020, https://www.nytimes.com/2020/11/10/business/biontech-covid-vaccine.html.

8. Neri Karra, Paul Tracey, and Nelson Phillips, "Altruism and Agency in the Family Firm: Exploring the Role of Family, Kinship, and Ethnicity," *Entrepreneurship Theory and Practice* 30, no. 6 (November 1, 2006): 861–77, https://doi.org/10.1111/j.1540-6520.2006.00157.x.

9. Frances Frei Solomon and Anne Morriss, "Begin with Trust," *Harvard Business Review*, May-June 2020, https://hbr.org/2020/05/begin-with-trust.

10. For more in-depth exploration on this topic, see Karra, Tracey, and Phillips, "Altruism and Agency in the Family Firm: Exploring the Role of Family, Kinship, and Ethnicity."

Chapter 7: Principle 4: Generate Profit the Right Way

1. Luis von Ahn, "reCAPTCHA and Duolingo: Luis von Ahn," *How I Built This with Guy Raz*, NPR, May 25, 2020, audio, https://www.npr .org/2020/05/22/860884062/recaptcha-and-duolingo-luis-von-ahn.

2. "Duolingo (DUOL) Market Cap & Net Worth —Stock Analysis," Stock Analysis, n.d., https://stockanalysis.com/stocks/duol/market-cap.

3. Neri Karra Sillaman, "The Unsustainable State of Fashion — It's Time for a Change | Opinion," *Newsweek*, February 10, 2023, https://www .newsweek.com/unsustainable-state-fashionits-time-change-opinion-1779598.

4. Karen Becker-Olsen and Sean Potucek, "*Greenwashing*," in Springer eBooks, 2013, 1318–1323, https://doi.org/10.1007/978-3-642-28036-8_104.

5. Milton Friedman, "A Friedman Doctrine—the Social Responsibility of Business Is to Increase Its Profits," *New York Times*, September 13, 1970, https://www.nytimes.com/1970/09/13/archives/a-friedman-doctrine-the-social-responsibility-of-business-is-to.html.

6. Colin Mayer, *Capitalism and Crises*, Oxford University Press eBooks, 2023, https://doi.org/10.1093/oso/9780198887942.001.0001.

7. "First Find Purpose, Then Profit," Oxford Alumni, January 4. 2024, https://www.alumni.ox.ac.uk/article/first-find-purpose-then-profit.

8. Hamdi Ulukaya, "Why True Success Goes Beyond Profit with Chobani Founder Hamdi Ulukaya (Transcript)," TED Talks, May 2, 2024, https://www.ted.com/podcasts/ted-interview/why-true-success-goes-beyond-profit?version=preview&preview_token=edcefc6829fc211bc d94473493d1a8.

9. Lois Alter Mark, "As the Cronut Turns 10, Dominique Ansel Reflects Back and Looks Ahead," *Forbes*, May 11, 2023, https://www.forbes .com/sites/loisaltermark/2023/05/10/as-the-cronut-turns-10-dominique-ansel-reflects-back-and-looks-ahead/.

10. Isaac Getz and Laurent Marbacher, "A Lesson in Creating Successful Companies That Care," Strategy+Business, June 10, 2020, https://www.strategy-business.com/article/A-lesson-in-creating-successful-companies-that-care.

11. Valeria Giacomin and Geoffrey Jones, "Spiritual Philanthropy in Emerging Markets," *Harvard Business School* Working Paper 21-117 (2021), https://www.hbs.edu/ris/Publication%20Files/WP21-117_d8d4e428-4065-444f-918d-fb69379f6df6.pdf.

12. "Luis Von Ahn Foundation," Luis Von Ahn Foundation, n.d., https://www.luisvonahnfoundation.org/.

Chapter 8: Principle 5: Build Community

1. The information on Hamdi Ulukaya in this chapter is taken from the following three sources: Hamdi Ulukaya, "Chobani's Secret to Scale: Tap into Community," *Masters of Scale*, 2024, audio, https://mastersofscale.com/hamdi-ulukaya-chobanis-secret-to-scale/; "Why True Success Goes Beyond Profit with Chobani Founder Hamdi Ulukaya (Transcript)," TED Talks, n.d., https://www.ted.com/podcasts/ted-interview/why-true-success-goes-beyond-profit?version=preview&preview_token=edcefc6829fc211bcd94473493d1a8; "Chobani Founder Hamdi Ulukaya on the Journey from Abandoned Factory to Yogurt Powerhouse," *Harvard Business Review*, April 25, 2022, https://hbr.org/2022/04/chobani-founder-hamdi-ulukaya-on-the-journey-from-abandoned-factory-to-yogurt-powerhouse.

2. This quotation and the following two are from Ulukaya, "Chobani's Secret to Scale: Tap into Community."

3. "Chobani Founder Hamdi Ulukaya on the Journey from Abandoned Factory to Yogurt Powerhouse."

4. "Company | Etymology of Company by Etymonline," Etymonline, n.d., https://www.etymonline.com/word/company.

5. Rachel Sussman, Carl Zimmer, and Hans Ulrich Obrist, *The Oldest Living Things in the World*, 2014, https://doi.org/10.7208/chicago/9780226057644.001.0001.

6. Suzanne Simard, *Finding the Mother Tree: Discovering the Wisdom of the Forest* (Penguin, 2021).

7. Michael Hill, "Profile Interview: Dug Song," *Infosecurity* magazine, August 16, 2024, https://www.infosecurity-magazine.com/magazine-features/profile-interview-dug-song-1/.

8. This quote and the previous one from Karim Faris are both from Omar Sofradzija, "The Co-founder of Duo on Building His Business in Michigan," *Hour Detroit* magazine, January 13, 2021, https://www.hourdetroit.com/technology-topics/tech-entrpreneur-duo-dug-song-on-why-he-couldnt-build-his-business-anywhere-else/.

9. "Instagram," February 13, 2020, https://www.instagram.com/p/B8hlgRRn6BH/.

10. "Instagram," February 13, 2020, https://www.instagram.com/p/B8hlgRRn6BH/.

Chapter 9: Principle 6: Reframe Rejection

1. Tope Awotona, "How I Built This."

2. The Immigrant Learning Center, Inc., "Tope Awotona < the Immigrant Learning Center," The Immigrant Learning Center, September 13, 2024, https://www.ilctr.org/about-immigrants/immigrant-entrepreneurs/hall-of-fame/tope-awotona/.

3. Amy Edmondson, *Right Kind of Wrong: The Science of Failing Well* (Random House, 2023).

4. Luana Marques, *Bold Move: A 3-Step Plan to Transform Anxiety into Power* (Hachette UK, 2023).

5. "Vanderlei Cordeiro De Lima — Curtain Going Up!," Curtain Going Up!, September 1, 2018, https://josmarlopes.wordpress.com/tag/vanderlei-cordeiro-de-lima/.

6. Max Levchin, "How I Built This Podcast with Guy Raz: E418: PayPal: Max Levchin (Part 1 of 2)," Wondery — Feel the Story, n.d., https://wondery.com/shows/how-i-built-this/episode/10386-paypal-max-levchin-part-1-of-2/.

7. "Tope Awotona — A Founder Story," April 16, 2018, https://www.atlantatechvillage.com/buzz/tope-awotona-a-founder-story.

8. *The Guardian*, "The Tragedy and Triumph of Diane Von Fürstenberg," *The Business of Fashion*, July 2, 2024, https://www.businessoffashion.com/articles/luxury/diane-von-furstenberg-wrap-dress-50-years/.

9. Tope Awotona, "How I Built This."

10. S. Tamer Cavusgil, "Lessons in Longevity from an 88-Year-Old Zipper Company," *Harvard Business Review*, March 2, 2022, https://hbr.org/2022/03/lessons-in-longevity-from-an-88-year-old-zipper-company.

11. Haim Saban, "Power Rangers: Haim Saban," *How I Built This with Guy Raz*, NPR, September 24, 2018, https://www.npr.org/2018/09/21/650524515/power-rangers-haim-saban.

Chapter 10: Principle 7: "Fry in Your Own Oil"

1. "Homicide in World Cities," *Wikipedia: The Free Encyclopedia*. Last modified September 20, 2023, https://en.wikipedia.org/wiki/Homicide_in_world_cities#1980s_by_rate_per_100,000.

2. "Deaths from Conflict and Terrorism per 100,000," *Our World in Data*, accessed October 12, 2024, https://ourworldindata.org/grapher/deaths-conflict-terrorism-per-100000?time=1985.

3. This quote is from the following podcast episode: Beto Perez and Alberto Perlman, "Zumba: Beto Perez and Alberto Perlman," Interview by Guy Raz, *How I Built This*. Podcast audio, February 1, 2017, https://podcasts.apple.com/lu/podcast/zumba-beto-perez-alberto-perlman/id1150510297?i=1000396023154.

4. Pura Conscientia, "Neville Goddard — Blake on Religion," December 9, 2022, https://www.youtube.com/watch?v=wxw8mYZ_XzY.

5. Dominique Ansel, "How I Built This Podcast with Guy Raz: E632: The Cronut and Dominique Ansel Bakery: Dominique Ansel," Wondery — Feel the Story, June 17, 2024, https://wondery.com/shows/how-i-built-this/episode/10386-the-cronut-and-dominique-ansel-bakery-dominique-ansel/.

6. Fadi Ghandour, "Part II: 'In Fact, My Brain Was Not Black or White, It Was Supremely Colourful.' Aramex Founder Fadi Ghandour on the Limitations, Risks and Rewards of Building a Heritage Company," Apple Podcasts, October 13, 2022, https://podcasts.apple.com/ae/podcast/part-ii-in-fact-my-brain-was-not-black-or-white-it/id1487299655?i=1000582526077.

7. "How Fast Should Your Company Really Grow?," *Harvard Business Review*, July 15, 2024, https://hbr.org/2024/03/how-fast-should-your-company-really-grow.

8. Yves Van Durme et al., "Deloitte 2023 Global Human Capital Trends," *Deloitte Insights*, February 2, 2023, https://www2.deloitte.com/us/en/insights/focus/human-capital-trends/2023/future-of-workforce-management.html.

9. Jan-Emmanuel De Neve, Micah Kaats, and George Ward, "Workplace Wellbeing and Firm Performance," *Wellbeing Research Centre* (University of Oxford, May 12, 2023), https://ora.ox.ac.uk/objects/uuid:8652ce7e-7bde-449f-a5e7-6b0d0bcc3605/files/s6d56zz16v.

10. "2024 Global Human Capital Trends," Deloitte Insights, n.d., https://www2.deloitte.com/us/en/insights/focus/human-capital-trends.html.

11. "How Fast Should Your Company Really Grow?," *Harvard Business Review*, July 15, 2024, https://hbr.org/2024/03/how-fast-should-your-company-really-grow.

12. "Patagonia Shows How Turning a Profit Doesn't Have to Cost the Earth," McKinsey & Company, April 20, 2023, https://www.mckinsey.com/industries/agriculture/our-insights/patagonia-shows-how-turning-a-profit-doesnt-have-to-cost-the-earth.

Chapter 11: Principle 8: Dare to Play Your Hand

1. "Intel Keynote Transcript: The Charlie Rose Show," Intel, November 15, 2001, https://www.intel.com/pressroom/archive/speeches/asg20011115.htm.

2. Dominique Ansel, "How I Built This."

3. Karen C. Houghton, "Tope Awotona — A Founder Story," July 16, 2018, https://www.linkedin.com/pulse/tope-awotona-founder-story-karen-c-houghton/.

4. Malina Saval, "Variety," *Variety*, March 22, 2017, https://variety.com/2017/biz/spotlight/haim-saban-poor-kid-middle-east-power-rangers-scion-1202013534/.

5. Alex Coad and David J. Storey, "Taking the Entrepreneur Out of Entrepreneurship," *International Journal of Management Reviews* 23, no. 4 (June 2, 2021): 541–48, https://doi.org/10.1111/ijmr.12249.

6. Aracely Soto-Simeone, Charlotta Sirén, and Torben Antretter, "The Role of Skill Versus Luck in New Venture Survival," *International Journal of Management Reviews* 23, no. 4 (May 28, 2021): 549–56, https://doi.org/10.1111/ijmr.12262.

7. Saval, "Variety," March 22, 2017.

8. Dominique Ansel, "How I Built This."

9. "Intel Keynote Transcript: The Charlie Rose Show."

10. Angela Duckworth, *Grit: The Power of Passion and Perseverance* (Random House, 2016).

11. Christian A. Tekwe, "Exploring the Influence of Grit on Small Business Survival Among Sub-Saharan African Immigrant Entrepreneurs in the United States — ProQuest," n.d., https://www.proquest.com/openview/6a7f68c87b76c61c3d9bddf0bbfb877d/1?pq-origsite=gscholar&cbl=18750&diss=y.

Conclusion: Our Future, Together as One

1. "On One Foot?" American Jewish University, January 27, 2016, https://www.aju.edu/ziegler-school-rabbinic-studies/our-torah/back-issues/one-foot.

2. Adam Grant, *Give and Take: A Revolutionary Approach to Success* (Phoenix, 2014). For other books on this subject see: Bob Burg and John David Mann, *The Go-Giver* (Penguin, 2010); Rajendra Sisodia, David Wolfe, and Jagdish N. Sheth, *Firms of Endearment: How World-Class Companies Profit from Passion and Purpose* (Pearson Prentice Hall, 2003); Kim S. Cameron and Marc Lavine, *Making the Impossible Possible: Leading Extraordinary Performance — The Rocky Flats Story* (Berrett-Koehler Publishers, 2006).

3. Theodore Roosevelt, "TR Center — Man in the Arena," n.d., https://www.theodorerooseveltcenter.org/Learn-About-TR/TR-Encyclopedia/Culture-and-Society/Man-in-the-Arena.aspx.

4. Mary Oliver, *New and Selected Poems* (Beacon Press, 1992).

Acknowledgments

Pioneers took six months to write, but it is the culmination of two decades of research and practice. Along this journey, I have been supported and inspired by more people than I can list here, yet each deserves heartfelt gratitude. This book is, in every way, a collective effort, and I am deeply thankful to everyone who played a role in its creation.

Brian Neill—for taking a chance on an unexpected LinkedIn message that said, "I saw that you viewed my profile, and I have a book idea I would love to talk about." Thank you for your open mind, for believing in my vision, and for being the very reason *Pioneers* exists.

David Hagan—my editor and right hand in this process, for your professionalism, attention to every detail, and dedication to helping bring *Pioneers* to life. Your invaluable input shaped this book, and it wouldn't be what it is without you.

Julie Kerr—my developmental editor, for your invaluable guidance and insight throughout this process. Thank you for being a thoughtful sounding board and for offering the honest feedback that pushed this book to its best. Your expertise and support were indispensable.

Gabriela Mancuso—my go-to at Wiley, thank you for your steady support and for being a constant presence throughout this process.

Thinkers50—to Stuart Crainer, Des Dearlove, and Monika Kosman, for including me among the top 30 up-and-coming management thinkers in the world, and for putting me on the 2024 Radar List. Your platform is truly a family and community, one that brings people together to spark new ideas and possibilities. This book would not have been possible without your belief in me.

The University of Miami, London School of Economics, Sabancı University, and Cambridge Judge Business School—as an 11-year-old refugee at the Bulgaria-Turkey border, I made a commitment to pursue a good education. I am deeply aware of how fortunate I am that I was able to realize that dream at your brilliant institutions. The first-class education you provided allowed me to live in multiple countries, pursue interests in entre-preneurship and academia, and ultimately write *Pioneers*. My interest in business longevity and immigrant entrepreneurship was nurtured by the extraordinary professors who supported and guided my research. Thank you for shaping and inspiring my journey.

I owe a special thanks to Mel Robbins, whose podcast episodes often accompanied me on my daily walks to pick up my son, and particularly to her conversation with Dr. Luana Marques, which sparked the very first proposal for this book—a journey that began with rejections but ultimately led to *Pioneers* as it stands today.

I would also like to thank ESCP Paris and the University of Oxford—two inspiring institutions that allow me the freedom to pursue what I love doing: teaching, advising, and tutoring the leaders of tomorrow.

Claire Sullivan—your talent and dedication brought the book cover to life in such a beautiful way. Thank you for your flexibility, professionalism, and willingness to adapt to the last-minute changes.

To the poets who inspired me—Vladimir Levchev, Warsan Shire, Ae Hee Lee, Juan Felipe Herrera, Elif Sezen, Shin Yu Pai, and the Adrienne Rich Literary Trust. Thank you for graciously allowing me to share your work in these pages; your words are woven into the heart of this book.

The Sillaman family—Grammy Elena and Pappy Jimmy—how lucky I am to have you as my parents-in-law—Anne and Lesley Sillaman, my bril-liant sisters-in-law, Aunt Caroline, Uncle Bob, Aunt Rose, Uncle Jack, Anne E. Ketchen, Amy Flynn, Erica Bower: your love, support, and unwavering encouragement have meant the world to me. I am grateful to be a part of your family.

My parents—to my mother and father, who taught me the meaning of resilience, integrity, and determination, and who sacrificed so much to build a life for us. You are the reason I know the meaning of an immigrant's dream, and your example will forever inspire me. I owe so much to all of you. To Fahri and Ece, thank you for your support.

Bryan, my Bebinski—words are not enough to convey my love and endless gratitude to you. You (and Flynn) are my whole world! Thank you for your support, patience, and understanding throughout this journey and for planting the seed for this book with your suggestion, "Why don't you write about what you know? You are an immigrant entrepreneur!" You believed in me from the very start, and every time I doubted myself (which was too often), you lifted me up. You and Flynn are my greatest blessings. Every day, I am grateful for the path that led me to both of you.

And to our son, Flynn—for your endless energy, love, good humor, and curiosity. Thank you for understanding when Mommy couldn't always pick you up after school or play with you and for being so adaptable when our August vacation turned into a staycation with Nene and Dede. You bring me (and us) so much joy and light, and I am only able to do what I do because of you and Daddy. Thank you for coming into our lives.

Finally, to the pioneers whose journeys inspired these pages—thank you for the example you've set through your courage, vision, and resilience. Your stories are the heart of this book, and it is my hope that I have done justice to the legacies you have built and the lessons you offer to others.

Albert Bourla (*Pfizer*)
Alberto "Beto" Perez (*Zumba Fitness*)
Alberto Perlman (*Zumba Fitness*)
Ahmed Rahim (*Numi Tea*)
Andrew Grove (*Intel*)
Artem Petakov (*Noom*)
Diana Verde Nieto (*Positive Luxury*)
Dominique Ansel (*Dominique Ansel Bakery*)
Dug Song (*Duo Security*)
Eren Bali (*Udemy*)
Fadi Ghandour (*Aramex*)
Haim Saban (*Saban Entertainment*)
Hamdi Ulukaya (*Chobani*)
Hernan Lopez (*Wondery*)
Isaac Larian (*MGA Entertainment*)

Jan Koum (*WhatsApp*)
Jane Wurwand (*Dermalogica*)
Karan Bilimoria (*Cobra Beer*)
Larry Liu (*Weee!*)
Luis Von Ahn (*Duolingo*)
Max Levchin (*PayPal*)
Noubar Afeyan (*Moderna*)
Oktay Caglar (*Udemy*)
Özlem Türeci (*BioNTech*)
Reem Hassani (*Numi Tea*)
Saeju Jeong (*Noom*)
Severin Hacker (*Duolingo*)
Tope Awotona (*Calendly*)
Uğur Şahin (*BioNTech*)

Thank you for embodying resilience and purpose and for paving a path that redefines what's possible. May this book serve as a tribute to the strength and vision immigrants bring to the world, inspiring others to dream, to build, and to leave their own enduring legacies.

About the Author

Dr. Neri Karra Sillaman is a globally recognized advisor, speaker, and author, recently named to the Thinkers50 Radar List for 2024, placing her among the top 30 emerging management thinkers worldwide. She serves as an Entrepreneurship Expert at the University of Oxford and as an Adjunct Professor at ESCP Paris. Neri is also the founder of Neri Karra, a global luxury leather goods brand with more than 25 years of partnerships with leading Italian labels. She holds a PhD from the University of Cambridge, an MBA from Sabancı University, and a BBA from the University of Miami.

A former child refugee, Neri's journey fuels her passion for resilience, cultural innovation, and ethical business practices. Her thought leadership has appeared in *Harvard Business Review*, *Forbes*, and *Fast Company*, sharing insights on strategy, entrepreneurship, and leadership. She has also been quoted in publications such as the *Financial Times*, *Newsweek*, *Vogue Business*, *Bloomberg*, *Business of Fashion*, and *WWD*.

Neri has spoken at notable organizations, including Apple, Credit Suisse, Bernstein, the University of Cambridge, Forbes France, Baker McKenzie, the International Bar Association, and the Global Leaders Summit. A three-time TEDx speaker, she inspires leaders to build businesses that balance purpose with profit for lasting impact.

Neri lives in Paris with her husband and their five-year-old son. When not assisting with her son's "experiments," she enjoys reading, cooking, and occasionally, gardening.

Index

229